Minnesota Lunch

Minnesota Lunch

From Pasties to Bánh Mì

EDITED BY

James Norton

MINNESOTA HISTORICAL SOCIETY PRESS

www.mhspress.org

The Minnesota Historical Society Press is a member of the Association of American University Presses.

Manufactured in the United States of America

10 9 8 7 6 5 4 3 2 1

♾ The paper used in this publication meets the minimum requirements of the American National Standard for Information Sciences—Permanence for Printed Library Materials, ANSI Z39.48—1984.

International Standard Book Number
ISBN-13: 978-0-87351-807-9 (paper)

**Library of Congress
Cataloging-in-Publication Data**
Norton, James R.
  Minnesota lunch : from pasties to bánh mì / James Norton.
      p. cm.
  Includes bibliographical references and index.
    ISBN 978-0-87351-807-9 (pbk. : alk. paper)
    1. Luncheons—Minnesota. 2. Cooking, American—Midwestern style. 3. International cooking. 4. Food habits—Minnesota. 5. Minnesota—Description and travel. 6. Cookbooks. I. Title.
  TX735.N67 2011
  641.59776—dc22

                                                    2010047472

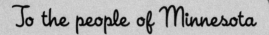

To the people of Minnesota

may your lunch breaks

always be a leisurely escape

to somewhere with

both soul and flavor

Contents

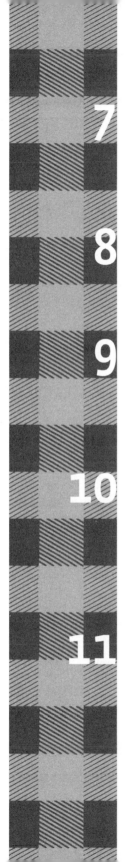

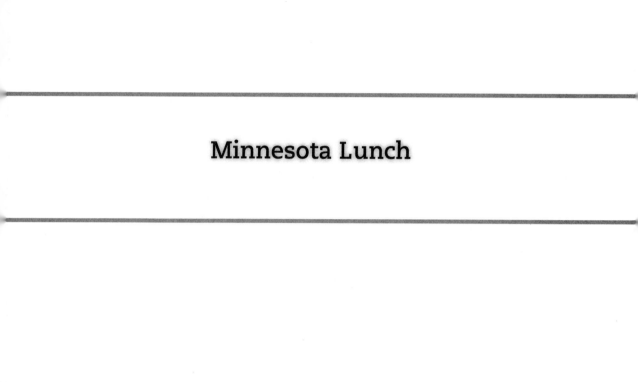

Minnesota Lunch

Introduction

Think about Minnesota for a moment. Probably you're going to imagine woods and water: the primal beauty of the Boundary Waters, mammoth Lake Superior and the mighty Mississippi, the game fish that fill some of those storied ten thousand lakes. You may also think of the busy streets of Minneapolis and the quiet urban elegance of St. Paul, the industrial waterfront of Duluth, the Red River fertility of Moorhead, the Bohemian dignity and raucous polka of New Ulm. You're probably not thinking about sandwiches. And yet, to tell a story of the state, that's where we—writers and photographers from the *Heavy Table,* an upper midwestern online food magazine—started.

Why Sandwiches?

The authors of this book have heard that question time and again, in a cascade of minor variations, since starting work. Here I'll take a whack at providing an answer, an explanation that goes to the heart of what we've tried to accomplish.

You'd be hard pressed to find a less sexy topic than sandwiches. They are seen as everyday food, not celebration food; as simple, not gourmet; as fuel, calories on a hard roll, to be eaten and forgotten. Merely lunch, nothing more. The general indifference to sandwiches extends even into the world of those who make them. More than once, our inquiries were met with puzzlement or silence from people who couldn't or wouldn't understand how something as mundane as meat and bread could be worthy of a book. But that's precisely the point.

If you want to tell the story of a place—in this case, the state of Minnesota—it helps to travel within its borders and get to know what a day in the life of an average person looks like. And for the average person working in the field, or in an office, or in a shop, most days revolve around a little oasis called lunch. Journalist James Lileks put it this way when writing about leaving an office job in May 2010: "The only thing you really miss is lunch. Where you went, who you went with, what you said and did, your private jokes. The peculiar, intense, and inevitably evanescent bond of people who are putting up with someone else's crap."

In a word, lunch is an escape, and the food is part of it. "For someone like me, who works in an office and gets fifteen minutes for lunch, that's probably the best fifteen minutes of my day," says Teddy Hobbins of his job at a Minneapolis ad agency. Hobbins writes about his daily bread for *City Pages* and his own blog, but his interest in the lowly sandwich is the exception, not the rule. In a way, that's the beauty of the food: beyond a few sensational cases (the ju(i)cy lucy war between Matt's and the 5-8 Club in South Minneapolis, for example), sandwiches are not endlessly deconstructed, studied, criticized, and analyzed. There aren't a lot of books about them. They're not newly chic, like cupcakes, or revered by serious foodies, like the baguette, or relentlessly trendy, like bacon.

But they are, in fact, the way we get through our collective days. They're old friends in a lunch box; they're about where we're from; they're comfort from home. And even as classic versions linger on, they're the front lines of culinary change. Sandwiches are how cultures mingle. Think of the bánh mì, the inexpensive sandwich that's gone from being an obscure ethnic specialty in the Twin Cities to a go-to for the urban working class and even a vehicle of high-end gastronomic exploration. "You look at a bánh mì," says Hobbins, "and there are textures and ingredients and pick-

ling that people might at first be averse to. But when you think of a bánh mì, something that takes French influences and Vietnamese influences and unites them, that's really cool—and it's accessible."

A great sandwich is also something that's easy to overlook. It's rarely about using an expensive, hard-to-find ingredient or applying a cooking technique that takes hours or even days to accomplish. It's about balance. It's about freshness. It's about editing: what you leave out is as crucial as what goes between the slices. Making a great sandwich is an art, not a science.

And while we explore the artwork, both historic and contemporary, of the food traditions that have given birth to and further developed the state's iconic sandwiches, we'll explore some of the ethnic and farm-to-table trends that have been driven in recent years by a newfound interest in great local food. "Minnesota farmers are feeding the Twin Cities in ways they didn't do ten years ago," says Rick Nelson, restaurant critic for the Minneapolis *Star Tribune*. "We're really fortunate here."

What Is a Sandwich?

Most of us have heard the Earl of Sandwich story about the food's birth, but here it is again, in the broadest possible strokes. While gambling, an eighteenth-century English aristocrat wanted some kind of hand food so that he could stay at the table. He ordered meat sliced and put between two pieces of bread. And voilà—John Montagu, Fourth Earl of Sandwich, starts a trend.

That no one had ever before thought to combine meat and bread—food items, let's remember, that have been with us for quite a while—is ridiculous. *The Life and Teachings of Hillel* by Yitzhak Buxbaum recounts that the Jewish sage Hillel the Elder put together something quite sandwich-like by combining lamb and bitter herbs between two pieces of unleavened

bread during Passover. Buxbaum writes, "The Talmud explains that Hillel and some other rabbis disagreed about how to eat the three Passover foods. Hillel said they should be eaten all at once, wrapped together; the other rabbis said they could also be eaten separately." And this improvisation occurred, well, right around the time of Jesus's birth, historically speaking.

More useful than trying to pinpoint the sandwich's murky origins is wrestling down some kind of definition. Hobbins offers an expansive one that we happen to like: "It's something that's portable; it's something that's convenient; it can be something you have to pick up with both hands . . . to me it's much more than just something between two pieces of bread; it's more a loose sense of principles that you can build something on." He continues, "It's something well rounded, something convenient, something you can get a complete meal from in your hands. Maybe it's a couple pieces of rye, maybe it's a tortilla, maybe it's a steamed bun like a bao. It's completely different from culture to culture, and I'm completely open to that. I don't think it needs to be bologna and American cheese."

Thus, the Minnesota lunches explored in this book are not bound by a narrow view of the sandwich. Our selections range from the stuffed dumpling-like sambusa to the meat pocket known as the pasty, all the way to the melted pile of delicious, cheesy mess that is the DeGidio's hot dago.

What's the Minnesota-Sandwich Connection?

We look at the sandwich as an opportunity to explore the changing face of the North Star State, from the original Native American inhabitants to the Scandinavian and German settler roots to the Italians and Slavs on the Range to the African and Southeast Asian and other newer waves of immigrants to urban areas who have given the state its body and soul. With sandwiches as the jumping-off point, we'll also dig into some of the industrial and cultural institutions—such as the state fair—that help define Minnesota.

The story we'll tell, starting from bread and meat and radiating out into immigration, culture, oral history, and geography, is not meant to be comprehensive. What we hope to do with *Minnesota Lunch* is to tell some road stories, share some great local food, and prime the palate for deeper exploration. We hope you'll enjoy what became, for us, a deeply personal journey into the history of a great American state. On that note: pull up a chair, grab something to eat, and let's hit the road.

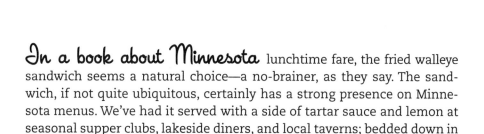

1 The Fried Walleye Sandwich
The Fish That Very Nearly Got Away

SUSAN PAGANI / PHOTOGRAPHS BY KATIE CANNON

𝓘𝓷 𝓪 𝓫𝓸𝓸𝓴 𝓪𝓫𝓸𝓾𝓽 𝓜𝓲𝓷𝓷𝓮𝓼𝓸𝓽𝓪 lunchtime fare, the fried walleye sandwich seems a natural choice—a no-brainer, as they say. The sandwich, if not quite ubiquitous, certainly has a strong presence on Minnesota menus. We've had it served with a side of tartar sauce and lemon at seasonal supper clubs, lakeside diners, and local taverns; bedded down in a delicate celery root slaw at a French bistro; daubed with wasabi aioli at an Asian fusion joint; and, our favorite, buried under a pile of bright red, pickled cabbage.

And then there's the walleye itself, a native fish so particularly Minnesotan, so beloved of diners and fishermen alike, that it was named the state fish in 1965. No one could tell us exactly when it arrived: perhaps it came ten thousand years ago with the last glaciation. We do know that it thrives in Minnesota's deep, large lakes and snaking river systems.

What does a walleye look for in water? It prefers cool temperatures—neither the cold of Lake Superior nor the warmer waters down south will do—and lots of structure for spawning. It is particularly well suited to our big northern lakes, such as Red Lake, Leech Lake, Mille Lacs, the Gull Lake chain, and Lake Winnibigoshish, which feature excellent spawning structure: rocks and gravel for the eggs to attach to as they sink, and large, windswept areas with flowing water to help keep them well aerated.

The walleye, it seems, was made for us, and we were clearly made for it.

So it came as a complete surprise when several people—people various-ly in the know about walleye and the state's culinary history—expressed serious misgivings, or at least confusion, about including a fried walleye sandwich in this book:

○ "It's surprising to me that walleye fits into that category: I don't think of it as a sandwich."
○ "One question: why would you ever do that to a walleye? I suggest fingerlings on a salad."
○ "Fried walleye sandwich, really? How did you land on that one?"
○ "I don't think that's a historic sandwich. I think that's a critter of the fast-food era—something you can eat on the go without a knife or a fork. I don't remember seeing it until maybe fifteen years ago."

So, let's say these folks were right. It wouldn't be the first time the main ingredient stole the story. If the fried walleye sandwich doesn't have a long and fascinating history, the fish itself has plenty of stories to tell us about Minnesota.

The Ice Fisherman: More Elusive than the Walleye

Fishermen are great ones for stories about fish, naturally, so we thought we'd start there. As it was midwinter, that meant going ice fishing. So, on a sunny Saturday afternoon, we headed out to White Bear Lake with Vic Stark, our amiable guide. According to bait shop intel, the lake had been stocked with walleye for the governor's fishing opener, and folks were still catching walleye out there.

While Stark set up his red, rather sharp-looking tent-style portable fishing shelter—this involved unpacking his ice auger, fish-finder, bait, small rods, Coleman lanterns, minnow bucket, heater, and snacks—we trundled out across the lake to knock on some ice shacks.

This was a completely misguided approach.

It turns out that men go ice fishing to not only catch fish but also to drink beer, eat beef jerky, smoke a cigar perhaps, and experience the tran-quility that comes with peering into an ice hole for hours. In other words, to get away—not, it seems, from all of society but from the society of women specifically. Imagine their stoic Minnesotan horror, then, when two women showed up at the door, one taking photos, the other firing off questions.

It went "yes" or "no" for many an interview, with apprehensive fishermen revealing little more than that they had been ice fishing all their lives, the walleye weren't biting, and, yes, they liked a walleye sandwich now and then—made at home, not in a restaurant, preferably in a Shore Lunch batter with mayonnaise, possibly tartar sauce. One fellow let slip that his father brought him and his brothers ice fishing so that their mother could get some housecleaning done.

Then, on the other side of the lake, we saw what looked to be a little house with smoke billowing from the chimney and an ice rink beside it. We imagined it to be one of those deluxe ice shacks you read about, with a full kitchen and HDTV. Once we hiked over to it, through knee-high snow, we discovered it was about the size of a large closet. The door opened, and a gust of hot air greeted us. Inside, it was a veritable sauna. There, Don Tembruell held court over three youngsters—his teenage daughter and her friends—from an easy chair parked directly in front of a full-size woodstove! On each side of the stove were fishing holes, and as we talked, Tembruell's daughter pulled several sunnies out of them.

Ice fishing shacks on White Bear Lake

Tembruell and his family had been parking the ice house on White Bear Lake since 1990. In all those years, he had caught only one walleye. It was a Sunday. He and his father were fishing either side of the woodstove. The latter hooked a fish and then lost it as it fought through the hole—only to see Tembruell pull it up, two seconds later, on the other side of the stove. "His eyes got huge," said Tembruell. "It was a nice, four-pound fish that would have paid for his gas, but I says, 'No Dad, this one is mine!'"

Tembruell's daughter seemed to love the ice shack and answered our demands for details with stories of childhood winters spent making root beer slushies, building snow forts, ice skating, and riding dirt bikes—the rink doubles as a dirt bike trail. It sounded pretty fun.

Satisfied with our catch, we headed back to Stark and the little red ice tent. Inside, it was surprisingly commodious and cozy warm. The ice holes were a couple feet deep, and in the dim light their walls took on a blue glow, both eerie and beautiful. Stark gave us each a beer and showed us how to read the fish-finder, a mesmerizing device. I do not know how long I sat there, nibbling cheese and crackers, sipping cold beers, and watching the hovering red line of a fish—perhaps a walleye!—seemingly nose to nose with my minnow. I do know that it was very, very peaceful.

Bait shops are the switchboard operators of their world: they know who's catching fish, where, on what, and when. We decided to check in at the bait shop in White Bear—a real pleasure, since bait and fly shops have an appeal similar to hardware stores. "Yeah, I always thought it was neat," says Ron Hansen, owner of Little Bear Bait and Tackle. "I used to go into bait stores as a little kid. I was fascinated with the places that were just wall-to-wall fish and tackle. You had to kind of scoot down the aisles 'cause there was so much stuff, and that's the way my store is."

Hansen has been in the bait business for twenty-five years. He reports that walleye fishermen are only about 25 percent of his business, a big decline from previous years. "It used to be a lot more; I used to cater to a lot of people who went to Mille Lacs, for example, and I'd sell two hundred pounds of leeches a week," he says. "Now, I sell maybe seventy-five pounds a week." The drop-off, he explains, is due to regulations, which is something we heard from other bait shops along the way. On Mille Lacs, for example, fishermen are restricted to fish below eighteen or above twenty-eight inches, a limit of four, with only one of those permitted in the larger category. "There are just too many restrictions. You can catch a nice, big fish, but you can't take it home or eat it. People don't like that," says Hansen.

Bait shop near Mille Lacs

He also notes that there are fewer walleye in the lakes, making them harder to find and catch. "I've been fishing White Bear Lake since 1952, and I can go out there and get skunked any day. It's just one of those things," he says. "If you do find them, you've got to figure out what they want to eat—you might throw a thousand times before you get a hook." Hansen has given up walleye fishing: he already has a thirteen-pound trophy on the wall, which he figures he can't beat. In fact, he's stopped going for bass and northerns, too. "I fish panfish because I have grandkids and nephews, and they all go fishing with me," he explains. "You have to

How to Properly Prepare a Walleye Sandwich

HELLO SUSAN!

Though I have never seen it featured on a menu, it so happens that I, myself, have already perfected the walleye sandwich! Without giving away any family secrets, I can lay out the premise of the soon-to-be-famous Uncle Vic's Fishwich for your culinary imagination. I make my fishwich with a fillet, pan-fried in a "Shore Lunch" style coating and served on a bakery-style white hoagie bun that is smothered in a sweet, creamy coleslaw. Sounds simple? The devil is in the details.

Actually, how you prepare the fish itself isn't the most important thing; just stick to the basic idea. I like to trim the rib cage away from walleye to balance the fillet so it will fit nicely within a cradle-like bun. It should go without saying: there can be no bones in this fillet! When your diner hits one bone, all confidence will be lost; they will ask for a fork and then systematically dissect your near-perfect creation.

No heavy breading or batter on the fillet. That is what the bun is for. Don't get crazy with any seasoning; a little salt and pepper is enough. Don't use a "flavored" breading or coating on the fish. Let the flavor of the walleye be the star. If you are not going to use a quality fillet, then you should make soup or fish patties instead. Concentrate on a good piece of fish that is properly cooked: Bake it, broil it, grill it, deep-fry it (if you know how to do it right: hot and fast). It doesn't matter—just make sure it is hot when it hits the bun.

The bun is just the vehicle to get the fish and slaw into your mouth without a fork or your fingers. However, the right bun is really important, too. Cooked fish falls apart. If your bread is tough or chewy, the fillet will be mashed and torn apart as you try to tear off a hunk of your sandwich. Big and soft is the requirement inside this bun. At the same time, you don't want your fingers to sink through the crust; a bun that wimpy won't last through the meal, and then you will need that fork. If you wanted fish on a plate, you would have made that and served coleslaw on the side with a dinner roll.

You need a bun that you can get easy, clean bites of bread, fish, and slaw without having to work so hard. One that soaks up the extra juices and keeps everything tied together until it is all gone. Buttering and lightly toasting or grilling the open faces of the bun is a small but invaluable touch. It shows that you care.

Now, the real secret is in the slaw: It replaces that tired, heavy, and lame tartar sauce, cools any blistering steam or oil from the cooked fish, adds plenty of dressing to moisten a dry mouthful of bread and (oops) overdone fish, and adds a crispy-crunchy texture to counterpoint the firm fish. Make the slaw fresh. One day ahead lets it mature, but you risk losing the crispness. Keep it cold and drain it well. The bun will soak up some extra liquid, but it isn't easy to lick dressing off of your own elbows. Try it. You'll see.

This all may seem overly complicated for a fish sandwich. It probably is. But hey, perfection isn't always easy. To me, it is so simple: fish, bun, and slaw. All those little details are just common sense and second nature, aren't they?

Oh, don't forget to garnish with a zesty, crunchy dill pickle. I have pickle issues and will judge a cook, chef, or restaurant harshly on this point. Whenever you bother to serve a pickled cucumber, make sure it has a backbone and character. A soft, lazy pickle is a sad, sad thing. I have lost respect for many sandwich purveyors over this single point alone.

Looking forward to fishing, Vic ○

have action when you have kids. You want to spoil a kid for fishing, take 'em out walleye fishing for a day and catch nothing. All my relations love fishing, and that's because they are used to catching fish." This level of success is important to Hansen, who has worries about the next generation of fishermen. "We need to keep trying to get more kids involved," he says. "When I was a kid, you went with mom and dad. Lately, I'm seeing more kids out fishing with grandma and grandpa—mom and dad are just too busy to take them."

Hansen does not eat walleye, sandwiches or otherwise, unless someone gives him one. They are, however, his wife's favorite fish. "She orders that walleye amandine, and I get frustrated because I don't like to pay that kind of money for fish," he says, laughing. "I mean, I'm having prime rib and she's having walleye and they are the same price. They're good eating, but I'd rather eat sunnies or crappies any day." Really? That sounds like piscatorial heresy! "Oh, yes, they're delicious."

Hansen's shop may just fare better in the coming years: the Department of Natural Resources (DNR) sold more than 565,000 licenses in 2010, a 13 percent increase over the previous year—and the highest number in ten years. Not only that, but sales of the walleye stamp surpassed 23,000, four times that of 2009. Still, he's not alone in thinking that the state's walleye fishing, and therefore the sport fishing and tourism industry, is suffering under the overregulation of slot limits—we heard this complaint again and again.

Giant walleye statue in Garrison, billed as the Walleye Capital of the World

Regulations and the Return of the Red Lake Walleye

Yet there are also people who don't see it that way. "I used to go up to Red Lake to go fishing, and it drove me crazy to hear people complaining that they caught forty walleye, but they were all over eighteen inches, so they had to throw them back," says Pat Brown, a fisheries biologist for the Red Lake band of Ojibwe. "What? But you caught all those fish! Where else in the state of Minnesota can you catch that many fish and have that much fun? It's just like pan-fishing 'cause the rates are so high." But, he adds, "I think that's the older generation. Hopefully the younger generation is starting to get the fly-fisherman mentality. They are starting to get it."

Brown has been part of a highly successful program to rehabilitate the Red Lake Fisheries, the state's only commercial walleye fishery and the only freshwater fishery left in the United States. Apparently the fishery began in 1917 when a bunch of anglers lobbied the state to allow them to fish without seasons or limits. There was a war on, Minnesota had a food shortage, and meat was expensive—people were hungry. Instead, the state formed small commercial fisheries on some of its larger lakes— Lake of the Woods, Winnibigoshish, and Red Lake—which it used to pro- duce inexpensive fish meat for Minnesotans. The state ran the Red Lake Fisheries until 1929, when it was essentially turned over to the Bureau of Indian Affairs, which managed it as a fishing cooperative for tribal band members.

The Red Lake band of Ojibwe owns 85 percent of the lake; the DNR owns 15 percent. Historically, the sections have been managed separately— at least until 1996, when Red Lake's walleye population collapsed, falling to only 200,000 pounds. "That sounds like a lot of fish," says Brown, "and it would be, if not for the fact that Red Lake is the sixth-largest lake in the U.S.—we have almost 285,000 acres of water." The Red Lake Fisheries co- operative had to decide, at that point, whether to keep fishing the lake. "They had seen that they weren't catching anything," explains Al Pember- ton, tribal council member and director of the Red Lake DNR. "The fisher- ies board told them it was depleted of walleyes, but there were still lots of perch in the lake. They voted to stop fishing."

Before the collapse, the average number of fishermen was two hun- dred, rising to as many as seven hundred in some years. Pemberton told us that he grew up fishing and, as a child, helped his father and grandfa- ther with the nets. "When I got older, I stopped fishing with nets," he says. "I fished hook and line, but I just figured that if I got another job, for me, it wouldn't feel right if I fished with a net and took away from someone who needed it, that had kids and that's all they did for a living."

A year after the Red Lake band made its decision, chairman Bobby Whitefeather met with the state of Minnesota, which had continued to fish the lake. "He said, 'We have to do something to bring the lake back,'" explains Pemberton, "and they ended up signing an agreement." That agreement formed the Red Lake Fisheries Technical Committee, a group of biologists and citizens representing the Red Lake band, the Minnesota DNR, the U.S. Fish and Wildlife Service, the Bureau of Indian Affairs, and the University of Minnesota.

"I think when they first sat down at the table, they didn't trust each other," says Pemberton. "One of the first things I said when I got there was, 'There's enough finger-pointing going around, there's enough.'" According to Pemberton, some people blamed the Red Lake band for the collapse, citing overfishing with gill nets and black market fishing. Others accused sport fishermen of *tripping*—taking one's limit several times a day on multiple trips.

We met a sport fisherman who, while not guilty of tripping, told us that he held himself accountable for having taken too many walleye—and so had stopped fishing anything but catch and release. Bob Nasby caught his first walleye sometime in the early 1960s: "I said, 'Oh boy, is this a nice fish!' I was so impressed, I started fishing for them seriously. I had myself pictured as the king of the walleye fishermen in Minnesota." And so it was. Nasby and his brother developed a habit of fishing sundown to sunup—a practice now banned on some lakes—when there were fewer people out and the fish were most active. And they fished exclusively for large fish, deploying eight- to ten-inch minnows, the size generally used for northern pike. "Most people were out fishing bobbers and leeches, stuff like that. With our minnows, we would catch these huge walleye," he remembers. "You know, twelve-pound walleyes—that's a thirty-one-inch fish! Now that's a sandwich!"

For two decades they fished obsessively, bringing in the state's largest opening day limits for several years running. "As young guys, we would get a lot of attention, and we thought that was pretty cool," recalls Nasby, "but more than anything, we loved to do it. If you've ever been out on a lake at night, it's magic. It's totally silent, you can hear the loons, and everything is illuminated by the stars." About two years in, an old fellow on Stony Lake in Hackensack saw the folly in their ways: "He said, 'You guys better quit: you're gonna ruin this lake.' And he was right: we took too many adult walleyes and we ruined it."

Tips from Bob Nasby, Nonprofessional Fisherman

ASK BOB NASBY about his fishing experiences, and he'll tell you that he has been fishing for fifty years, that at one point he and his brother were considered the kings of walleye fishing—in fact, they developed a regrettable addiction to the sport—and that today he regularly guides clients on fresh- and saltwater fly-fishing trips in Minnesota, Wisconsin, Michigan, and Florida.

But for all that, he won't be called a professional. "There's no such thing as a professional fisherman," he says. "That's just a bunch of nonsense the industry comes up with to try to sell you a bunch of stuff. Really, there's just guys that get to fish more, so they have more experience. I pull my pants up just like everybody else." Yet, in his heyday, Nasby regularly brought in the biggest opening day limits statewide. Here he gives us the benefit of his experience with some tips for hooking the big walleye.

1. Walleye are predators, so Nasby prefers live bait, such as a fathead minnow. Jigs are also a favorite: a quarter ounce is a good all-around walleye size; go heavier in deeper waters or high winds and lighter in shallower. He carries yellow, white, and black. Nasby says you can tip them with a minnow or worm, but "a good fisherman doesn't need to; he can make it move like a minnow." Take that as you will. He'll also fish stick bait and suggests all manner of Rapala, including straight, jointed, floating, sinking, deep diving, and countdowns.

2. With all of those baits, trolling is the way to go. In terms of structure, look for drop-offs.

3. Nasby says bobbers can be a bit boring, but "they work and some people like them." He suggests setting up over a rock pile and dropping night crawlers and leeches.

4. Nasby recommends fishing the low-light hours, predawn and from 7 PM to sundown. Personally, he prefers to fish the middle of the night, and always during what he describes as the dark side of the moon: "There's ten good fishing days in a thirty-day period, five of which are questionable—which leaves five truly good days. So then you gotta figure out which days they are. In my opinion, it's the days just prior to a full moon and the days just after."

5. Don't load up on tackle: "If you take a big box of stuff, you are going to spend the whole day messing around, trying to come up with the right lure. Taking a small selection allows you to really learn that tackle and become effective with it. In the U.S. Navy survival kit, they just have some jigs and a line." ●

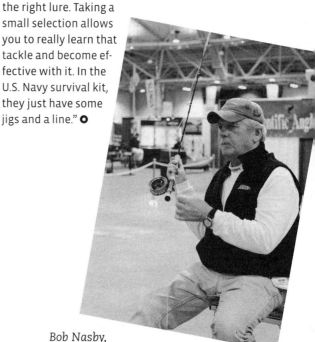

Bob Nasby,
nonprofessional fisherman

The epiphany came on a seven-day fishing trip. Nasby and his brother kept each night's catch—something like eighty-four fish—in holding boxes beside the dock. "At the end of the trip, we had to knock them in the head, and they're watching us," Nasby says. "And I realized: this is gross. It's like clubbing seals. We don't need this much fish—and I stopped." Today Nasby is a well-known fly-fishing instructor. He fishes only catch and release. "I can't kill fish," he says, "but I don't think there's anything wrong with taking fish home to eat. Just use discretion—take what you need, and don't be a pig. I mean, how many nine-pound walleye can you eat?"

Nasby's experience brings home some of the decisions the Red Lake Fisheries Technical Committee has made since it formed in the fall of 1997. First, it ended all walleye fishing on Minnesota and band waters. Then, it increased enforcement to ensure that any regulations put in place would be followed. And, finally, it began stocking the lake, adding some 120 million walleye fry over the course of five years.

And it worked. The fishery rebounded from 200,000 to 12 million, and it's sustaining that population. Both the Red Lake band and the state opened fishing again in 2006, "which is remarkable because some of us thought it would take twenty years," says Brown. He continues, "I think there were a couple of factors that really helped us out. The band and the state biologists really got along well, so we were able to work closely. And then, probably the biggest thing was compliance. We just have a couple of wardens for these huge basins, so without public support it wouldn't have worked."

"Before, the right hand didn't know what the left hand was doing because we never asked the state what they were doing and they never asked us," adds Pemberton. "Now we are all taking care of the lake, scientifically." Regulations similar to those on other large, Minnesota walleye lakes are in place. On both the Minnesota and band sides of the lake, it's hook-and-line fishing only, and the size limit is anything below twenty or above twenty-eight inches. Why protect the Nasbian lunkers? Brown explains that female walleye don't start laying eggs until they're almost eighteen inches. He likes to wait a year—so their eggs have more yolk and the fry a better chance of surviving—and then give them the opportunity to reproduce five or six times.

All of this is great news for fishermen—and for the Red Lake Fisheries, which are back up and running. So far, Pemberton reports, three to four hundred people are fishing. In addition, the fisheries now fillet and process all of their own fish, which has helped keep money and jobs on Red Lake.

or, The Difficulty of Farming Walleye

CONSIDERING the fish's popularity in entrées, it seems surprising that some enterprising producer hasn't farmed walleye and presented its flaky white flesh and sweet flavor to the world.

Apparently, it's not that easy. "It's certainly one of those fish that everyone wants to culture," says Jeff Gunderson, director of the Minnesota Sea Grant, which facilitates public education and research of Lake Superior and Minnesota's aquatic resources and associated economies. "It's a high-value and highly desired species, and it's not being produced in the U.S. It's just proved not to be economically viable at this time. It may be eventually."

According to Gunderson, walleye are dedicated predators, and it's nearly impossible to get them to eat formulated feed—in fact, they've been known to food strike, starving to death before they touch a pellet. "That's been the trick all along," he says. "Some of these fish are just genetically programmed to eat live prey, so if you put something in front of them that's not moving, it's hard for them to recognize it as food." They definitely recognize other walleye as food. In fact, they are such cannibals that aquaculture folks like to joke that if you try to put a bunch of them in a culture system, all you'll end up with is one big walleye. "I think they've got it to the point where they can get them to eat the pellets and not each other," says Gunderson, "but it's just a very costly process."

Indoor tanks in research aquaculture facilities are expensive and labor intensive to maintain—light, water quality, and feed have to be tightly controlled. The high-protein food is pricey, and even the walleye that can be trained to eat it have a mortality rate between 50 and 90 percent. Those that survive grow relatively slowly, requiring a couple of seasons to reach stock size. So, Gunderson says, researchers are still working on it.

In the meantime, "the stocking racket," as Gunderson calls it, continues to stock lakes all over the state, including those that produce walleye naturally and those that don't. "There's been a big management push in the state, primarily directed by recreational fishermen, to stock lakes," says Gunderson. "In some cases, they've stocked them in lakes where walleye aren't native, lakes that don't have the spawning habitat. You can do that, but the fish won't reproduce, and so a lot of those lakes have to continuously stock."

Today, all stocked walleye are produced from wild populations. Walleye will often spawn in river systems. In the early spring, just after ice-out, walleye—a cool-water fish—leave lakes and head into rivers, looking for good spawning ground. They like flowing, well-aerated water and gravel. The egg-taking facilities are waiting: the migrating fish wander into the nets, and their bellies are squeezed for eggs or milt. Fertilized eggs are mixed with clay so they don't clump and then put into jars for a couple of weeks, until they hatch. Those fry are then stocked into—ideally—empty, natural ponds. "We have a unique situation in Minnesota," says Gunderson. "Both the DNR and private producers use wetlands, which tend to freeze out every year. These are shallow, productive ponds that have such low oxygen levels during the winter that any fish are killed off."

And that's a good thing because any walleye left over from the previous year would be six to eight inches long—they'd make quick work of the tiny fry. Of course, that also means producers have to purchase fathead minnows to feed the burgeoning walleye, an   ❍

expensive practice. "So this allows us to produce a lot of walleye," says Gunderson. "We have a huge aquaculture industry in the state. The DNR produces walleye, but there are also private fish farmers selling not only to the DNR but also to private lake associations, out of state, or to people that just want to stock walleye in their lakes. So they don't raise them as food fish or anything; it's just basically to stock them into the lakes for angling."

If he sounds less than enthusiastic about the process, it may be that to some degree he mourns the loss of commercial food fish produced in Minnesota. In Ontario, for example, where much of our commercial walleye come from, Gunderson says there are more lakes, fewer people, and much less pressure from sport fishermen. "They tend to value the commercial fishing a little bit higher than we have in the United States," he explains. "When you have a commercial fishery pitted against a recreational fishery, the recreational fisher has taken over—it's just political pressure. The recreational fishermen can motivate a lot of support from the industry, people who sell boats, rods, tackle, and all that."

"The clientele for commercial fishing are the people in the restaurant," he continues, "but they don't necessarily make the connection: they want to eat some fish, and they don't care if it came from Red Lake, Canada, or Lake of the Woods. It's not entirely dead, but I think we've lost a tradition and a heritage, especially along the North Shore of Minnesota. I mean, that's why a lot of people moved here, to participate in commercial fishing."

On a more positive note, Gunderson reports that researchers are working on a hybrid fish, a cross between the walleye and a sauger, which is often mistaken for a walleye. "It may have potential for aquaculture," says Gunderson, "and it will taste similar to a walleye." Interesting: will we one day be eating fried wauger or saugeye sandwiches?

When it comes to taste, Gunderson explains there is actually some science in the walleye's popularity for cooking and eating. Walleye are very low in fat, which allows them to be stored in the freezer for longer periods of time. "The fats in fish are unsaturated and polyunsaturated, which is what makes them so healthy to eat," says Gunderson. "But those fats oxidize faster. So with fattier fish, like lake trout, you'll notice an off flavor—especially if you don't handle it well—after about two or three months."

"The term *fishy* really bothers me," he adds. "It is a fish, so it should taste like fish. What people really mean when they say that is the fish is rancid—it's spoiled, not fishy. Walleye will last a long time in the freezer and still taste good. And I think the color of the fish has something to do with it, too. It has nice white, flaky flesh, it's fairly firm . . . it just kind of really fits the bill for eating and storing." **○**

The fisheries have also been buying and processing walleye from Ontario, but those packages are labeled differently. "The Red Lake fish is way better tasting," Pemberton says. "It may be the sandy bottom of the lake, I'm not sure, but they have a cleaner, sweeter taste. I have friends who don't eat fish—they don't like the flavor—but I took them some walleye, cooked it for them, and they ate it. Said it didn't even taste like fish."

Tavern on Grand: The Classic, if Somewhat Gloomy, Fried Walleye Sandwich

Red Lake's walleye hasn't shown up on restaurant menus yet, but it's probably only a matter of time. Brown reports that the band is exploring other opportunities, such as a fish stand at farmers markets. That'll be great news for the Tavern on Grand in St. Paul, which once featured Red Lake walleye exclusively. Whether or not Minnesotans living in the metro area believe in the sandwich's historic significance, if you say, "fried wall-eye sandwich," they will most assuredly reply, "Tavern on Grand." And so it was that we tried like mad to get an interview with the current owner, Steve Munyon, who would not return our increasingly pleading calls or notes. Somehow, he seemed like the missing piece, the oracle of walleye.

On a Saturday—the walleye opener, which seemed significant some-how—we decided to just stop by the restaurant. If nothing else, we could get a photo. To our glee, Munyon appeared at our table in minutes, say-ing, "Oh, isn't that funny. You sounded like an old woman on the phone." And then he sat down and proceeded to chat our ears off for the duration of lunch.

Dave Wildmo opened Tavern on Grand twenty years ago. He imagined it as the epicenter of all things walleye, a concept he introduced with an all-you-can-eat walleye fry for just $5.95—a risky thing to do, Munyon says, because at the time, it wasn't that easy to get walleye. Apparently, the gambit worked. The restaurant sells a thousand pounds of walleye a week, some of them in sandwiches, which Munyon believes were on the menu from day one. And that pretty much makes it the oldest fried walleye sandwich recipe we've sampled. Historic? Potentially so.

Tavern on Grand, St. Paul

Walleye sandwich at Tavern on Grand, St. Paul

The recipe has not changed a bit since Wildmo's time: "Oh, no! After about a month, I kiddingly told my partner, we're going to have to change some of the walleye recipes, and [I] put her on for a while, until she pulled a gun on me. No, you don't change those." The walleye is fried in a cracker crumb—more than that, he wouldn't tell us. The tartar sauce is old school, but Munyon has replaced the bun with a softer ciabatta that suits the fillet perfectly. "It's a nice light bread, basically just water and air," he says. "It was such [a] breakthrough, but when I changed to that, oh my god, I thought people were going to have me assassinated." But eventually the tavern's regulars came around, as they have to other small changes Munyon has introduced, including a jalapeño tartar sauce, a béarnaise, walleye cakes, blackened walleye, and Portuguese walleye. "We do try to change it up," says Munyon. "Our customers like to see new things, and I hope it brings in a younger crowd. It's getting to be, well, these people are starting to get older and they are going to die off—I mean, do you guys eat walleye?"

We do now.

Like everyone, Munyon buys his walleye from Canada. "We use only six- to eight-ounce walleyes," he said. "It's the best-tasting walleye there is, and believe me, I've tasted them."

"And why is it so tasty?" we asked.

"Because they haven't grown nasty through the years and grumpy, like I am," he answered. "They just get more bones. Walleye live to be nine years old, and they will die just about at nine years to the day, too."* Though we were starting to notice a disturbing trend in Munyon's conversation, we soldiered on, wondering if, in lieu of a recipe, he might provide the home cooks with some advice. "Well, I think it's best just to keep it simple," he said. "You want the walleye to come out and just be walleye—just be you."

---

*Actually, Mr. Munyon, they live for decades, but we didn't have the heart to ruin your somewhat fatalistic opinion of the walleye.

Preserving History, Hot Summer Nights, and Cold Beer

WALKING INTO Fisher's Club in Avon on a Friday night is a little like stepping back in time. The walls are covered in that honey-colored knotty pine so particular to midwestern lake houses of the thirties, except over the bar, where some ancient red wallpaper, wilted and billowing, has been lovingly stapled in place. In the corner, a 1939 popcorn machine is furiously churning out hot, fluffy kernels, and everywhere there are curiously labeled wooden boxes—Bottle Club lockers, you'll discover, if you hang around long enough. And you just might: this place feels familiar and welcoming, like you could settle in for an evening of table hopping and chatter. And that's pretty much how the current owners—a group of twelve that includes Lake Wobegon's Garrison Keillor—wants you to feel.

According to restaurant lore, George "Showboat" Fisher opened the club in 1932. Having recently retired from playing major league baseball, he thought a seasonal club—open in the evenings from May to October—would be just the antidote to an all-day, year-round job that might keep him from hunting and fishing. Fisher's featured a jukebox, cold beer, and slot machines. If music and gambling did not appeal, Ol' Showboat had another plan to lure in customers. "He'd make his sons, George Jr., Dick, and Lewis, go out and fish for sunfish all week," says Colleen Hollinger-Petters, co-owner and manager of the restaurant. "Then they'd fry them up and give them away for free on Friday and Saturday to get people to drink." Apparently, Showboat's wife, Flo, fried all that fish in a tiny kitchen behind the bar.

One night a "savvy nightclub owner" from St. Cloud, a lady as the story goes, convinced Showboat he should sell the fish. "He came up with a secret recipe for the breading," Hollinger-Petters says, "the same one we use today, and then eventually there were more people than sunfish, and he switched to walleye. We have one menu from every year, and walleye and northern pike show up in the 1940s."

The other thing Fisher's started in the forties, just after World War II, was the Bottle Club. Essentially, the idea was to bring in your bottle of gin, bourbon, vodka, or what-have-you, and the bartender would supply the setup. At the end of the night, you'd write your name on the bottle and leave it in a locker or you'd take it home.

In the late 1950s, George Jr. and wife Sally took over the restaurant, adding the current, larger kitchen and, perhaps more notably, a potato salad that is still served in its original form. In fact, the restaurant recently tried to substitute in a precut potato, to the displeasure of its regulars. "If you mess with it, they'll tell you the next day," says Hollinger-Petters's uncle, Karl Petters. "They said, 'This is awful.' I couldn't tell the difference, but everyone else could."

Fisher's became the sort of supper club people flocked to all summer long. Each week, they came on the same night and sat at the same table—which might be named for them: beware the intruder who tried to squat there. The walleye could take three hours to roll out of the kitchen, so folks spent long evenings dancing, drinking, and visiting with their neighbors and friends.

Into the midst of this culturally rich summer community stepped Garrison Keillor. "He had lived on a farm kind of near Freeport," says Hollinger-Petters. "He would come in, order a cup of coffee, and just sit and listen; that's where he got the accent. He still gets a lot ◗

of material—I mean, he must have stacks of spiral-bound notebooks." In 2003, Keillor, a longtime friend of the Petters family, asked them to let him know if George and Sally were going to retire. "He said, 'It would be a shame to lose such a tradition,'" recalls Hollinger-Petters, "'and it would be kind of nice to have a place where kids in the area can have a job that they can ride their bikes to.' So, it was kind of more altruistic on his part rather than wanting to own a restaurant."

George Jr. and Sally did retire in 2005, after forty years. The Petters family and Keillor stewarded the process of buying the restaurant from them: "We talked to longtime customers and fans of Fisher's Club and asked them if they wanted to buy shares." In the end, they formed a limited liability corporation. Keillor holds the majority share, and there are eleven other partners, including the Petters family, who basically run the place.

Not surprisingly, the group made an effort to keep things pretty much the same as they have always been. The Bottle Club license is still active, and Fisher's serves beer and wine, including California, European, and South American vintages. "We've learned from the wine reps," Hollinger-Petters reports, "that you just have to carry Beringer white zinfandel and no other; people who drink white zin only want Beringer."

They've expanded the dinner menu to include plates under ten dollars—and a walleye sandwich! "We were sensitive to the price of the walleye dinner, and some people didn't want that much food," Hollinger-Petters says, adding that she was inspired by a halibut sandwich she had in Key West. "And, for the survival of supper clubs, you need to keep your signature items, but you need to appeal to the peripheral crowds so they become your people," she concludes.

Though Fisher's people seem to enjoy the food, some are none too pleased that Chef Pat gets dinner out of the kitchen in twenty minutes, upsetting the program. "It's like the country club of rural America, no pretensions," says Hollinger-Petters. "People come and they stay. If you look in any etiquette book, it says that table hopping is bad, but at Fisher's everybody table hops because there are people here you haven't seen since last summer. There are people who have moved away, come back after ten years, walked in, and seen people they know—so this is really the history of the community."

Still, Hollinger-Petters and her partners are working on building new clients, the Fisher's people of tomorrow. She notes that Keillor's notoriety and the proximity of the Lake Wobegon Trail have helped to boost business. Specifically, they are seeing more book groups and young people. "There's been a resurgence of all ages," says Hollinger-Petters. "We're slowly seeing a new generation bringing their kids back; they love to be able to sit here and have a martini and see their kids out on the beach." ◗

Walleye Po'boy from the Blackbird Café, Minneapolis

WHEN I DIE, BURY ME WITH A SIDE OF PICKLED CABBAGE. Early in 2010, a fire heavily damaged the retail block Blackbird Café inhabited, destroying the restaurant and four other well-loved businesses. [Blackbird reopened in a new location in November 2010.] We were devastated to lose the Blackbird, which served an eclectic menu featuring everything from pork tenderloin tacos to gnocchi in lobster cream and bánh mì to, yes, walleye po'boy. About the latter, we had heard tales of a spicy cornmeal breading and an exotic pickled cabbage. It sounded fabulous: the perfect foil to what could, in its lesser incarnations, be a rather bland sandwich.

But Blackbird's walleye po'boy no longer existed—or did it? Amazingly, just weeks after losing their restaurant, Chris Stevens and Gail Mollner were willing to create the sandwich for us in one of our home kitchens.

Chef Stevens has a remarkable way of blending ingredients, of balancing textures and flavors so that each comes through, yet the whole is harmonious. When we asked him if he applied a formula to creating dishes, he said it was more unconscious than that. "You taste things and you know you need to add a sweet, sour, salty, or spicy to balance it all out," he explains. "For sure, I've got a pretty acidic palate, so I prefer vinaigrettes, and we've got a ton of pickles—there's a pickled cabbage on the po'boy."

"I just love textures," he adds. "I like having a variety of options, so it's not like eating the same thing constantly. You know, the spicy peanut noodles are fun because you've got these little piles of greenery: radish sprouts, cilantro—I think phở, with that little plate of stuff that you can add, that was the inspiration. Sweet is a good component, but it's kind of overdone in our culture, and then there's salt and, it doesn't always happen well, but I like to work in bitter—just to clean things up a bit."

"Like preserved lemon or radicchio," chimes in Mollner.

"Yeah," he agrees. "And I don't know if we push the envelope on spicy, but that's always something we try to incorporate. It's just such a nice thing: sprinkle some Thai chilies on something or habanero here or there, that sort of thing."

It's a funny way to start a conversation about walleye sandwiches because, as a genre, they can tend toward bland, relying heavily on tartar sauce and lemon to carry the day. So why would a restaurant beloved for its flavor profiles offer a fried walleye sandwich?

Mollner says that, as a native, the fried walleye sandwich is, "a—well, duh—Minnesota thing. It's what you eat when you are camping or on a canoe trip. You catch a fish, you crack the saltine bread crumbs, fry it up in whatever Griswold pot of oil you've got, and then stick it in bread to sop up the oil." Yet, they agree the walleye's popularity might be rooted in the fact that, while it can have a certain sweet flavor all its own, for folks averse to eating fish, it isn't "fishy."

"Freshwater fish are nice, but they are kind of plain; they don't have a complex flavor profile," Stevens says. "It's this thing you do and eat and it's good. As a kid, it makes sense to have it fried all the time, but fish and chips, that seems kind of lame. It's like, what else can we do with this?" The answer: let's put it on a sandwich. And that's how the walleye po'boy was born: "We ran it as a special. We just wanted it to be a really simple, really delicious fried fish sandwich. We call it a po'boy because it's got some southern influences, a lot of black pepper and cayenne, thyme," says Stevens. "And it just stuck."

The walleye po'boy developed a huge following, with regulars stopping in every week to eat one. It is simple, but it comes together unbelievably well: the fish holds up to the frying, and it has a great texture. It's not incredibly moist, but that's the job of the cabbage and a moderately spicy Cajun mayonnaise.

The pickled cabbage makes the difference at Blackbird Café, Minneapolis

The walleye Blackbird serves, like most of what you find in restaurants today, comes from Canada, which, as Stevens points out, is still more local than any marine seafood. "I think it is awesome that we can still get fresh walleye," he says. "Even when we were working at Table of Contents [in St. Paul], we would never use walleye because, back then, you could eat any kind of fish; they weren't considered fished out yet. I mean, that's when Copper River salmon was huge."

Mollner laughs, "Yeah, why would you eat walleye when you could have swordfish? You could eat a dolphin!" She pauses. "I'm sorry: that was terrible. I don't mean it!"

"You know, with our business model," she adds, "we aren't trying to reach up and impress people who are really into food.

If anything, we are kind of trying to collect those people who are used to eating really bad walleye sandwiches and say, 'Hey, try this one, you might like it.'"

And perhaps you can: Mollner and Stevens have resurrected Blackbird Café in Minneapolis's Kingfield neighborhood. Cheers!

Walleye Po'boy

Makes 6 servings

Cajun Mayo

2 teaspoons black peppercorns
½ teaspoon whole fennel seed
½ teaspoon whole mustard seed
1 clove garlic, finely minced
½ tablespoon minced fresh thyme
½ tablespoon minced fresh sage
½ teaspoon smoked paprika
1 pinch cayenne
1 cup mayonnaise
Salt to taste

In a dry skillet over medium-high heat, toast peppercorns, fennel seed, and mustard seed until fragrant, about 3 to 4 minutes. Allow spices to cool, then grind in a spice mill. Combine ground spices and remaining ingredients (garlic through salt). Refrigerate until ready to use.

Pickled Red Cabbage

1 medium red cabbage, shaved (about 4 cups)
½ medium red onion, shaved
½ cup sugar
½ cup champagne vinegar
¼ cup water
1 tablespoon salt
½ teaspoon black pepper

In a large bowl, combine cabbage and onion. Set aside. Combine remaining ingredients (sugar through pepper) in a saucepan and bring to a boil

over medium heat. Cook, stirring occasionally, just until the sugar and salt is dissolved. Pour hot liquid mixture over cabbage. Let cool for a few hours before using. Use a slotted spoon to scoop the cabbage onto the sandwiches so that you can retain the pickling juices.

Fried Walleye Fillets

¾ cup finely ground Parmesan cheese
½ cup fresh bread crumbs
½ cup cornmeal
3 tablespoons minced flat-leaf parsley
1 teaspoon smoked paprika
½ teaspoon ground cumin
2 cloves garlic, minced
1 teaspoon salt
½ teaspoon black pepper
All-purpose flour
3 eggs, beaten
Canola oil for frying
2 (1-pound) walleye fillets, pin bones removed, flesh cut into equal
    portions

Combine first nine ingredients (Parmesan through pepper) on a plate. Place flour on a separate plate. Place beaten eggs on a third plate. In a deep fryer, heat oil to 350°F. Dredge fillets in flour, then egg wash, and finally cornmeal breading. Fry fillets until golden brown; when finished cooking, they should float. Remove to paper towel–lined plate.

Assembly

Salted butter, at room temperature
6 focaccia or ciabatta rolls, halved lengthwise

Butter each side of halved rolls and broil, butter side up, until golden brown and toasted. Spread Cajun mayo on each roll to taste; add a walleye fillet and pickled red cabbage to taste. Enjoy!

The Chef Shack's Streetwise Tartar Sauce

STREET FOOD IS HOT, HOT, HOT in the Twin Cities. Suddenly, there are all manner of hot dog school buses, smart car espresso bars, tiny taco trucks, and portable pizza ovens parked if not on the street proper then inside neighborhood farmers markets. The adoring public has been only too happy to take their meals curbside, eating standing up, perched on a park bench, or squatting in a stairwell—anywhere, so long as it's tasty.

No one has done more to feed this veritable revolution than Minneapolis's Chef Shack, brainchild of chefs Lisa Carlson and Carrie Summer. The Shack, as it is affectionately known, is parked outside the Kingfield and Mill City farmers markets on weekends and brings lunch to the workers of St. Paul during the week. On any given day, the chalkboard menu boasts everything from not-so-humble Thousand Hills hot dogs to pulled pork quesadillas, beet salad with fried green tomatoes, the odd chicken foot, and, yes, a sublime fried walleye sandwich.

Served on a baguette made by fellow farmers market vendor Sun Street Breads, the sandwich balances a lightly battered walleye fillet atop a trifecta of pickled cabbage, dressed salad greens, and pickled-ramp tartar sauce. While all of the elements blend into a delicious whole, we were particularly struck by the brightness of the tartar sauce and its sweet-and-sour ramps. Somewhat famous for her condiments, Chef Carlson agreed to share her recipe, which came about out of necessity. "Honestly, the ramp is a challenge," she says. "The season is only about a month long, so they are a little pricey. And, you know, they're roots, so they come into the kitchen caked with earth, and they are tricky to cook—it's easy to overdo it. So, they are labor intensive, expensive, and you don't want to ruin them, but you get this delicacy in the end." ⊙

Pickled Ramp Tartar Sauce

Contributed by Lisa Carlson and Carrie Summer, chefs
Makes 8 to 16 servings

PICKLED RAMPS

1 cup white balsamic or plain white vinegar
1 cup organic sugar
1 cup water
2 pounds ramps, well cleaned, tops clipped

Mix first three ingredients (vinegar through water) together in a medium saucepan and bring to a boil. Remove from heat. In a separate pot of boiling water, blanch ramps until limp, about 30 seconds. With a slotted spoon or tongs, remove ramps from boiling water and shock in an ice bath to stop the cooking process. Place ramps in jars, cover with brine, let cool, and refrigerate until ready to use, up to two weeks.

TARTAR SAUCE

2 tablespoons lemon juice
1 tablespoon grainy mustard
½ small onion, minced
1 small clove garlic, minced
3 tablespoons minced pickled ramp
1 tablespoon chopped washed capers
1 cup mayonnaise (follow standard recipe or use organic store-bought mayonnaise)
Chopped fresh herbs: may include a mix of dill, parsley, tarragon, cilantro, and chives
Salt, pepper, and cayenne to taste

In a medium-sized container, combine lemon juice, mustard, onion, garlic, ramp, and capers. Let rest five minutes to infuse. Fold in mayonnaise, herbs, and seasonings. Refrigerate until ready to use.

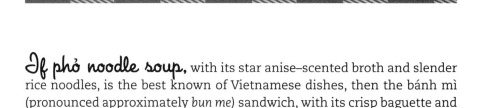

The Vietnamese Bánh Mì Sandwich

2

Darling of the Twin Cities Foodie Scene

LORI WRITER / PHOTOGRAPHS BY KATIE CANNON

𝒪𝒻 𝓅𝒽ở 𝓃𝑜𝑜𝒹𝓁𝑒 𝓈𝑜𝓊𝓅, with its star anise–scented broth and slender rice noodles, is the best known of Vietnamese dishes, then the bánh mì (pronounced approximately *bun me*) sandwich, with its crisp baguette and layers of creamy pâté, crunchy vegetables, and savory cold cuts, might be the most mysterious.

Isaac Becker, executive chef and owner of 112 Eatery in Minneapolis, says, "I've always loved them. To me, it seems like the kind of thing cooks might eat. I saw a recipe a couple of years ago. Before that, I didn't know what was in them." Chris Stevens, chef and owner of Blackbird Café in Minneapolis, says of bánh mì sandwiches, "When we first had them, we would need to eat lunch quick just to stop and go. We always just hit places on University [Avenue in St. Paul]. And we thought: 'Gosh why doesn't anyone know about this sandwich?'"

Stevens continues:

It's this great amalgamation of cultures. It's a French sandwich, but all of these Vietnamese ingredients. It's so awesome. There's different kinds of pork, spicy chilies, and pickled carrots. But then it's on a baguette and it's got pâté on it. I just think it's really fun. It's a pretty rich sandwich with the mayonnaise on there, but I like that you can bite into it and at one point get a jalapeño that is super spicy. And that kind of lingers with you. And the cilantro's super fresh. And you get the tartness of the pickled vegetables and the meat is just kind of there as a nice base. Sometimes you get a lot of the liver flavor in there. It's a super-fresh sandwich, I think, as opposed to a big greasy burger or something.

Says Peter Phan Nguyen, owner of Ala Francaise French Bakery in St. Paul, "It's cheap and easy. If you order it, you can get it right away; you don't have to wait. It's fast food, just like a hamburger here [in America]. You can walk, eat. You can sit down, eat. Watch TV, eat. Playing around, you can eat. And on the bus you can eat. At the office, you can eat."

In the thirty-five years since the fall of Saigon in April 1975, when waves of Vietnamese refugees fled their homeland and started arriving in the United States, Vietnamese cuisine in general and the bánh mì sandwich in particular have captivated Minnesotans' palates. Anthony Bourdain, chef, author, and host of the Travel Channel's culinary tourism program *No Reservations*, told *Minnesota Monthly*'s James Norton in 2007, "Minnesota has some of the best Vietnamese food in America." The cuisine was virtually unknown in Minnesota in the early 1970s, but by the early 1980s Vietnamese restaurants were flourishing. And by 2010, the bánh mì sandwich, surfing high on the crest of a charcuterie wave sweeping the nation, crossed over into the mainstream and started splashing onto menus all over the Twin Cities.

Bánh mì sandwiches appear today not only on menus of the Vietnamese establishments that introduced them to Minnesota but also on the menus of high-end Minneapolis restaurants. Examples of the former, serving traditional sandwiches, include those dotting St. Paul's University Avenue, such as Saigon Restaurant and Bakery and Trung Nam French Bakery, and those clustered along Minneapolis's Nicollet Avenue, better known as "Eat Street," including Jasmine Deli and Quang Restaurant. Fine dining establishments offering contemporary interpretations of the sandwich include Minneapolis's 20.21 Restaurant and Bar by Wolfgang Puck in the Walker Art Center and 112 Eatery in the warehouse district. At a moderate price point, the bánh mì sandwich is a cornerstone of the menu at Blackbird Café in Minneapolis, is on the lunch menu of Ngon Vietnamese Bistro in St. Paul, and appears occasionally as a special at delis around the Twin Cities. There are even vegan interpretations of the sandwich.

To tell the story of the bánh mì sandwich is to explore a general culinary history of Vietnam. Vietnamese cuisine is a gastronomic patchwork that reflects a thousand years of domination by the Chinese; nine centuries of independence while fending off European, Mongolian, and Chinese invasions and pushing southward into the Mekong River delta, annexing Cham and Khmer territory; and seven decades of French colonization that ended in 1954. The Chinese, Mongols, and French have retreated, but their influence on the cuisine lingers. *Bánh* is the Vietnamese word for "cake" or "bread." The bánh mì sandwich uses a French baguette as its foundation and calls for mayonnaise, butter, or both—also introduced by the French. Chinese-inspired char siu pork also appears as a frequent filling in Vietnamese sandwiches. The French introduced modern food processors that enabled Vietnamese home cooks to make pâté, no longer the exclusive domain of specialists, who mixed it in vast quantities using mortar and pestle.

Bánh mì components at Vina Vietnamese Restaurant, Richfield

Fresh ingredients are a hallmark of Vietnamese cuisine. Caroline Nguyen Ticarro-Parker, cofounder and executive director of the Catalyst Foundation in Northfield, which provides humanitarian relief programs in Vietnam and sponsors annual culture camps for families that have adopted Vietnamese children, says, "In Vietnam, in general, everything is fresher. Everything was either picked that day or made that day. There is no option for storage. You have to be a wealthy family to own a fridge, and even then, it would be very small. You buy what you need for the day and cook it immediately, like [in] Europe." Ticarro-Parker, who frequently travels to Vietnam, adds, "There's something about buying it from a street vendor. Every vendor is in competition. There's a lot of drama trying to maneuver through traffic to your favorite vendor."

Ticarro-Parker left Vietnam with her parents and three brothers in April 1975, arriving in the United States in November. "I turned five en route," she recalls. As far as availability of ingredients, Ticarro-Parker says it's difficult even today to find what she needs outside of the Minneapolis–St. Paul metropolitan area, explaining, "It's two hours round trip from Northfield. It's a field trip. Cilantro is the only thing I can find [locally]." She muses, "I don't know how my mom did it. She grew a lot of herbs herself, though she didn't know how to keep them alive in winter. She didn't want to bring them inside, but it's hard to keep them outside in Minnesota. My mom would be totally appalled to see me pull lemongrass out of the freezer."

The *St. Paul Pioneer Press and Dispatch* reported on June 12, 1985, that the newly arrived Vietnamese first introduced their food to Minnesotans at the Festival of Nations in 1976. Ngo Nhung, of Phoenix Restaurant on Grand Avenue, was one of the first Vietnamese restaurateurs, but he soon faced fierce rivals. Ngo reportedly told the *Dispatch*'s Eleanor Ostman, "Competition is getting tough. Vietnamese restaurants are opening all over town."

First Impressions

Thuy Nguyen, owner of Vina Restaurant in Richfield—and the founder's daughter—believes Vina was the first in Minneapolis–St. Paul to call itself a "Vietnamese" restaurant. Nguyen was eighteen in the summer of 1980 when she fled Vietnam in a boat with her parents and four siblings. After enduring seven months in refugee camps, first in Thailand, then in the Philippines, the family flew to Minnesota, where Nguyen's maternal uncle lived. "Refugees are prioritized by relationship," she explains. The Nguyens considered moving to Louisiana, where two of her paternal aunts lived, or to California, where another maternal uncle lived. But, upon seeking advice in the camps, they were told, "If you want a good education, go north." So, Nguyen, concludes, "my uncle did the paperwork." She continues, "We came in 1981. And my cousin owned a Vietnamese restaurant already in Minnesota called Que Viet Village House in Northeast Minneapolis. At the time, if I remember correctly, there were about four or five Vietnamese restaurants, but none of them said 'Vietnamese restaurant.' They always said 'American-Chinese restaurant.' I think in 1980 Minnesotans didn't know anything about [Vietnamese food]."

The day after Nguyen arrived in Minnesota, she began working at her cousin's restaurant, which offered an American breakfast menu mornings from six to eleven and a Vietnamese menu alongside an American menu from eleven to seven. Nguyen explains, "[My cousin] was afraid they would not accept our food." But, when Que Viet became very popular about a year after the Nguyens arrived, Yen Bui, Nguyen's mother, opened her own restaurant, Vina on Cleveland Avenue in St. Paul's Highland Park neighborhood—without an American menu.

"My mom had a restaurant in Vietnam. She had already been in the restaurant business since 1964–65. So she had plenty of experience," says Nguyen. "If we were going to open a restaurant, we were going to say 'Vietnamese' because they learn and accept it. And that's how we were probably the first one to say 'Vietnamese restaurant.' Before, they would always say 'Chinese' or 'Chinese-Vietnamese.'"

Nguyen recalls that Vina struggled at first:

My mom opened the restaurant in December '82. And I remember it was really cold. And nobody came to the restaurant. I walked to the *Highland Villager,* the local paper, and I dropped my business card. And my English was so poor. But, [I said:] "I want you to come to try. If you like it or you hate it, just try it, our new restaurant." They never showed up. We were begging them to come, but they never showed up.

I think about a half year later, the *Star Tribune* or something came. And they wrote a glorious paper about us. And they interviewed [restaurateur] Leeann Chin . . . and asked her what restaurant she would go and try. She said, "Vina." Boom! That's when the whole thing started.

And I remember '83 or '84, our restaurant was about two or three doors from the Highland Cinema theater. And there's a line going to the theater, and a line going to Vina. It was so cold, but people waited in line. It was always busy.

Eventually, Yen Bui opened four locations. The second, in Richfield, is the only one that remains in the family today, the others having been sold to employees over the years. Nguyen attended the University of Minnesota, where she earned a double major in chemistry and chemical engineering. She worked at 3M before returning to school for an MBA. After working for the Radisson Hotel in Washington, DC, and downtown Minneapolis, then for Hennepin County/Environmental Management, Nguyen was persuaded by her mother, who has since retired, to rejoin the family business. "My parents are snowbirds now," Nguyen chuckles.

Nguyen says that the success of Vina, Que Viet, and Lotus restaurants fueled a trend in the 1980s of opening new Vietnamese establishments. According to *20 Years After—The Resettlement of the Vietnamese Refugees in Minnesota,* "In the late 1970's there were only a few Vietnamese restaurants like Kim Long, Bamboo or Phoenix in St. Paul[. However,] by 1995 there are already over 70 such establishments in the Twin Cities—which averages out to one restaurant per 250 Vietnamese Minnesotans, a ratio that is almost twice as dense as in the general population." Similarly, Ostman's *Pioneer Press and Dispatch* article reported, "Just as the exodus of the best chefs from Communist China in the late 1940s made Hong Kong and New York the capitals of Chinese cooking, the best Vietnamese food may ultimately be found in the United States. The Twin Cities, after an extraordinary influx of refugees, have at least as many Vietnamese restaurants as any areas in this country—probably more."

Vina Restaurant does not offer bánh mì sandwiches on its menu, although advance orders are taken on occasion. "We don't have [it] every day. In order to have a good sandwich, it has to be fresh. You cannot have leftover bread from the day before, and to maintain that freshness, if you're selling one or two a day, it's not worth it," Nguyen explains. Vina's specialties are crispy egg rolls and hot and spicy chicken.

Ha Nguyen, owner of Que Nha Vietnamese Restaurant in St. Paul, says her restaurant no longer serves bánh mì, despite the beautiful display of full-color sandwich photographs lining the wall behind the counter. "Too labor intensive," she says. Nguyen made the photos when she was a university student. "I have to take those down," she says.

Peter Phan Nguyen, owner of Ala Francaise French Bakery in St. Paul's Frogtown neighborhood, believes his bakery, which he originally opened at Lexington and University avenues in 1985, was the first in the city to offer bánh mì sandwiches to the public. He says, "Maybe we are the first one to get the sandwich." Nguyen was a seminary student, not a baker, in Phan Thiết, a city in southeastern Vietnam, before he fled the country, alone, in July 1976, when he was twenty-six. "When I escaped the communists, [it was] very hard to take the whole family. The communists tried to catch me and put me in prison. I had to escape somewhere. Finally, I escaped by boat." Nguyen and thirty-seven others spent two days afloat in the ocean, until they were rescued by an English ship, which transported them to a camp in Brunei. Nguyen spent six months in Brunei before flying to Minnesota, which he chose on a friend's advice: "I got

Peter Phan Nguyen, owner of Ala Francaise French Bakery, St. Paul

a friend of mine here, who lived here. That's why I connect with him." Nguyen continues, chuckling, "I didn't know [Minnesota had] a lot of snow. When I got off the airplane, I thought, 'What?' The whole city was white. I didn't know. I thought maybe the sand was white."

Nguyen went to college and then joined Catholic Charities as a social worker. "When you live somewhere you know environment here. That's why you don't want to leave it. I worked at Catholic Charities . . . helping many people to resettle to Minnesota here. I helped them to find a job. And [I was] interpreting, and [helping them] look for housing. Looking for employment. That's why a lot of people know me. That's why I don't want to leave them."

Nguyen got into the bakery business when a friend in Seattle came to Minnesota to show him how to make sandwiches. Nguyen flew to France

Bánh mì sandwiches prepared at Ala Francaise

for lessons in making croissants. He estimates the bakery's daily output at fifteen hundred crisp French baguettes—three hundred of which are used to make bánh mì sandwiches—and a couple hundred buttery, French-style croissants. Bread making—mixing, shaping, proofing, and baking the dough—begins at four o'clock in the morning and lasts until nine.

Ala Francaise makes only one style of sandwich, and that's the classic bánh mì thịt nguoi "special," with julienned carrots and daikon, barbecued pork, mayonnaise, a sprig of cilantro, a slice of jalapeño, and, of course, the crisp baguette—all prepared in-house. Ala Francaise purchases the banana leaf–steamed pork sausage, the ham (headcheese), and the pâté from California because they are hard to "get just right." Ala Francaise's bánh mì sandwich is an exercise in restraint, with only smudges and pinches of each ingredient layered onto the baguette.

Nguyen says that the most important part of a bánh mì sandwich is "what's inside." As far as the baguette, the interior should be soft and the exterior "crispy and flaky. Not chewy." At Ala Francaise, the key to the crusty baguette is baking with steam. Baguettes in Vietnam are very light. They rise quickly, says Nguyen, "due to the weather." Nguyen says that though most bakeries in Saigon use electricity, some bakeries in Vietnam bake by wood fire. "It makes a different taste," he explains.

Ala Francaise no longer sells directly to the public. Its customers today are restaurants and grocery stores, such as Shuang Hur in both Minneapolis and St. Paul and Sun Foods in Brooklyn Park. "Even from Wisconsin," says Nguyen. In 1995, Nguyen bought the building on University Avenue in which his bakery operates today, moving his giant Swedish double oven, the size of a walk-in closet, with him. Tam Phan, a freelance journalist and former Vietnam News Agency reporter who accompanied us on our tour of Ala Francaise, gestures to Nguyen with a grin, "Someday, he'll own all of St. Paul."

Vina isn't the only Vietnamese restaurant operating under the management of a second generation of restaurateurs. Saigon Restaurant and Bakery on University Avenue is also being led by the next generation. But Hai Truong took a different path. In 2007, Truong and his wife opened Ngon Vietnamese Bistro, "a modern Vietnamese restaurant" with "seasonal fusion entrées [that] stay true to the flavors of Vietnamese cuisine, while providing a contemporary twist to traditional dishes." *"Ngon,"* says Truong, "is Vietnamese for 'delicious.'"

Truong was born in Saigon but immigrated to Minnesota with his family in 1979, when he was five. He grew up in the Riverside community in Minneapolis, "where most of the Vietnamese were," and remembers being struck by the tall buildings. Today, Truong lives two blocks from his restaurant, which is located on St. Paul's University Avenue in the space formerly occupied by his father's Caravelle Restaurant. Truong, who bused tables growing up, believes Caravelle was one of the first Vietnamese restaurants to open in the neighborhood, which in 1984 was otherwise dominated by stores such as Crazy Louie's Surplus City. Operating a restaurant back then, says Truong, was "what was available as part of immigrant jobs, and what you needed to do to provide for your family."

Asked why bánh mì sandwiches have recently become the darling of the foodie scene, Truong comments, "Sandwiches are trendy in this economy. People are looking

The sandwich at Ngon Vietnamese Bistro, St. Paul

for cheap eats and good flavors." Though bánh mì sandwiches are "traditionally a small snack food, almost like fast food," Truong wanted "to create a heartier, meal sandwich" for Ngon's weekday lunch menu, "using the same components" of the classic bánh mì, but with "more meat than bread." Ngon's sandwich begins with a baguette from Ala Francaise because Truong likes the structure and consistency "crispy and a little soft. We use the long baguettes and cut them up instead of using the small [six-inch] ones, so you don't end up with just the ends." Ngon's cooks prepare everything else for their sandwich, including the sweet potato fries and spicy aioli that accompany it, from scratch: marinated and grilled Duroc natural pork loin, pâté, and pickled vegetables. Truong chose pork loin over the classic red Chinese char siu pork or grilled pork shoulder because it offers "less fat and a lot more flavor. Sometimes shoulder is chewy." The pâté, according to Truong, is the most difficult to get right in terms of consistency and flavor. "You want a buttery spread," he explains.

Crossing into the Mainstream

Husband and wife team Chris Stevens, chef, and Gail Mollner, manager, launched Blackbird Café, offering "traditional bistro classics, and comfort foods with a twist," in South Minneapolis in 2007. Blackbird, and its bánh mì—barbecued pork, liverwurst, pickled vegetables, and jalapeños on focaccia bread—were embraced as neighborhood favorites nearly immediately. Stevens and Mollner were inspired to include a bánh mì sandwich on their menu because they'd enjoyed the ones they'd tried at the various Vietnamese establishments in St. Paul along University Avenue, near where they live. Stevens says, "It's cool going to Saigon in St. Paul and you pay three bucks for a sandwich and it's a good deal, but it's not always like the best quality meat. So I was thinking I wanted to make one that would be super tasty and delicious."

Stevens says Blackbird's bánh mì is

> pretty typical in terms of the different kinds of ingredients that are on there. We do use really nice-quality pork—we get Berkshire pork from Six Point Farm in southwestern Minnesota. We use shoulder. Then we put a spice rub on it—it has a lot of ginger, a lot of garlic, cumin, coriander, maybe some cinnamon and a few other things in it—then let that sit on it for twenty-four hours. And then we slow braise it six, eight hours, until it's falling apart. Then we shred that meat and use that on the sandwich. We get a nice liverwurst—we were using Nueske's for a while; then we were getting one out of Milwaukee, Usinger's. Just put that on the bottom of the bun, then the shredded pork, then we got some carrots that we pickle in lemon juice, ginger, and a little bit of sugar and tamari. Then there's cilantro, jalapeños, cucumbers, a little bit of mayonnaise. We kind of put it all together.

As far as the bread, Stevens says that, at first, they purchased the baguettes from Trung Nam French Bakery, near their home, but the bakery didn't open early enough. "It was a nightmare logistically," explains Stevens. "So we get these little focaccia rolls from New French that work really well. Not super traditional, but I don't think it really matters."

Stevens and Mollner credit the flagging economy and the maturing of Minnesota's food community for driving the recent increased interest in bánh mì sandwiches. Says Stevens,

> My sous chef, Adam To, his dad worked with Leann Chin in her original restaurant—his dad is from Vietnam. They used to eat bánh mì and bánh bao and all of the stuff that we're getting used to now when [Adam] was a kid growing up, and that would be lunch. It's really weird how it's finally filtered down.
>
> In '05, '06, and before everyone had to stop and check themselves on how much they are spending on eating out, [the bánh mì] wasn't a big deal because it was just a sandwich and there [were] other things that people were intrigued about in terms of cuisine from Vietnam. People are now figuring out how to lower their price point and make things be a really good value.

He continues, "When we first did it, we costed it out, and we said, 'We're going to have to charge nine dollars for this thing,' but part of it is that you're using expensive meat and that sort of thing, and it's a bigger sandwich than you might find at Saigon or for a street food kind of a thing, so that was part of it. It's upscaling it, using higher-quality ingredients and making it a more substantial sandwich rather than just a snacky thing."

Mollner adds, "The food community in the last seven, eight years has changed dramatically. We used to be the only white people eating in a restaurant on University. The only place [where white people ate] before used to be Krua Thai, before they changed ownership. Now, with Ngon opening [. . .] people are now more comfortable thinking of bánh mì as a comfort food, as part of their food identity as a white person. It's not high art cuisine." Stevens concludes, "It's great to see the food culture really grow up."

Isaac Becker, executive chef at 112 Eatery in Minneapolis's warehouse district and finalist three years running for the James Beard Foundation's prestigious Best Chef: Midwest award, says his inspiration for the duck pâté bánh mì sandwich came when he "saw a recipe for one. And the head chef at 112 had just made a duck pâté and didn't know how to get it on the menu. It was a nice, elegant, refined pâté, and I thought it would be a nice twist to combine with all of the spices and vegetables in a bánh mì sandwich." The eatery's bánh mì sandwich, which is small but rich, starts with a baguette from New French Bakery that is crisped in the oven, brushed with sesame oil and soy sauce, smeared with mayonnaise, heaped with a finely shredded napa cabbage and carrot slaw, loaded with a generous slab of pâté, topped with fresh cilantro leaves, pierced with a toothpick, sliced, and then served with a ramekin of spicy house-made pickles.

At 112 Eatery, Minneapolis

"We have a whole street food section on our menu," says Becker. "The veal tongue with soba noodles, the bacon, egg, and harissa sandwich, the hamburger. All kinds of small snack-sized dishes. We only charge five or six dollars for [the bánh mì sandwich]."

Executive chef Asher Miller of the stylish 20.21 Restaurant and Bar in Minneapolis says 20.21's bánh mì pork sandwich, with pickled vegetables, country-style pâté, and fingerling potatoes, is at sixteen dollars "the fanciest one, and the most expensive one, I've ever seen." As Miller renovated 20.21's lunch menu, he "wanted to come up with a sandwichy, more casual kind of lunch . . . Bánh mì sandwiches seem to be the new thing right now, and it sort of makes sense. It's an Asian restaurant, and you think, what's an Asian sandwich? And that's the bánh mì." Miller collaborated with Scott Drewno, executive chef at Wolfgang Puck's the Source Restaurant in Washington, DC, and, of course, Puck himself, the Los Angeles–based Austrian celebrity chef, to develop the sandwich.

If Ala Francaise's bánh mì sandwich is an exercise in restraint, 20.21's is the polar opposite, an application of lush decadence. Miller says he's "trying to make every ingredient really, really good. There's so much more than just a Vietnamese sandwich going on. There's the French pâté, French roll, Korean chili paste [used in one of the two mayonnaises with which the sandwiches are dressed], Szechuan-style potatoes on the side, and the American pickles, and the Asian vinaigrette."

One key ingredient in 20.21's version is "a French country-style pâté, which means it's chunky." The pâté is wrapped in Nueske's applewood smoked bacon, which, Miller says, "is really consistent. Some bacons are all fat and just a little meat, whereas Nueske's is consistently mostly meat." Miller adds, "It's [rare] to see a really well-executed, traditional pâté."

Miller tries to keep a balanced pairing of sweet and spicy, which is "Wolfgang's concept" and the "jumping-off point" for everything the restaurant does. "Sweet and spicy," says Miller, "appeals to a lot of palates. The trick is not to be too strong in either direction." His restaurant's sandwich has "a lot of sweet things going on, even with the pickles." The Asian vinaigrette, in which the scallions and cilantro leaves are tossed, "has a hint of sweet." The Korean kalbi-style mixture in which 20.21 marinates its pork begins with pureed onions and Sprite.

Says Miller, "The most important part of the sandwich is the bread. If you have crappy bread, it doesn't matter what you put on it: it's going to be a crappy sandwich." And so 20.21's cooks experimented with eight different baguettes until finally settling on New French Bakery's par-baked six-inch sourdough roll. They even experimented with baking their own, but, Miller explains, "when you only make four or five sandwiches a day for lunch service, it's impossible to get consistent good results." He adds, "The trick is to have a really crusty, crumbly outside and a soft and warm, toasty inside. That's a common theme in all bánh mì sandwiches."

Bánh mì sandwiches, once unfamiliar to many Minnesotans, are no longer just for the 20,570 individuals of Vietnamese ancestry who live in the state today. Bánh mì have worked their way into mainstream consciousness. Sometimes it's hard to know whether they have become more American than Vietnamese, like the people who brought their traditions with them over the seas thirty-five years ago. One of those refugees, successful restaurateur Thuy Nguyen, observes, "I now dream in English."

photo by BECCA DILLEY

EXECUTIVE CHEF/OWNER Isaac Becker, 112 Eatery, Minneapolis: "I always get them from **Quang Deli**. Love the bread. The baguette at 112 is fine, but theirs is great. Their sandwiches are quite a bit bigger, full of more stuff."

Executive chef **Asher Miller**, 20.21 Restaurant and Bar by Wolfgang Puck, Minneapolis, tried his first bánh mì sandwich at **Jasmine Deli** on Nicollet in Minneapolis: "It was really good." He says, "I like to buy sandwiches for the kitchen crew at **Shuang Hur** grocery store [which are from Ala Francaise Bakery, St. Paul] in Minneapolis. Only two dollars in the grocery line." But Miller's all-time favorite was at **Blackbird Café** in Minneapolis, before the restaurant was destroyed by fire in February 2010. "Their bread was really good," says Miller, speaking in spring 2010, before Blackbird Café reopened in their new location that fall. "They put more attention into the simple elements. Really solid." Of 20.21's own sandwich, Miller says, "The La Belle Vie guys have discovered it. That's a good thing, right?"

Chef/owner **Chris Stevens**, Blackbird Café, Minneapolis: "I like Isaac's a lot at **112**; that's really good. I haven't had the one at 20.21, yet; that would be really fun. I like when they are made fresh, when they are still warm. **Saigon's** is good, but they are hit or miss." Of Saigon's atmosphere in its former location, he remembers, "The old Long John Silver's space. They totally came in and just slapped some paint on the walls. They still had the ropes on there. It was just so fun to get in line. They made it right in front of you. That was my favorite. To go in there and have them make it for you."

photo by BECCA DILLEY

Chef/owner **Karen Cross**, Black Cat Natural Foods, Minneapolis, which introduced a vegan bánh mì sandwich at the Mill City Farmers Market in the spring of 2010: "I think the best bánh mì is at **Saigon** on Uni and Dale. I also like to sample a different bánh mì in the food court at the **Hmong market** off of Como and Rice in St. Paul every time I'm there—if I'm not already stuffed with laab and Hmong sausages."

CEO **Nick Nguyen** of the Tea Garden, multiple locations in the Twin Cities metro area: "My favorite is from **Saigon** restaurant. Their grilled pork sandwich. Their bread is freshly made: crispy and soft. They give you the right proportion of meat and veggies to bread, something that a lot of restaurants don't do. And the way they grill and marinate the pork makes my mouth water just thinking about it."

Contributing writer to *Mpls.St. Paul Magazine* and James Beard Foundation award-winning host of the Travel Channel's *Bizarre Foods* **Andrew Zimmern** wrote in a Twitter post: "Bahn Mi sandwich on new menu at **20.21** in mpls is OFF THE CHARTS . . . street food meets fine dining!" He elaborated in a post on his blog *Chow and Again:* "Their Banh Mi is the best in the Twin Cities, hands down. Superb, high quality ingredients (especially the pate) make this version of my fave Vietnamese street food snack so very tasty, indeed."

Chef/owner **Hai Truong**, Ngon Vietnamese Bistro, St. Paul, likes the pork sandwiches from **Saigon** on University Avenue or the ones he can pick up at the grocery store because "they are quick and convenient." Says Truong, "That's the premise of the whole sandwich. You don't travel far for a bánh mì sandwich." ◐

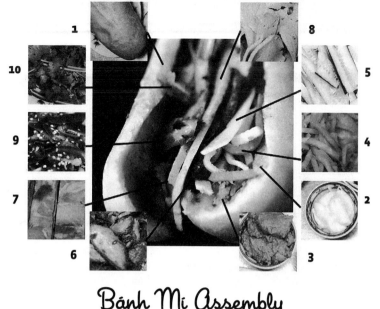

Bánh Mì Assembly

1. Baguette (bánh mì): six-inch French baguette, crisp exterior, soft interior, split with a serrated knife. Contemporary bánh mì sandwiches, such as 20.21's, often call for New French Bakery's sourdough baguette or ciabatta, sliced clean through and toasted. Minneapolis-based New French Bakery distributes its products through a variety of retail grocery and specialty stores throughout Minnesota and the United States.

2. French mayonnaise: a swipe of smooth and rich egg yolk mayonnaise or of butter. Vina Restaurant uses egg yolk whipped with butter. Contemporary sandwiches use multiple or flavored spreads, such as 20.21's drizzle of jalapeño aioli and kochujang aioli or 112 Eatery's brush of soy sauce and sesame oil.

3. Pâté: a smear of smooth and creamy pork liver pâté, spiced with pepper, garlic, or star anise. Contemporary renditions: 112 Eatery uses a thick slice of duck pâté; 20.21 loads its sandwich with two juicy slices of chunky pâté de campagne. Braunschweiger is a good substitute for either the classic or contemporary pâté: Blackbird Café uses Nueske's.

4. Pickled carrots and daikon radish (đồ chua): a pinch of crunchy, sweet, and tangy julienned carrots and daikon radish.

5. Cucumber: a spear or thin slice of cool, crisp cucumber, skin on.

6. Barbecued pork (heo xá xíu): two or three thin slices of Chinese-style barbecued pork cushion, skin on. Contemporary sandwiches, such as Ngon Bistro's Vietnamese-style pork sandwiches, typically use heartier portions, leaner loin, and nontraditional marinades.

7. Headcheese (giò thủ): one thin slice of peppery headcheese, traditional sandwiches only. Asian markets, such as United Noodles Oriental Foods, Inc., in Minneapolis, stock Phủ Hu'o'ng brand giò thủ, "head loaf," in the freezer case.

8. Steamed "silky" pork sausage (chả lụa): three thin slices or a pinch of julienned mildly salty and fish-flavored spongy sausage, which Ticarro-Parker calls "Vietnamese bologna," traditional sandwich only. Asian markets, such as United Noodles Oriental Foods, Inc., in Minneapolis, stock chả lụa (giò lụa) in the freezer case.

9. Jalapeño pepper: a thin slice or spear of jalapeño, traditional sandwich only. Contemporary sandwiches typically include a slaw in lieu of the jalapeño.

10. Cilantro: a sprig of fresh cilantro to brighten the flavors. Contemporary sandwiches use leaves only.   [LW]

Traditional Bánh Mì Sandwich

Various component parts make for a complicated sandwich. Follow the recipes provided here, and consult the detailed photograph on page 39 to construct your own version of the bánh mì.

Ala Francaise French Bakery's Mayonnaise
Contributed by Peter Phan Nguyen, owner

Thanh-Mai Phan, University of Minnesota student and daughter of free-lance journalist Tam Phan, believes this sauce is the secret ingredient that makes Ala Francaise's bánh mì sandwich her favorite: "My dad gave them to me when I was little," she says. At Ala Francaise, Nguyen's wife is in charge of making the mayonnaise, in batches large enough to last a week. If you are uncomfortable eating raw eggs, you may want to skip this recipe.

3 egg yolks
⅛ teaspoon salt
¾ cup corn oil (or other vegetable oil)

Place egg yolks and salt into bowl of electric stand mixer fitted with whisk or single beater attachment. (Or use a regular bowl and an electric hand mixer.) With mixer set on high speed, gradually pour in a thin stream of oil, whisking continuously for approximately five minutes, until the mayonnaise becomes thick and concentrated and all of the oil has been used. Make sure the oil is being incorporated as you pour; if it starts to pool, pour more slowly. Cover and refrigerate overnight.

Ala Francaise French Bakery's Pickled Carrots and Daikon Radish (Đồ chua)

Contributed by Peter Phan Nguyen, owner

This recipe yields vegetables that are mildly pickled and still crisp. According to Nguyen, the amount of sugar is flexible depending on who prepares it and whether they prefer the vegetables "more sour or more sweet." Let the marinade cool before pouring it over the vegetables, or they will spoil.

2–6 tablespoons sugar
¾ cup distilled white vinegar
1⅝ cups water
1¼ pounds carrots, washed, peeled, and julienned manually or using a
   mandolin
¼ pound daikon radish, washed, peeled, and julienned manually or using a mandolin.

1. Add first three ingredients (sugar through water) to a saucepan, cover, and bring to a boil. Boil for several minutes, then turn the heat to low and simmer, covered, an additional 15 minutes. Remove marinade from heat and let cool.
2. Place julienned carrots and daikon in a large bowl. Pour cooled marinade over carrots and daikon. Stir. Cover and refrigerate overnight.

Vina Restaurant's Roast Pork (Heo xá xíu)

Contributed by Thuy Nguyen, owner

This roast pork is fragrant with the scent of star anise from the five-spice powder. The food coloring gives the pork its characteristic red hue. It's traditional to leave the fat on for added flavor and juicer texture, but you can remove it if you wish.

1 teaspoon five-spice powder
½ teaspoon baking soda
½ teaspoon salt
3 teaspoons soy sauce
1 teaspoon sesame oil
A few drops red food coloring (optional)
2 pounds pork butt, sliced into two or three pieces and skin thoroughly
   cleaned (optional: remove skin)

1. Mix first six ingredients (five-spice powder through food coloring, if using) together in a small bowl. Rub mixture evenly over pork. Place pork in a dish and cover with plastic wrap. Refrigerate 5 hours or overnight.

2. Preheat oven to 350°F. Place pork in a roasting pan, cover with aluminum foil, and roast on center oven rack for 40 minutes, or until cooked through. Cool to room temperature.

Ha Nguyen's sister, Thu, emigrated from Saigon nine years ago and brought these recipes with her. Though Que Nha no longer offers bánh mì sandwiches at the restaurant, the family prepares sandwiches, with all the fixings, at home. Ha Nguyen recommends making more than you need, then storing the leftovers in the freezer.

Thu Nguyen's Chả Lụa (also Giò Lụa) (steamed "silky" pork sausage)

Contributed by Ha Nguyen, owner, Que Nha Vietnamese Restaurant

In her book *Into the Vietnamese Kitchen: Treasured Foodways, Modern Flavors,* author Andrea Nguyen writes, "Giò Lụa is the most widely eaten of all of the Vietnamese charcuterie." Caroline Ticarro-Parker refers to it as "Vietnamese bologna."

Traditionally in Vietnam, the meat paste was pounded by hand with a stone mortar and pestle, a task left to skilled professionals. This modern recipe for home cooks suggests using a food processor instead. Most Asian markets carry the pink packets of Alsa brand baking powder.

1 pound fresh lean pork, ground twice
¾ teaspoon sugar
¾ teaspoon salt
1 tablespoon fish sauce
½ cup canola or vegetable oil
1 tablespoon tapioca flour
1 packet (11 grams) baking powder, Alsa brand preferred
½ cup water
Banana leaf, rinsed and wiped dry (or substitute plastic wrap)

1. In a large bowl, mix together ground pork, sugar, salt, fish sauce, and oil. In a separate bowl, mix flour, baking powder, and water. Fold flour mixture into pork mixture. Cover and rest in refrigerator overnight, at least 6 hours.

2. Grind mixture in food processor until very smooth. Dollop onto a banana leaf (or plastic wrap) and roll into a tube shape about 5 inches long. Twist ends so mixture cannot leak out.

3. Fill a wok or large pot with 2 inches water, insert steaming rack, and set over medium-high heat. Bring water to boiling. Place tube on rack, cover, and steam 20 to 25 minutes. Allow sausage to cool. Discard banana leaf (or plastic wrap) when ready to serve.

Thu Nguyen's Pâté (Pa-Tê)

Contributed by Ha Nguyen, owner, Que Nha Vietnamese Restaurant

This recipe produces a creamy, spreadable pâté, which will keep up to ten days in the refrigerator.

2 egg yolks
3 teaspoons sugar
1 teaspoon black pepper
1 teaspoon salt
½ teaspoon star anise powder
1 head garlic, peeled
1 pound pork (or duck or chicken) liver, cut into 1-inch chunks
½ pound fresh lean pork, ground or cut into 1-inch chunks
½ pound pork lard (fatback, skin removed)

1. Using a food processor, work in batches to mix all ingredients (egg yolks through pork lard) together until smooth. Pause occasionally to scrape insides of food processor bowl with a rubber spatula.

2. Fill a wok or large pot with 2 to 3 inches water, insert steaming rack, and set over medium-high heat. Bring water to boiling. Spoon mixture into ceramic bowl, cover with foil, and steam in covered wok or pot for 30 minutes. Allow to cool; then chill at least 12 hours before serving.

Thu Nguyen's Giò Thủ (headcheese)

Contributed by Ha Nguyen, owner, Que Nha Vietnamese Restaurant

Headcheese, which despite its name is not a type of cheese, is traditionally made from the pieces of meat from a pig's head, cooked with gelatinous liquid, formed into a mold, and chilled. To simplify matters for the home cook, this recipe calls for pork shank, pig ears, and pig tongue rather than

the entire head of a pig. The skin, tendons, and cartilage, Ha Nguyen explains, break down to serve as the "glue that holds it all together."

1 pound pork shank, cleaned, skin and tendons intact
½ pound pork ears, scraped clean of stray hairs
½ pound pork tongue, scrubbed and rinsed thoroughly 2 to 3 times
1 ounce dried wood ear mushrooms (also called black fungus), shredded
1–2 tablespoons canola oil
1 head garlic, peeled
½ teaspoon sugar
½ teaspoon salt
½ teaspoon ground black pepper
1 teaspoon black peppercorns
½ tablespoon fish sauce
Banana leaf, rinsed and wiped dry (or substitute plastic wrap)

1. Boil pork shank in an uncovered stock pot over medium heat 15 minutes until cooked about three-quarters of the way through. Drain. When cool enough to handle, slice into ¼-inch-thick pieces the shape and size of a pink rubber eraser.

2. Boil pork ears in an uncovered stock pot over medium heat 15 minutes. Drain, rinse, and let cool. Slice each ear in half lengthwise and then into ¼-inch-thick strips.

3. Boil pork tongue in an uncovered pot over medium heat 3 minutes. Drain, rinse, and then clean tongue again, removing the white top membrane layer from tip to back with a sharp knife or vegetable peeler. Boil tongue for an additional 15 minutes. Drain, rinse, and let cool. Slice in half lengthwise and then into ¼-inch-thick slices.

4. Soak shredded wood ear mushrooms in warm water 1 hour. Drain.

5. To a wok preheated over high heat, add canola oil and then garlic and heat until fragrant. Add pork shank, pork ear, and pork tongue and cook 2 minutes. Add sugar, salt, pepper, peppercorns, fish sauce, and drained mushrooms and cook 15 minutes, stirring frequently, until the gelatin from the ears releases and the meat feels tacky to the touch.

6. Lay down a piece of banana leaf. Cover leaf with a layer of plastic wrap. Pour hot meat mixture onto plastic and form into a loaf shape about 5 inches long. Wrap up loaf into a tight roll. Fold both ends, then enclose in another layer of plastic wrap. Refrigerate overnight. Discard banana leaf. Slice and serve.

Though we have halved and quartered 20.21 Restaurant and Bar's recipes, some of the yields, such as for the Korean kalbi-style marinated pork loin, are still large by home-cooking standards. Given the amount of effort involved in preparing all of the sandwich elements, much of which must be done in advance, we envision home chefs will prepare these sandwiches when entertaining a small crowd. Executive chef Asher Miller suggests shopping Clancy's Meats and Fish or United Noodles Oriental Foods, Inc., both in Minneapolis, for any ingredients not available in your local supermarket. He prefers Diamond Crystal kosher salt because it does not contain an added anti-caking agent.

Contributed by Asher Miller,
executive chef

Jalapeño Aioli

2 cups mayonnaise
1 cup quick pickled jalapeño (recipe follows), chopped

Stir mayonnaise and pickled jalapeño together in mixing bowl. Refrigerate until ready to use.

Quick Pickle

½ pound jalapeño peppers, sliced into ⅛-inch rings (do not remove
    seeds) OR ½ pound carrots, julienned OR ½ pound daikon, julienned
2 cups unseasoned rice wine vinegar
1 cup sugar
½ cup water
1 tablespoon Diamond Crystal kosher salt

Place jalapeños, carrots, or daikon in 1-quart glass canning jar. Set aside. Stir remaining ingredients (vinegar through salt) together in a stainless-steel saucepan. Bring to a boil and let simmer, uncovered, 5 minutes. Pour mixture over vegetables and seal jar with lid. When cool, place jar in refrigerator. Marinate 1 week before using.

Kochujang Aioli

Korean kochujang, also called gochu-jang, kimchi paste, or kimchi base, is a thick, salty paste made from ground chili peppers, fermented soybean paste, and glutinous rice flour. Look for it in jars on the shelves of Asian grocery stores.

1½ cups mayonnaise
½ cup kochujang (Korean chili pepper paste)
2 tablespoons honey
1 tablespoon sesame oil
2 teaspoons superior soy sauce (Miller recommends Pearl River brand)
1 teaspoon mushroom soy sauce

Stir together all ingredients (mayonnaise through mushroom soy sauce) in mixing bowl. Refrigerate until ready to use.

Pâté de Campagne

This pâté is rich, moist, and chunky, with a hint of five-spice powder. Chef Miller says, "It's important to keep everything [tools and ingredients] really cold at all times, or it will turn into a greasy mush." In the book *Charcuterie: The Craft of Salting, Smoking, and Curing*, authors Michael Ruhlman and Brian Polcyn agree: "Until your pâté goes into the oven, you must do all that you can to keep the meat cold. Don't let your ingredients and tools get warm. You don't have to be fanatical about it [. . . ,] but do be slightly paranoid about it." Chill your bowls, blades, and paddle in the freezer, and keep ingredients refrigerated when you're not working with them.

1 large yellow onion, finely diced (about 1 cup)
1 tablespoon unsalted butter
1 teaspoon chopped fresh thyme
¼ cup heavy cream
1 egg
1½ slices white bread, crusts removed and discarded
1/4 pound skin-on fatback, cubed (leave on any tendons)
1 pound pork butt, divided
¼ pound bacon, cubed, divided
½ pound pork liver, cubed, divided
3 cloves garlic, chopped (about ½ tablespoon)

2 tablespoons cognac

1½ tablespoons Diamond Crystal kosher salt

3¾ teaspoons sugar

½ teaspoon black pepper

⅜ teaspoon five-spice powder

Pinch allspice

Bacon slices to line terrine mold (20.21 uses Nueske's Applewood
Smoked Bacon)

1. Preheat oven to 300°F. In a skillet over medium heat, sweat onions in butter until soft. Stir in thyme. Remove from heat and allow to cool. In a small bowl, stir together cream and egg. Lay bread slices in a small dish. Pour cream and egg mixture over bread and set aside.

2. Grind all of the fatback, half the pork butt, half the bacon, and half the pork liver on ¼-inch meat grinder setting. Set aside in the refrigerator or freezer. Grind remaining pork butt, bacon, and pork liver; garlic through allspice; cooked onions; and bread mixture on 3/16-inch grinder setting. Set aside in the refrigerator or freezer.

3. In an electric mixer fitted with paddle attachment, mix first reserved meat mixture until thoroughly combined, and then add in reserved meat, spices, and bread mixture. Chill until ready to use.

4. Brush inside of terrine mold with oil, then line with plastic wrap, allowing several inches to overhang. Line with bacon slices until inside of mold is completely covered. Using a spoon or rubber spatula, dollop or thwack mixture into mold, then cover surface with additional bacon slices. Fold over plastic wrap to cover. Place either terrine lid or aluminum foil over the top.

5. Place terrine mold in a bath of hot tap water, covering the sides of the mold by 1 to 2 inches, and then place on the middle rack of preheated oven. Cook until a temperature probe at the terrine's center shows an internal temperature of 150°F. Remove from oven and cool to room temperature. Drain water bath and weigh terrine down lightly with a rolling pin. Refrigerate until ready to use. Slice ¼ inch thick for bánh mì.

Korean Kalbi-style Marinated Pork Loin

Chef Miller uses a Korean-inspired kalbi marinade, more typically used for grilled short ribs, to marinate the pork loin in this recipe. The Sprite in the marinade serves to balance the kochujang chili paste, making this dish neither overwhelmingly spicy nor overwhelmingly sweet.

¼ cup Sprite soft drink
½ medium white onion, chopped (about ½ cup), pureed in food processor until smooth
5 pounds pork loin or pork butt, trimmed of sinew and fat, cut into 1-ounce segments, pounded to ⅛ inch thick
1 cup sugar
½ cup sesame seeds, toasted
1 tablespoon coarse-ground Korean chili flakes
8 stalks green onion, greens and whites thinly sliced
12 cloves garlic, finely chopped (about ¼ cup)
2 tablespoons ginger root, finely chopped
1¼ cups soy sauce
1 cup plus 2 tablespoons honey
1 cup Chinese rice wine
1¼ cups toasted sesame oil
½ cup kochujang (Korean chili pepper paste)
Peanut oil
Diamond Crystal kosher salt

1. Stir Sprite into white onion puree. Layer pork in baking dish and cover with onion mixture. Cover with plastic wrap and refrigerate 24 hours.
2. Stir together next eleven ingredients (sugar through kochujang) in large bowl.
3. Remove pork from pre-marinade; discard pre-marinade. In a new baking dish, layer kalbi marinade and pork. Cover with plastic wrap and marinate, refrigerated, at least overnight or up to 3 days.
4. Lightly coat a skillet with peanut oil and place over low heat. Add marinated pork slices to skillet in a single layer and season lightly with salt. Cook 1 minute, then flip. Season lightly with salt. Cook 1 additional minute, until no pink remains. Remove from heat and serve.

Asian Salad

2 tablespoons roasted white and black sesame seeds
1 tablespoon Diamond Crystal kosher salt
½ teaspoon white pepper
1½ cups ginger vinegar (recipe follows)
1¼ cups peanut oil
¼ cup sesame oil
2½ tablespoons chili oil
Scallions, bias sliced
Cilantro leaves

Make vinaigrette by combining first seven ingredients (sesame seeds through chili oil) in a large bowl; mix well. Toss scallions and cilantro in vinaigrette. Set aside.

Ginger Vinegar

This vinegar will last two months in the refrigerator.

¾ cup sugar
16 ounces unseasoned rice wine vinegar
6 ounces ginger root, peeled and sliced into paper-thin ribbons with a
    knife or Japanese mandolin

In medium saucepan over medium-high heat, stir together sugar and vinegar and bring to a simmer. Do not allow mixture to boil. Remove from heat and stir in ginger. Allow to steep for 2 to 4 hours. When cool, refrigerate mixture in glass container.

3 Pasties and Porketta
The Soul of the Iron Range

JAMES NORTON / PHOTOGRAPHS BY BECCA DILLEY

> "Pasties and porketta represent seminal historic demographic changes that changed the face of the Range . . . and state history, when you get down to it."
>
> *Aaron Brown,* WRITER AND FIFTH-GENERATION IRON RANGER

"Melting pot" surely ranks among the most potent two-word expressions of American identity, right up there with *Second Amendment* and *World Series*. In three short syllables, you conjure up discussions of race, class, ethnicity, immigration, culture, and civic identity. At the same time, you've expressed the still controversial and complicated idea that America is a place where people immigrate, full of hope, and become part of a culture that blends a potent new brew from the citizens of the world.

But when you hear the words *melting pot,* you're almost certainly transported to a big city on the East Coast, circa 1920 or 1930. You're probably in the Lower East Side of New York, among the tenements, where clothes are hung out to dry on lines stretched between buildings and where the honking of the newly popular car horn is just beginning to assert itself over the singsong sales pitch of the roaming sidewalk vendor. What you're probably not thinking about is a string of mining and lumber towns splayed out across northeastern Minnesota.

And yet: the allure of stable work and educational opportunities for the next generation made the Range a destination for successive waves of immigrants. They hailed from forty-three nations by one count, according to author Ann L. Burckhardt, writing in *A Cook's Tour of Minnesota*. Ore was first noted in the region in the 1850s, but at that point the main appeal of the Range was still primarily as a source of massive stands of white pine. Logging would take off near the end of the nineteenth century: by 1901, thirty thousand lumberjacks were working the forests. And as that boom faded, mining claimed its place as an engine of settlement and commercial activity.

Completion of the Erie Canal in 1832 and the Sault Ste. Marie locks in the middle of the nineteenth century opened the world market to Minnesota. The first major commercial shipment of Minnesota iron ore was made in 1884 from the Soudan underground mine on the Vermilion Range, which stretches between Tower and Ely; it wasn't long before the Mesabi Range came on line in 1892, followed by the Cuyuna in the early part of the twentieth century. As mines began to drive and then dominate the local economy in northeastern and north-central Minnesota, the industry acted as a magnet for immigrants, a number of whom began to turn to labor activism as sometimes brutal conditions became intolerable. Despite the struggle over the economic fruits of the mines, however, business boomed. By 1950, Minnesota was providing 62 percent of the iron ore consumed by the nation, an enormous technological and commercial achievement that fueled the U.S. effort in World War II and long-term development of the Iron Range itself.

While mining is never a piece of cake, early conditions were particularly brutal. Author and Iron Range native Mary Ellen Mancina-Batinich talked to Santino "Sam" Aluni—a miner and grocer from Virginia, Minnesota—about the early days for her book *Italian Voices: Making Minnesota Our Home*: "Working conditions were terrible and the men went out on strike in 1907. The company brought in lots of men from the Balkans—Slovenians and Montenegrins—and put them to work. They killed 'em like flies. They were green, you know, they never worked in a mine. There was terrible hatred for the mining companies. They were terrible people when they began here."

Aluni, who participated in a landmark 1916 strike against the mining companies, put the experience of working on the Range in stark terms: "The federal government was against the people. The state government was against the people. The county government was against the people. Our own city police worked alongside the company gunmen and arrested and clubbed the strikers. The businessmen were even against the workers and sided with the company. They were mad because when the miners went on strike, they didn't make no money so they couldn't spend no money."

Aluni was part of the Italian wave of workers who, along with Slavs, followed on the heels of Finnish workers. Tom Forti, the flinty and deeply knowledgeable owner of the Sunrise Deli in Hibbing, has a perspective

Porketta sandwich (featuring Fraboni's porketta) at Zimmy's, Hibbing

on the region's history—and its melting pot character—that's informed by multiple generations of commerce and life on the Range. "Isn't it strange that the Italians would come to this godforsaken cold place?" Forti asks at the beginning of our conversation. "The first settlers here after the loggers were Scandinavians to work the mines. The Scandinavians, as you know, have a more socialistic mindset. And they formed unions."

Aaron Brown, an author and blogger from an old Range family, studied the history of the region for his book *Overburden: Modern Life on the Iron Range.* I met Brown in downtown Hibbing's Bob Dylan–themed restaurant, Zimmy's, where we both ate porketta sandwiches while he talked about the past, present, and future of the Range. "The first big strike was 1907," says Brown,

> It was led by the Finns, who were 90-something percent literate, coming out of Finland, compared with virtually no literacy among immigrants from other countries. They were able to say, "Hey! Look what they're doing: they're pitting immigrants against one another, they're underpaying us."
>
> The Finns lead the first strike, and it's crushed. The Finns are blacklisted here for about ten years. They moved out to places like Cherry, where I'm from, and they farm—well, they grow rocks. They live off the land to some extent. The Finns get beat because the other groups would cross the picket line—the Italians, the Slavs.

Knowledge of sophisticated underground mining comes only with time, and at a high price paid in both blood and money. Therefore, when the Iron Range began its life as an ore-exporting region, experienced foremen were brought in to oversee the operations on-site. Fortunately for mine owners, a tremendously qualified workforce was becoming available. Cornwall, England, was home to some of the world's most experienced underground miners, and their diaspora (to places including Mexico, South Africa, and the desert Southwest) was key to the Range's development into a mining powerhouse. "The first mines up here were underground," says Forti. "The Cornish had experience in underground mining. They first came to Michigan to work the copper mines, and then they found iron. Then when underground mines [were developed] here, they came here."

Brown, of Cornish descent, uses his own family history to explain the development of the Range's mining culture and economy. "In 1860–1890ish, Cornwall, England, all the mines are shutting down—they're running out of work," he says. "A hundred thousand young men who are all experts in mining are running out of work at one place in the heart of the British Empire. They have huge families, in general. Maybe the father has six sons. They're all miners. They're not married yet. You've got six unemployed young men between the ages of sixteen and twenty-five." The solution: emigration.

"You can go to South America, or Australia/New Zealand, or Canada, which is what my family did. And you go from [the mines of] Canada to U.P. [Upper Peninsula] Michigan until the copper ran out . . . but then the Mesabi Iron Range was opening up. There's a lot of people around here whose ancestors came that direct line. U.P. to Canada to Cornwall."

The Cornish brought with them more than mining knowledge. The Cornish pasty (PASS-*tee*, not PAY-*stee*)—a simple, usually lard-based half-moon pastry pocket filled with hearty stuff like potatoes, ground beef, carrots, and/or rutabagas—is ready-made for the mine environment. Over the decades, it has become a signature dish of Upper Peninsula Michigan (home to turnips, carrots, and even suet) and the Iron Range. Some Cornish found themselves in Wisconsin, where pasties remain a staple in the southwestern Mineral Point/Platteville part of the state. *Star Tribune* columnist Jim Klobuchar memorably described the pasty as "the only recognizably good food produced in Great Britain in more than 2,000 years."

Many (if not most) world cuisines have some kind of meat-stuffed pastry item, varying from soft and delicate Asian steamed buns through the empanadas of the Latin world to the piirakka of Finland/Karelia, and innumerable others. But the tough, monstrously big pasty is uniquely suited to life in the mines. At its best, the pasty is the very essence of "meat and potatoes," a warm, savory stew in a hearty crust that can crush the fiercest hunger on the coldest day. Ideally, the pasty isn't overly salty, balances its meat, potatoes, and other veggies, and contains enough soup stock–like moisture to please the palate without disintegrating the crust.

"The Cornish pasty is the mother food of the original European miners who came here," says Brown. "There were a lot of Scandinavians who came for logging in the mid- to late 1800s, also Germans—they were transient. But miners came and built houses or were assigned houses." He continues, "The Cornish mining professionals brought the pasty with them, and it kind of got institutionalized because it's such a great miner's food."

Brown nails the importance of the pasty: "It keeps," he says. "You can eat it cold; you can eat it hot. You can make a bunch of them at once. You can keep it in your pocket, and it doesn't fall apart. It's compact. You can just eat in a very short lunch break, if you get a break—you can eat it while working if you have to. And it's LADEN with calories. Potatoes, meat, vegetables, butter—it's all there." A perfect hand food and workday companion, the pasty has become one of the region's defining folk foods, a dish that still plays an important part in the way people eat, socialize, and define themselves.

"All the immigrants who came here didn't get along, but their kids married each other," says Brown. On a similar note, and with a great deal of sincere passion, Sam Aluni told author Mancina-Batinich,

> I look back on my life here on the Iron Range and what we went through. The American born, they hate all of us. So everybody had his own corner—the Finn, the Polish, all of us separate. So what the change was, the young people later on they didn't care. The Italians, they jumped the fence and picked Polish girls and Polish men picked Italian girls. See that's a wonderful mixture now. I married my wife 64 years ago and they thought it was terrible that I married a Polish girl. Why, God almighty, I couldn't have got a better woman . . . I got a jewel.

And as families began to meet and intermingle over the decades, so did their foods. "We all shared each other's foods," recalls Eleanor Ostman, a journalist and cookbook author originally from the Iron Range. "Slovenians, Finns, Swedes, Italians . . . Everybody understood and liked all these foods."

A World Apart

"The difference with the Range is that this is a geographically isolated place," says Brown.

> You drive up here from the Cities and you notice that things are changing—the roads get smaller, the leafy trees become the pine trees—it's topographically higher, so you're driving up a hill to get here . . . and until recently it was not uncommon to be born in Virginia or Hibbing and never really travel more than fifteen miles from home. You didn't need to. Driving down to Duluth or the Cities was a very rare thing you did when someone got married or got drafted in the military. It wasn't really until the sixties that that changed.

The feeling of entering another country is palpable even for uninitiated visitors making their way north from the Twin Cities. On a February day, the pavement and green highway signs are the only visible color; snow-blasted pines and birch trees line the road, and the sky is a uniform mass of gray, descending to the ground in the form of wispy fog. Only ninety miles out of Minneapolis, the landscape and weather have conspired to create a place that feels like Finland or Canada—it staggers belief that the road we're driving on, if taken far enough south, also touches Texas.

With isolation came a sense of independence that would be unusual for a state, to say nothing of a region within a state. Scott Kuzma, writing in the quarterly *Minnesota History,* detailed an event that might be the high-water mark of independence in a stubbornly independent region: the secession of the Iron Range town of Kinney and the creation of the "Republic of Kinney."

Kinney was built at the edge of a mine, Kuzma writes, "solely to serve the interests of the mining company. Built between 1901 and 1903, it was intended to be a temporary site with an approximate lifespan of 25 years . . . By the early 1970s, Kinney's water pipes were choked with heavy deposits of iron and manganese." Decrepit infrastructure combined with increased population meant the water system was falling apart by July 13, 1977, the date of Kinney's secession. Previous efforts to obtain the $186,000 needed to repair it had failed, so the secession was dreamed up as a way to attract a bit of attention, under the theory that foreign countries receive more U.S. aid than American small towns. Tough, stubborn, independent—these are Ranger qualities that typified the only half-joking secession of Kinney, which, it should be noted, accomplished its goal of obtaining grants to fix the water system by the end of 1978.

The distinct identity and independence of the Range, Brown explains, is part of the reason it has been able to preserve so much of its own heritage. "All the ethnic music, and traditions—the accents—they've stuck around. The Iron Range accent is different from the Minnesota accent."

When the topic of ethnic traditions was broached, Tom Forti of Sunrise Deli recalled, "When I used to walk to high school, I'd walk about a mile. In the spring or early fall, walking down the street, I'd see groups of old men talking, and I might hear eight or nine different languages. This really was a melting pot." Greeks and Jews, now largely gone from the Range, contributed to the cosmopolitan feel of the boom town that was mid-twentieth-century Hibbing. Talking about the converted theater that houses his business, Forti refers to the now well-known Jewish family that originally constructed the building. "It was built in 1946," he says. "Bob Dylan's three uncles on his mother's side—Sam, Max, and Julius—built this theater." The original name of the theater was Lybba, after Bob Dylan's great-grandmother.

"It only had a drop of four feet, so it was not a great theater," says Tom. "This was a crying room," interjects Tom's wife, Mary, referring to the office in which the interview is taking place. "Or a make out room," says Tom, smiling. "Depends on your station in life."

The Fortis bought the theater in 1983, it having passed into the hands of the Mann theater chain before that. "Mann Theaters bought this theater from the Edelsteins, and then they divided it into two theaters, and they had it that way for three to four years before they moved out to a mall." Not coincidentally, the Forti business—which dates back to the original founding of the Sunrise Bakery in Hibbing in 1913—does a pretty good trade in Cornish pasties. When asked what sets their pasties apart from the crowd, Mary is quick to respond: "Flaky crust."

"That's what distinguishes our pasties," says Tom. "It's a semi-puff pastry. A good puff pastry will have between eight and eleven hundred layers, and ours don't have that many, but it is flaky. It's not mealy."

Sunrise sold pasties through the Vermont Country Store catalog and website in 2009–10, distributing more than two thousand all over the country. "We'd send them to Florida, California—all over," recalls Mary. "And we were getting phone calls back from people saying that people really liked them a lot. We had a woman from Arizona tell us she'd come from Minnesota, so they brought back memories for her."

The jump to mail- and Internet-ordered pasties is, not surprisingly, a quantum leap from the origins of the business, which had its roots in the very personal customs of local commerce up on the Range. "When I was a young kid, my father's business would deliver wholesale," recalls Tom. "He had twenty-two stops in Chisholm, and sixteen of those were grocery stores. There were three grocery stores I remember where you'd walk into someone's house and a bell would ring and they'd walk out of their living room. You ever seen a grocery store like that? There were so many . . . but then Piggy Wiggly came to Chisholm, and that was the end."

The Great Northern Church of the Pasty

The connection between churches and pasties is not immediately obvious. A church is both a physical place of worship and a spiritual community that revolves around religious observance and fellowship. And a pasty is a Cornish meat pie. But *community* is key to understanding the church/pasty link. A number of churches on the Range (and even some off of it) use pasty bakes as fundraisers, as community outreach, and as a way to celebrate social bonds among the faithful.

Tom Forti at work, Sunrise Deli, Hibbing

"It's a fellowship," affirms Don Peterson, head of the pasty committee for the Grace United Methodist Church in Pequot Lakes, located west of the Range in lake country but very much part of the pasty tradition. "We'll have twenty-five people in here making pasties together . . . and it's loud with laughter. We had talked about getting a machine to roll the dough, because it takes five gals to do that . . . and they said, 'Don't you dare. That's the fun of it, is being there.'"

"It's only once a month, and people get a chance to chat," says one volunteer. "We get a break every now and then. The baker controls when the break is. At the point where he's taking the batch out, he rings the bell, and that's when we have fun."

Grace United Methodist has been making pasties since 1997, and Peterson attributes some of the rebounding of the church's congregation to the success of pasty bakes and the community connections that are forged as they sell meat pies to the public. The church averages about six hundred pasties per gathering, once a month every month except for February. (This sounds like a lot—and, sure, it is a lot—but it's worth considering the words of Tom Forti at Sunrise, who says, "Three of us, when we make a good-sized batch of pasties, that's about 320. And we make it in about fifty-five minutes.") The church recently hit a milestone, baking pasty number seventy thousand. Beyond that, Grace United brings people together for pasty dinners. "We have two a year," says former committee head Bob Macnamara. "In May and in September we have a dinner open to the public. We put the round table out here with about six different toppings—you can have hot gravy, barbecue sauce, ketchup, sour cream, salsa . . . Don even made his own sauce, a glorified ketchup."

"I think the variety of condiments make those dinners a success," Peterson chimes in. "By themselves, pasties are much too dry, I think."

The business, as it is, is booming. "This July, we're taking on a dubious job," says Macnamara. "The chamber of commerce is hosting a fifteen hundred–person bike rally for MS [multiple sclerosis] in July—they'll be in town for overnight—and they asked us, 'Can you host a dinner for 250 to 300 people?' Seating is our problem."

Quilt square, Grace United Methodist Church, Pequot Lakes

"We trade pasties for church advertising on the radio station, KLKS," adds Peterson. "They sell them on Saturday mornings at a discounted price." The pasties retail for four dollars apiece, a bargain for a mammoth meat pie that can easily feed two hungry diners. "We were considering a price raise last year, but with the economic downturn we decided to hold it," says Peterson.

The pasties themselves are heavy and convincingly classic, featuring creamy tasting potato and ground beef with a relatively durable and dry crust and a solid onion kick. "It's a combination of coarse-ground beef and pork, onions, rutabagas, potatoes diced, salt and pepper, and a lard crust," says Peterson, neatly summing up the dish. "It started out—our impetus was to get a fund to build a new church [building]," explains Peterson, recalling the beginning of Grace United's pasty gatherings. "The money from the pasties goes into the general fund of the church—everyday expenses and programs, whatever. If we exceed a certain amount in a given year, it goes into capital improvement."

The recipe used in Pequot Lakes comes from a sister church in Hibbing, which has been making pasties to raise money since near the start of the twentieth century. "When Hibbing gave us the recipe, we had to swear in blood that we would not give the recipe out," says Peterson, a serious look on his face. "A number of us went up there to see them and see how they do this, and there was a lady about four and a half feet tall that came and stood up in front of me and said, 'You will use lard.' We haven't dared change that." Peterson and his church crew are traditionalists about their pasties, taking seriously the recipe handed down by their comrades. "They told us in Hibbing that rutabaga is the thing, and we haven't seen the need to branch out or screw up our inventory," Peterson concludes.

The Hibbing connection is Wesley United Methodist Church, which claims as its own a recipe that goes back to around 1917. "We started them in North Hibbing, from the old English recipe," says Marge Clark, one of the church's many pasty volunteers. Clark's reference to North Hibbing alludes to the town's original location; the city was moved south in order to better facilitate mining, leaving a ghostly network of empty streets still intact near the world's largest open-pit mine.

"Our crust is exceptional," continues Clark. "We use a lard crust. I have checked other churches, and we use real chopped-up steak and pork, and a lot of others use hamburger. And we put a lot of meat in compared to some of the others." Fifty-one years ago, when she was three, Clark recalls her mother going to the same church pasty gatherings that she now attends.

The affair is both everyday and extraordinary. When we opened our car door on a cold winter day, a rich, savory smell—onions, and pastry, and meat—swept into our vehicle. We'd arrived at the right place. About twenty or so mostly older women (and a couple men, preoccupied with rolling out dough and shuttling heavy trays of pasties from kitchen to common area) busied themselves in the spacious basement, which had taken on the atmosphere of a rec room: warm, convivial, busy—and dedicated to the single noble purpose of turning out big old pasty after pasty.

Esther Mackey, another veteran of the pasty production line, reports that the numbers of pasties and workers both have declined in recent years. From a high of about fifteen to seventeen hundred per three-day bake period, she says the group now produces about seven hundred pasties. "You know, so many of our young women are working now, and there isn't the availability," she says. "You look at some of them who have done it for years and are in their eighties already. That was the big change."

Another woman chimes in: "The young are too busy with their families or working, and the older ones are dying off."

"In the fifties, when I was a teenager, my mom was at home, and this was the big day," Mackey recalls. "So many of the moms were home then and could make pasties. During the day it's really hard for them. That has changed."

Mackey says the process, which occurs over three days, has changed little through the years. Tuesday is dough-making day. Wednesday is when the balls of meat get made ("They weigh each ball of meat . . . so no one gets cheated," explains Mackey). The potatoes and rutabagas (*ru-*

Volunteers making pasties, Wesley United Methodist Church, Hibbing

tabeggies, in the local argot) also are prepped. Thursday, when we turned up, is the big bake day. An assembly line stretching from the left-hand side of the kitchen toward the ovens on the right pushes pasties through a serious of steps. First, the dough is rolled out. Then, meat and veggies are mixed together and put into the center of the dough. The dough is folded and crimped and docked and then finally baked. The kitchen is filled with sound: the squeak of rolling pins, the clattering of dishware, and the constant chatting of the volunteers—stories being told, jokes cracked, remarks tossed casually across the crowded room.

All of this looks easier than it actually is. While my dough-rolling skills commanded some charitable praise, the lady supervising the meat and veggie mixing station was outwardly peeved by my lack of mixing ability, pointing out that if I were on duty, it would be all week before the pasties got baked. "As a beginning mixer, I was told, 'make sure you spread that meat out so no one gets cheated!'" says Mackey. A lot of the excellence of the Hibbing church pasties is the even consistency of the filling and the lack of variance from pasty to pasty. The meat, a blend of pork and beef, is sticky, and it takes dexterity and focus to really break it up and mix it evenly with the vegetables.

The result of all this work: hundreds of handmade, roughly one-pound pasties that can keep a grown man working even in Minnesota's cold weather. I ask, credulously, if someone can take down an entire pasty, and Mackey laughs. "Oh yeah," she answers. "Some of 'em would take down two. They were big miners."

Carol Borvac, another volunteer, recalls, "The miners would heat up a brick and put it in their lunch pail, and the pasty would be on a heated brick, so the men would have hot pasties for lunch. The way you'd judge a good pasty is if the juice would run down your arm." She also volunteers that the Finnish church in town makes pasties, too. Are they different? "I've never had them."

"Most of them have carrots rather than rutabaga," interjects one of the other women, filling in some details on the mystery pasties.

One thing's clear about the pasties made at Wesley United Methodist in Hibbing: they're classic examples of the form, ravishingly tasty even minus ketchup (the traditional go-to condiment). Moister than you'd expect, the interior is generous on the meat but balanced in terms of filling, and the crust, while durable, is not chip-a-tooth tough. The pasties, in fact, won an Iron Range pasty bake-off in March 1999. "Our district superintendent knew of all the churches in the area that made pasties, so he organized a bake-off," recalls one of the volunteers. "All the Methodist churches all over the Range—from Chisholm, Duluth, and so forth—came. It was a good time. All the pasties had a certain number, no one knew which was which. We do have a plaque out here."

Porketta's Flaky Allure

Along with pasties, one of the most revered classics of Range cooking is the Italian porketta. More properly and classically rendered as *porchetta*, on the Range it's spelled with a k. Of all the many special ethnic foods still made and celebrated in Range towns like Hibbing and Chisholm, it may be the best loved. Essentially a fennel and garlic and/or thyme–spiced pork butt roast, porketta is traditionally slow roasted so that the meat can be pulled apart into delicate, moist, deeply flavorful little pieces. Properly done and served on slightly crunchy Italian bread or a hard roll that provides a textural contrast, porketta makes a sandwich that rivals the corned beef at Katz's Delicatessen in New York. The flavored pork almost melts in the mouth, conveying a deeply spiced flavor that is absolutely divine.

"I love porketta," says Rick Nelson, lead restaurant critic for the Minneapolis *Star Tribune*. "Years ago, when I was a camp counselor at Camp Warren in Eveleth, Minnesota, we used to sneak off camp and go to the drive-in up the road. They had an amazing porketta." Nelson didn't recall the name of the drive-in, but I knew it: it was the K&B on Highway 53, the very place whose pasty and porketta–focused menu piqued my original interest in doing a book to tell the story of Minnesota through hand food.

The K&B is a remarkable place, a way station of old-fashioned food done with care. And on the Range, "old-fashioned" includes porketta, brought over by Italian immigrants near the beginning of the twentieth century and turned into a commercial mainstay by grocery store butchers and the Fraboni Sausage company.

Mark Thune heads up Fraboni's, which supplies porketta to consumers and restaurants, including the K&B and Zimmy's in downtown Hibbing. That a man of Norwegian heritage manages an Italian specialty producer is typical of the Range's ethnic melting pot. Thune is proud of his product, which is distinguished in at least one important way. "The big thing on our porketta is that we are the only people who use fresh fennel," explains Thune. "We use fennel seed and grow our own fennel."

Thune, who has been with Fraboni's for thirty-five years, says the company dates back to 1920 or thereabouts as a small neighborhood grocery in Hibbing. The store was founded by Dominic and Palmina Fraboni, who arrived in Hibbing from Ancona, in Marche, a central Italian region northeast of Rome. Their point of departure isn't surprising: Iron Range Italians hailed mostly from central and northern Italian provinces, in contrast to most Italian Americans, whose origins are in the poorer southern part of the Apennine Peninsula, plus Sicily.

The Fraboni children all helped with the business. Leo and Rose stuck around Hibbing and made a major push to become a regional meat distributor in the 1960s, while Angelo ventured to Madison, Wisconsin, where he founded a successful and still popular Italian grocery store under the family name. "As far as I know, the Fraboni family was the first to put porketta on the market for resale, in the 1950s and 1960s," says Thune. "Before that, everybody made it at home—everybody had gardens." Leo passed away in the late nineties, and Thune bought out Rose (who still lends advice and support) five years after that.

The business now employs about thirty people between the Fraboni Sausage company and the food service and distribution company, which serves clients within a hundred-mile radius of Hibbing. The company sells a lot of sausage (including exotic varieties such as blood sausage and potato sausage), but it may be best known for its porketta, which shares a mining connection with the pasty. "It was originally for the miners: they'd cook it up and make sandwiches," says Thune. "Some would put mustard on it. If they wanted it warmed up, they'd put it on a piece of equipment. In them days, you didn't go out for lunch. You brought your lunch or you didn't eat. That porketta tastes different cold from hot. I actually think you taste more spice when it's cold."

Fraboni's makes their porketta by hand. One dexterous worker with a knife starts with de-fatted pork butts and debones them. The pork butts are then butterflied, slit, stuffed with fennel, rolled, and tied. "Porketta's all manual," says Thune. "There's no equipment to make porketta. Right now, it's made exactly the way it was when I was here [thirty-five years ago]—no change." Observing the process is like watching a martial arts

demonstration: every motion is efficient and deliberate, and the interaction between knife, spice, and meat is perfectly coordinated. In a few moments, a table full of pork butts have been converted into porkettas, ready for storage and sale.

The resulting roast is a staple of Range cooking, often served at weddings and graduation parties—any time when the people are numerous and the mood is festive. Caroline Garavaglia Hanson, a miner's daughter from Eveleth quoted in *Italian Voices*, recalls porketta as part of the spread at family gatherings. "Baptisms were

Making porketta, Fraboni's, Hibbing

a big event, of course, and one particular one that I remember is my own cousin, Margaret Simonetta . . . there was food galore, for instance—oh, God—ham and porchettas and spaghetti . . . we had some sweets, too, plus then your wine and your coffee, whatever, and then that took care of baptism."

Although Thune is one of a number of porketta makers on the Range—the porketta from the Super One grocery store has a number of fans, who like its more intense spicing—Fraboni's is the only federally inspected maker. "A lot of others use different cuts of meat," explains Thune. "Some don't take as many cuts of meat off, or they'll use parsley instead of fennel . . . and no one else uses fresh fennel." The company plants its fennel crop at the end of May and, in a good season, makes three harvests. When the color at the top of the plant turns golden, it's time to cut. The feathery leaves of the plant season porketta; Fraboni's never uses the bulb.

Other than Fraboni's and supermarket offerings (some of which make quite respectable porkettas), the meat can be difficult to locate. Fichtner's Sausage and Meats of Duluth did a well-regarded porketta sandwich in its day but shuttered its doors in the mid-2000s; Brotherson's Meats in South Minneapolis, also well regarded for its porketta made from an old Iron Range recipe, shut down in 2000. In the Twin Cities, however, the torch is still carried by, among others, Everett's Foods and Meats in South Minneapolis. The Clyde Iron Works Restaurant and event center in Duluth features a porketta sandwich that has a lot of fennel flavor but is otherwise a work in progress: overly soft bread and too-finely flaked meat make for a squishy texture, lacking the crispy contrast of the dish at its best. Still, the fact that a porketta sandwich plays a prominent role on the menu of a large new restaurant speaks to the real connection between the dish and the local population.

The New Face of an Old Meat Pie

As is so often the case, innovation takes place outside of a folk food item's stomping grounds. An intriguing cumin-based variant of porketta ("Red Porketta") is sold at Clancey's Meats and Fish in the Linden Hills neighborhood of Minneapolis, and a thoroughly reimagined pasty is sold west of the Iron Range, in lake country.

Baker Mark Schultz of Turtle River Pasties came to his current role through an unusual route. Schultz wasn't originally a baker by trade. He met his wife, Peggy, in Africa (via the Peace Corps) and used his degree in environmental studies from Bemidji State University to raise tropical fish, which he did at the University of Oklahoma and in upstate New York. He also made a stopover working as a wetland resource manager in Florida. Schultz and his wife moved to Turtle Lake, north of Bemidji, in 1999. In 2005, they started a home food-processing equipment business that evolved into a jerky and custom sausage business, which in turn—thanks to the influence of a meat smoker—morphed into a pasty bakery. Turtle River makes smallish (about ten ounces after baking) pasties with a gourmet twist.

"We found that our smoker was really made to do briskets," says Schultz. "So we started doing beef briskets, and they were so good—people really liked them." Schultz considered using the leftover meat in sandwiches, but that didn't strike him and Peggy as unique enough to thrive. Road trips provided an answer. "Peggy came from New York, and we'd travel back and forth, at least once a year for deer hunting," he recalls. The trips took them across the Upper Peninsula of Michigan. "We'd see all these shops, and at first we thought they were pastie shops, tacky novelty shops!" he says. "And finally, we figured out what they were and started stopping and trying them . . . Our kids loved them. On one of our drives back, we just said, 'I bet our brisket would be great in one of these.'"

Schultz adapted the traditional pasty recipe to suit his own taste and the meat produced by his smoker. Using tri-tip beef—its relative tenderness was an asset—he found he could make gravy with the drippings. "Pasties really are a

Mark Schultz, Turtle River Pasties, near Bemidji

dry thing, the way they're traditionally made," he explains. "People kept saying they were turning out dry, so we kept adding more and more gravy, until we were up to about a can's worth for a batch of sixty. At one point, we were adding a pat of butter to each pasty as we were folding it, and then I was putting flour in there so the flour and butter would combine as they were baking."

The first struggle Schultz tackled is familiar to anyone who's ever attempted to develop a good scratch pastry recipe. "It was so hard to come up with a dough that would work with the rollers," says Schultz, referring to his equipment. "For us, we have to have more water to get it more pliable. Generally, if you add more water, you're making the fat a little more homogenous, and it won't be as flaky as you want it. You want it pliable, but still with chunks of butter. It's an all-butter crust." Why butter, rather than the traditional lard? "I think the flavor is wonderful," explains Schultz. "You just can't beat butter. It's harder to get a flaky crust, because the water interferes with it, but it's worth it. And not that it's healthier, but I'd rather eat butter than vegetable shortening or lard."

Schultz's shop puts its effort into the meat and uses canned or frozen veggies, in contrast to Pasties Plus, a well-known pasty shop in Grand Rapids. "They were good," he says of the Pasties Plus meat pie. "They use ground chuck, and they peel their vegetables. They peel carrots, peel ruta-bagas, chop them every day, and put them into pasties. We didn't want to go that route. We wanted our meat to be really good, but we were willing to compromise on the vegetables."

More important, Schultz didn't stop with his unconventional butter crust/brisket-filled interpretation of a classic pasty. Turtle River offers a minimum of seven varieties at any given time, including a country-style sausage, egg, and cheddar cheese breakfast pasty that is perfectly balanced and mind-numbingly delicious, and a rightfully popular Reuben variety with lean corned beef, sauerkraut, Swiss cheese, and dressing.

The shop opened in May 2009 and was soon making waves, selling up to one hundred pasties daily during the holiday season and a steady thirty to forty on a typical day. North country food writer Sue Doeden re-interpreted the shop's approach for one of her columns. Of the pasties she tried in the Upper Peninsula, Doeden recalls, "They tasted dry, and I didn't really like them. Then all of a sudden this shop opened here in Turtle River." A friend brought her a couple of pasties to sample, and they made an immediate positive impression. "One was a Reuben, like the Reuben sandwich, and one was traditional with the beef and carrot and potato," she recalls. "And we baked them, and we loved them. And that's when I decided I might want to visit with Mark. For one thing the crust was so flaky and buttery and good, and the insides were moist."

Not surprisingly, Schultz has caught some guff from pasty tradition-alists with Range heritage. "We've been raided a few times by the pasty police, and they'll say, 'That's not a pasty: a pasty can't use smoked meat,'" laughs Schultz. "'A pasty is ground beef.'" Schultz defends his product by citing history and the pasty's own humble roots. "A pasty was whatev-er was leftover," he says. "And I don't think a miner sitting with another miner in tin mines would say, 'Hey! That's not a real pasty.' It was a lack of diversity in their diets that sort of set what the typical pasty became—it was real peasant food." He continues, "The beef brisket we use may be closer to the traditional pasty than ground beef, actually, because people didn't really grind beef in the same way back then, and they did a lot of slow cooking of meat over a fire or in a big pot."

And as unconventional as the pasties are, they've gained approval from some highly qualified experts from abroad. "We had a couple stop in while traveling across the U.S. from San Francisco to the East Coast, and one of them was from Cornwall in England, and the other was from Ireland," Schultz recalls. "But they saw the sign and they stopped, and they asked us to warm some up for them, and we did. And they sat in their motor home and ate them, and then they came back, and afterwards they said they would pass muster anywhere in Cornwall." Indeed, their sole critique could be read as a compliment: "The fellow said, 'You put too much meat in them! The English wouldn't put that much meat in them.'"

Regardless of his food's authenticity, which is always a debatable point, Schultz observes that the pasties have adapted nicely to the local lifestyle. "People buy them for ice fishing; some people have ovens out in their ice houses," he notes. "Deer hunters—they'll buy a bag full of pasties for their deer camps. You stick 'em in your pocket, break 'em in half—have one half for breakfast and have the other a few hours later. You've got so much time on your hands, you can savor each morsel, eating them real slow, sitting in your deer stand."

For his part, Sunrise owner Tom Forti has also experimented with the pasty, selling miniature portions of the dish as well as a pork and spinach variety. He also makes a German strudel version. "We take a piece of dough that's maybe nine pounds, and we stretch it over a table that's nine feet by five feet long," he says. "Then you take butter, you pull the whole thing, and we sprinkle bread crumbs so it holds the butter and gives you delineation between the rolls, and then we put pasty filling in and roll it up. It's really a good product, but it's slow to make."

While sometimes available in grocery store freezer sections, pasties are far less of a staple in the Twin Cities, with only Milda's Café in North Minneapolis having a local reputation for making and serving them. Available either frozen every day or hot three days a week (Monday, Wednesday, and Friday), the pasties at Milda's come with gravy for an extra buck, bringing the total price to $7.25. The crust was tender, not lard-tough, easy to pick apart with a fork. The filling was moist and potato-heavy, the whole pack-

Pasty at Milda's Café, North Minneapolis

age enhanced further by the use of gravy, which brought a bit of additional salt and moisture to the party.

And if you're hunting down pasties in the Duluth area, Penelope Pasties in Hermantown offers an interesting variation on a theme. Sold out of a refrigerator case from a BP station, Penelope Pasties are relatively small (ten ounces) and overwhelmingly ground beef filled—the potatoes come as delicate little cubes, swamped by the meat. They're actually a bit closer to piroshki, the Russian hamburger that's baked into a roll. Still, as is true with the local cheese and sausage snack packs sold in Wisconsin gas stations, the fact that pasties are a service station food staple reflects their part-of-the-landscape nature—they're food for people who work for a living.

The Range, Looking Forward

As the pasty evolves and the porketta endures, the future of the Range stands as an open question. For some residents, it's hard not to look at the raw population numbers and get discouraged. "We're losing our population," says Forti. "This town is as big now as it was in 1920. [Current mine] employment at full tilt is something like 3,650 guys. Back in 1978, it was 22,500. Those were high-paid union workers. That's not ever going to come back."

A lot of the math, Forti explains, relates to modernization of equipment and mining practices. As the operations become more efficient, fewer workers are needed to mine and process the ore. "When I was in high school, the normal haul truck was twenty-three tons," he recalls. "Now the trucks are between 230 and 250 tons. So it takes one truck to do what twelve trucks did . . . And the mechanics? They lease [the trucks], so if there's trouble, Caterpillar will fix 'em."

Visitors to the website of the *Hibbing Daily Tribune* can pick up on Forti's sense of an aging, shrinking population. The first two sections listed on the site are unsurprising—News and then Sports. But Obituaries takes the third slot. Fifth, after Opinion, is Milestones, a section that, on a recent visit, was largely focused on events for seniors. Newspapers know their audiences, and the *Daily Tribune* seems zeroed in on the older residents who make up an increasing share of the local population.

Aaron Brown comments, "Since the 1980 census, we have lost half our population. As I often say, population loss is [a] problem. As you lose population, it's usually the younger people who leave—and then your community becomes older, and less inclined to want to change anything. It's a vicious circle. I tell people I'm sick of all the good-bye parties, because I work at the college. All these doctors and technical people come, they find the community unwelcom[ing], and they get sick of it, take a job elsewhere, and leave. It's really hard to create a vibrant community under those conditions."

Brown also stresses history while explaining reasons to rally around the Range as a source of identity. "People don't recognize how important this region was to the nation's economy," he says. "They're proud that their parents worked hard for forty years in the mines, but they don't realize their parents are part of a small group of workers who won World War II by providing enough steel to make the weapons we needed to win." He adds, "The Iron Range had the highest enlistment percentage, in World War II and Vietnam, in the whole country. There's no sense of that . . . it's always, 'I'm proud of my parents and I'm proud of my family' . . . but it's never, 'Look at what we did, all together.' It's hard to get people to say that these days."

But Brown also offers some hope in his book, *Overburden*. Writing about the Range and his own story, he puts the region's uncertainty—and future prospects—in personal terms:

THERE ARE DISPUTES over what belongs in a pasty (carrots and rutabagas being among the most controversial and typical ingredients), how to crimp it (in the U.P., the crimp is on top; on the Range, it's to the side), and how to best approach the crust.

For some, simplicity makes the most sense. Duluth-based chef Rick Rodenwald, quoted in the *Duluth News Tribune,* says, "In my opinion a pasty is ground meat, potatoes, and diced onions. Anything else subtracts rather than adds. A pasty is by nature a simple comfort food. Why try to fix something that is not broken?"

The discussion can get delicate in a hurry if you're dealing with someone who has a personal connection to the pasty, which is north country soul food. In 1994, cookbook author Eleanor Ostman wrote a story for the *Pioneer Press* expressing her mild but distinct anguish over the reworking of her mother's pasty recipe by Lucia Watson in *Savoring the Seasons of the Northern Heartland.* A full sixteen years later, she voices much the same sentiment, indignation crackling over the phone line.

So, experiment at will, but adapt a loved one's recipe at your own peril. That caveat said, if you're working on your own pasty recipe, here are a few things to consider.

MOISTURE If you don't precook your meat and veggies, the interior of your pasty has a tendency to dry out as it bakes for a long period of time, which may require gravy or ketchup on the back end for an optimal dining experience. But a dry pasty has its advantages: it'll hold together better and be more durable for travel or long-term freezing. Ostman recalls that the meat would traditionally be placed atop the veggies in a pasty "so that the juices would travel downward." A pat of butter crowned the meat before the pasty was folded and crimped.

BALANCE A criticism of many substandard pasties is that they're largely potatoes with a bit of ground beef wedged into the cracks. A great pasty is a balanced pasty, in terms both of seasoning and of the ratio of potato to vegetables to meat.

MEAT MIXTURE Pork is often added to beef to provide moisture and flavor, and even the type of beef—from smoked cubed brisket to ground beef—can vary. Ground beef, common in store-bought frozen pasties, is usually considered the bottom of the barrel; good church pasties will usually use a steak/pork mixture.

CRUST Know in advance what you're going for—a tougher lard crust that makes a traditional pasty that can be picked up and carried or a tender butter crust that's more flavorful.

PERSONAL TASTE Above all, don't be afraid to start with an established recipe and innovate. The beauty of the pasty, despite its deep tradition on the Range, is that it responds so well to improvisation. As one of the original great Cornish leftover catch-alls, it's well suited to being designed to order—or to preserving, for the long haul, whatever happens to be in your refrigerator. ◖

The year 1979 was the best year ever for taconite production on the Iron Range. I was born that year. My dad said that on the day I was born, he saw no reason his first son couldn't spend his whole life making a good living on the Iron Range. New trucks and snowmobiles filled the garages of miners across the Mesabi. It could be argued that the other babies and I born that year or close to it were born into an Iron Range with only two possible destinies: one of innovation and survival, or one where our pessimism and feelings of entitlement would doom us. The first test of this theory came quickly, as the steel industry foundered shortly after I was born and struggled for the first fifteen years of my life. One of these "new" plants sitting on some of the richest ore, Butler Taconite near Nashwauk, closed in 1985. Things improved in the 1990s and then worsened at the turn of the 21st Century. Now they're OK, with great potential. Is this just the old up and down puppet show we've seen for a century, or is the Range really going to enter the future?

But regardless of what the future holds for the Range, its food traditions will no doubt continue to give the region a sense of identity, a tangible reminder of its past, and a hearty lunch.

Cornish Pasties

Makes 6 servings

Contributed by Inez Andrews, Cornish immigrant to the Iron Range, via the Minnesota Discovery Center (formerly Ironworld)

What makes this recipe "Cornish," as opposed to one more typical of the modern Iron Range, is that the vegetables are sliced onto a freshly rolled crust. Most Iron Range cooks would dice their vegetables into a bowl, mix all the filling ingredients together, and then scoop them onto their crust. Also, a true Cornish crust differs slightly from the version here; it would be made from dough so tough that it would be difficult to break.

1 cup lard
4 cups all-purpose flour, plus additional for rolling dough
1 tablespoon salt

1 cup cold water
3 medium potatoes, cubed (about 3 cups)
3 cups cubed round steak
2 medium onions, chopped (about 2 cups)
1 medium rutabaga, grated (about 1½ cups)
6 teaspoons butter
Salt and pepper

Preheat oven to 425°F. In a medium bowl and using a pastry cutter or two knives, cut lard into flour and salt until size of peas. Blend in water, mixing with a wooden spoon, until slightly sticky. On a lightly floured surface, roll mixture into six dinner plate–sized circles. On one half of each circle, divide and layer next four ingredients (potatoes through rutabaga) in that order. Top each mound with 1 teaspoon butter; salt and pepper to taste. Dampen edges of pastry and fold opposite side over filling. Crimp or flute edges to seal tightly. Bake 30 minutes; reduce oven temperature to 400°F, and continue baking 30 minutes, until slightly brown. Serve.

Not-so-traditional Pasties

Makes 6 servings

Contributed by Sue Doeden; inspired by Turtle River Pasties

Do not use filling that is still hot: it should be at room temperature or right out of the refrigerator. Baked and frozen pasties can be warmed in a 350°F oven until heated through.

Pastry

1⅓ cups all-purpose flour
¼ teaspoon seasoned salt or garlic salt
⅔ cup chilled butter, cut into small pieces
5–6 tablespoons ice water

Sift flour and salt into a large bowl. Using a pastry cutter or two knives, cut butter into flour until mixture resembles coarse bread crumbs. Add 1 tablespoon ice water at a time, gently tossing with a fork between additions, until the dough begins to come together. Shape dough into a ball, wrap tightly with plastic wrap, and refrigerate 30 minutes.

Filling

2 tablespoons olive oil
1 medium onion, chopped fine
1 medium red potato, peeled and diced
1 small rutabaga, peeled and diced
1 medium carrot, peeled and diced
1 tablespoon all-purpose flour
1¼ cups beef broth
2 tablespoons Worcestershire sauce
12 ounces cooked beef, cut into small chunks
Salt and pepper to taste

Heat olive oil in a large skillet over medium-high heat. Add onions and cook, stirring, for about 10 minutes, until soft and just beginning to brown. Add remaining vegetables (potato through carrot) and cook, stirring, another 10 minutes. Sprinkle flour over vegetables and stir and cook for 2 minutes. Add beef broth and Worcestershire sauce; simmer 15 to 20 minutes, until much of the stock has cooked away and thick gravy remains. Stir in beef. Season to taste with salt and pepper; remove from heat and set mixture aside to cool. (Filling can be refrigerated until ready to assemble pasties.)

Assembly

Flour for rolling dough
1 egg beaten with 1 teaspoon milk

1. Divide chilled pastry dough in half; return one half to refrigerator. On a lightly floured surface, roll remaining portion to ⅛-inch thickness. Use a 6- to 8-inch plate or bowl turned upside down to cut out 2 circles. Refrigerate scraps. Repeat process with remaining dough half. Combine and roll out scraps for 2 more circles, a total of 6 dough rounds.

2. Preheat oven to 375°F. Spoon a heaping ½ cup filling on half of each dough round, leaving a 1-inch border at edge. Moisten edges with beaten egg mixture. Fold pastry over filling and crimp to ensure a tight seal. Cut three small slits in the top of each pasty. Brush with egg mixture, covering completely. Bake on lightly greased or parchment-lined baking sheets for about 30 minutes, until golden brown. Serve hot, warm, or at room temperature.

Lunch-and-Dessert Pasties

Makes 4 servings

James Norton and Becca Dilley

Although difficult to impossible to find in contemporary recipe books, a cultural memory of pasties that were a clever combination of lunch and dessert exists. "A housewife would make pasties for underground miners," recalls cookbook author Eleanor Ostman. "There'd be a meat mixture for two-thirds of the pasty, and the last third would be filled with [fruit] preserves." Pressing down the dough between the two pockets of food helped keep them separate. Food writer Sue Doeden recalls pasties that were "Half full of a sweet filling, like jam, or apple pie filling. So they'd eat the first half, and they'd put the pasty back in their pocket and pull it out later when they were hungry for dessert."

We took a stab at creating a modern version of this archaic but delicious-sounding dish. Our version uses a butter crust and relies on the sweetness of sweet potatoes and the omnipresence of apple to smoothly blend the flavors of the lunch and dessert halves of this big, nontraditional pasty. We tried using a crimp to separate the two halves but eventually decided it wasn't worth the effort. While the apple pie aspect of this dish is a classic dessert, it can be freely mixed with the savory half—with no negative impact on taste.

Crust

5 cups all-purpose flour
1 tablespoon salt
2 cups (4 sticks) cold, unsalted butter, cut into ½-inch cubes
1 large egg
1 tablespoon apple cider vinegar
About 1 cup ice water

1. Combine flour and salt in a large bowl. With a pastry cutter or your fingertips, blend in butter until mixture resembles coarse meal with roughly pea-sized butter lumps. Using a fork, beat egg and vinegar in a 1-cup measure. Add water to measure 1 cup total. Add liquid mixture to flour mixture, stirring until incorporated.

2. Turn mixture onto a lightly floured surface and knead gently to bring dough together. Roll out into a 15x9-inch rectangle. Arrange dough with short side nearest you and fold into thirds, creating a 5x9-inch rectangle. Wrap dough in plastic and chill for at least 1 hour.

Pork Filling

¾ pound trimmed pork chop, cut into ½-inch cubes
1 teaspoon coarse (kosher) salt
½ teaspoon freshly ground black pepper
Pinch cayenne pepper (optional)
2 teaspoons vegetable oil
1 large white onion, chopped (about 1 cup)
2 medium Granny Smith apples, cut into ¼- to ½-inch cubes (about
    1 cup)
1 medium sweet potato, cut into ¼-inch cubes (about 1 cup)

Combine pork with salt, black pepper, and cayenne (if using). Heat oil in a skillet over medium-high heat. Add pork, cooking for 1 to 2 minutes and stirring constantly, until most of the meat's exterior has changed color. Remove meat to bowl. Reduce heat to medium low, add a bit more oil if necessary, and cook onion, stirring, until tender, 4 to 5 minutes. Remove from heat; add to pork. Combine apples and sweet potatoes with pork and onions. Set aside.

Apple Pie Filling

3 small to medium Granny Smith apples, cored and sliced
3 tablespoons sugar
1½ tablespoons brown sugar
1 tablespoon all-purpose flour
¼ teaspoon lemon zest
½ teaspoon lemon juice
Pinch salt
Pinch cinnamon

Combine all ingredients (apples through cinnamon) in a bowl and mix well. Set aside.

Assembly

Flour
Butter
Water or milk

1. Preheat oven to 400°F. Using one-quarter portion of chilled dough, roll out a 10-inch round on a lightly floured surface. Place about 1 cup apple mixture near left-center of dough round. Place about 1½ cups pork mixture near right-center of dough round. Divide a thin pat of butter, putting half atop each mixture.
2. Lightly brush edges of dough with water or milk. Fold over dough into a half-moon shape, and crimp sides using a fork or your fingers to seal. Use a knife to cut slits in the top: 2 slashes for meat, 1 slash for apples. Repeat process to make 3 more pasties.
3. Bake about 35 minutes. The apples should be bubbly and releasing liquid and the pork cooked through. Serve.

Slicing into a home-roasted porketta at the home of Sue and Dennis Doeden

Italian Porketta

Makes 16 servings

This *Cook's Tour of Minnesota* recipe is among the simpler ones available; more intricate preparations can involve as many as three different spice rubs, applied at different times and on different parts of the meat. Those who love porketta's flavor can also seek out turketta, a roast turkey variation on the theme. This boned, seasoned pork roast has become so popular in the Twin Cities that it is now available, ready to roast, in the meat departments of larger supermarkets. Traditionally, porketta is roasted until the meat falls apart. To serve old-world style, pull pork apart with fork.

1 (4-pound) boneless pork butt roast
½ cup chopped fresh parsley or 2 tablespoons dried parsley flakes
¼ cup fennel seeds
2 teaspoons salt
2 teaspoons freshly ground black pepper
½ teaspoon garlic powder
½ teaspoon onion powder

Preheat oven to 350°F. Halve roast lengthwise and open it like a book. Combine spices (parsley through onion powder) in a small bowl and rub mixture over both sides of meat, pressing fennel seeds into the pork. Fold roast back together, secure with string, and place in a shallow roasting pan. Roast 45 to 60 minutes or until meat thermometer registers 150 to 155°F. Let rest 5 to 20 minutes before slicing. Serve on toasted rolls or Italian bread slices.

4 The State Fair Turkey Sandwich
The Great Minnesota Get-Together Meets the Great Minnesota Poultry

JILL LEWIS / PHOTOGRAPHS BY KATIE CANNON

Colloquially known as the "Great Minnesota Get-Together," the Minnesota State Fair is a big deal. It brings together state residents and visiting guests for twelve days of food, games, rides, exhibits, and concerts near the end of every summer, and you'd be hard pressed to find a Minnesotan who hasn't come to St. Paul at least once in his or her lifetime for the extravaganza. Minnesota families have been known to plan their summer vacations around the fair, and the Minnesota State Fair has supported legislative action to mandate that state public schools don't start their academic years until the day after Labor Day, ensuring that families don't have to head home before the fair ends. It's a fair assessment to say that Minnesotans love their state fair.

In contrast, you might have to do some digging to find a critical mass of Minnesotans who can accurately tell you about the impressive scope of the state's turkey industry. Despite producing the most turkeys of any state in the Union, Minnesota is more known for its lakes, which number close to twelve thousand, than the 40 million–plus turkeys raised here each year. Though the turkey industry generates more than $600 million annually in income for producers, processors, and other related industries, according to the University of Minnesota's Department of Animal Science, it escapes the notice of many Minnesotans, especially those in urban areas, who are far removed from food production.

But once a year the Minnesota State Fair and the state's turkey industry come together at the fairgrounds, and residents reap the benefits of their partnership in the form of the popular turkey sandwich. Most fairgoers probably don't think about the economic and cultural impact of these two powerhouse industries as they enjoy their meaty, juicy sandwiches, but the fair favorite is more than just turkey and bun. It represents Minnesota's long history of agricultural excellence, dedication to research and innovation, and, of course, propensity to enjoy life to the fullest.

Happy Turkeys Come from Minnesota

Think about the word *turkey*: what comes to mind? Thanksgiving, likely, or perhaps the bourbon or bowling. But chances are you wouldn't think about Minnesota, which is a pity because it wears the crown of the highest turkey-producing state in the country. In 2009, approximately 46 million turkeys were raised on six hundred farms throughout the state, with Kandiyohi County in central Minnesota being the largest production area.

Why is Minnesota such a hotbed of turkey production? Steve Olson, executive director of the Minnesota Turkey Growers Association (MTGA) and the Minnesota Turkey Research and Promotion Council, points to four main reasons:

1. Proximity to affordable feed sources. As a state that produces large quantities of corn and soybeans, two crops that comprise the majority of turkey feed, Minnesota is well positioned to raise the birds in a cost-effective manner. Olson explains, "Feed is about 75 percent of the cost of raising a turkey. The fact that we've got a lot of corn and soybeans grown in Minnesota makes that part of it a little less expensive to raise turkeys here than in other parts of the country. It's also synergistic in that corn and soybeans are grown here, turkeys produce manure, their manure goes back on the fields in the form of fertilizer, so it provides nutrients to grow corn and soybeans."

2. Depth of turkey-raising knowledge. Just like crop and dairy farms, many turkey farms are family businesses that employ and pass their knowledge through multiple generations. "We've got guys who are second-, third-, and fourth-generation turkey farmers, so over time they've survived business cycles and have become very astute businesspeople, and they've learned from previous generations how to raise turkeys," Olson says.

3. Strong academic and government support. The University of Minnesota has several experts in avian and poultry genetics, nutrition, and management, and the state's board of animal health plays an active role in animal production. Says Olson, "When we have issues, whether it's a disease issue or an environmental issue, we've got people there who can help us understand what the issue is and to address it."

4. Ample processing facilities. Minnesota is home to turkey processors like Jennie-O, Northern Pride, and Turkey Valley Farms, which can reduce their costs by relying on turkeys raised close to their processing plants. "The processors need a supply of birds to come into their plants that are close by, and likewise, the turkey growers need to have an outlet for their product. In the process, they've been pretty aggressive in developing new products, and that helps increase the consumption of turkey," Olson reports.

Though the Minnesota turkey industry tends to fly under most residents' radar, Olson notes it's making a significant impact on the state's economy and sense of community. "Whether it's somebody who's working for Jennie-O on one of their farms or their processing plant, or if it's one of our independent growers who markets through Jennie-O or one of the other processors . . . these are real businesses. People don't realize these are multimillion-dollar farms. And whether it's an independent grower who has two barns or it's a larger company . . . they're adding to the social fabric of these rural communities."

In fact, the MTGA takes advantage of the Minnesota State Fair's reach to call attention to the strength of the state's turkey industry. In addition to the Turkey to Go restaurant, which serves the famous turkey sandwich, the association also sponsors an educational booth in the Dairy Building. The exhibit walks visitors through the turkey-raising process and provides new turkey recipes for consumers to try. "The state fair has been a part of who we are for most of our organization's history," Olson explains. "It started out as a great way to promote turkey, and it's one thing that's consistent with how we operated fifty years ago to how we operate today. We're trying to promote the consumption of turkey, and the state fair enables us to do that with a pretty broad audience."

The Evolution of Turkey Growing

In 1939 when the MTGA was founded, Olson notes, it took farmers twenty-eight weeks to raise a twenty-one-pound turkey. Today it takes only twenty-one to twenty-two weeks to grow a forty-five-pound turkey using less feed and fewer acres of farmland. How did this happen? A combination of advancements in breeding and nutrition has made turkey production more efficient in terms of cost and time, allowing fewer farmers to provide more meat for more consumers.

Sally Noll, a professor of poultry science at the University of Minnesota who specializes in turkey nutrition and production, traces the beginning of modern turkey-raising practices to the 1920s, when scientists identified vitamins, such as Vitamin D, that were essential for turkey health. Later, they developed ways to synthesize these vitamins and integrate them into turkey feed. In the 1940s and 1950s, animal scientists studied new breeding methods and recognized that one variety, a bronze turkey, grew faster and had broader breasts than other breeds. From this knowledge they developed the Broad-Breasted Bronze Turkey, but its dark-colored feathers left unappealing streaks of pigment on the turkey carcasses after they were plucked, so local turkey experts got the idea to breed a more consumer-friendly bird featuring lighter feathers.

"The University of Minnesota actually played a major role in working out the genetics of feather color for turkeys, and they found out that they could select for a turkey that had white feathers, so when the feathers were removed from the carcass, you didn't have that small piece of pigment that was left in the feather follicle, and it made the carcass look cleaner," Noll explains. "Now most of the commercial turkeys are of the white-feather variety, so we went from the Broad-Breasted Bronze to what is now called the Large White. At the same time, the birds were bred for larger size and for faster growth rates."

Throughout the 1980s, demand for turkey grew as it became less of a seasonal meat and new turkey products, such as turkey hot dogs, came to market. From a food-production stance, it made sense to raise larger birds from which processors could harvest more meat, Noll says, and average turkey size continued to increase. Once again, work done at the University of Minnesota was instrumental in this development, as researchers identified the optimal levels of protein and energy in turkey feed to spur additional growth. Today's turkey feed is a blend of corn and soybean meal, along with smaller quantities of canola meal, wheat, and distiller's dried grains with solubles—the material that remains after fermentation for the production of ethanol.

The supersizing of turkeys has resulted in more than just bigger birds, however. It has also spawned an industry focused on turkey reproduction. Conventionally grown turkeys must be artificially inseminated now because their larger size prevents them from successfully mating naturally. "One of the advantages of doing that is that you can select for what you call the 'elite males' in terms of whatever characteristics you're looking for in the progeny and then utilize the semen in the bird to inseminate many hens," Noll says. "You also get some savings, too, in the number of breeder toms you have to keep on hand. Under a natural mating system, you might be looking at one tom for every ten hens, which is a pretty typical ratio. With artificial insemination, you could go one tom for up to about sixty hens."

And as turkey production moved from a life cycle geared toward harvest for the fall and winter holiday season to year-round production, breeding moved indoors, for the most part. The switch temporarily increased the bird mortality rate, but now that figure has fallen as farmers have learned how to better manage the barn environment. University of Minnesota experts conducted leading research in the

Turkeys raised indoors, Lakewood Turkey Farm, Eden Valley

1970s and 1980s to define the best air and litter quality and acceptable levels of dust and ammonia in the barn for the turkeys' health.

Changes in turkey production have also had an impact on the environment. Increased production results in larger amounts of manure, which can often be used as a crop fertilizer at nearby farms or in more innovative ways, such as fuel for power plants. In 2007, the Fibrominn power plant, located in the west-central Minnesota town of Benson, became the nation's first poultry litter–fueled power plant. "A fertilizer produced from manure has a lot more benefits to it than a commercial-type fertilizer in terms of building up the soil material," Noll says. "But there are still areas where you have heavy numbers of all kinds of farm animals being produced, and in that case you can potentially run into a situation where you don't have the cropland available to spread all the manure. And that was the case for building that plant out in Benson."

The emissions from turkey barns—primarily ammonia—are also a cause of concern, one which has inspired researchers to develop new additives for turkey litter that lower its pH level and keep the ammonia in the litter rather than releasing it into the air. Ammonia can also stress the respiratory systems of turkeys, according to Noll, so scientists are studying how further changes in turkey feed can help to decrease the amount of ammonia that the birds excrete. In fact, turkey feed is one aspect of turkey production that Noll predicts will lead to future developments in the industry. She also foresees that new technology that can monitor barns for air quality and temperature will become more economical for farmers to install—but that it won't make the true expert, the farmer him- or herself, obsolete. "[Automated monitors] would be a very good management tool, but we're still going to be dependent upon having trained people who can go into the barn and look at the birds and say, 'Well, there might be something going on here,'" Noll says.

The Life of a Turkey and a Turkey Farmer

Though Noll probably doesn't know him personally, chances are she was thinking about someone like Mike Langmo, who owns Lakewood Turkey Farm in Eden Valley. Since 1960, the farm has welcomed day-old turkeys, called *poults*, from a hatchery and settled them into a 313-foot-long, 65-foot-wide brooder barn, where they will live for the next five to seven weeks among forty thousand birds. Later, they'll move into a similarly sized finishing barn for several more weeks as they grow to their harvest weight. From there they'll be transported to one of the state's turkey processors, such as Jennie-O or Turkey Valley, and then travel to dinner plates all over the country.

Like many Minnesota turkey farms, Lakewood began as a family business when Mike's father, Jim, founded it with his brother. Mike grew up helping out on the farm, pulling weeds and loading turkeys into the barns and trucks, and later took over ownership to raise three million pounds of turkey each year. "We're not a very large producer," Langmo says, though that number may seem impressive to those not involved in turkey production. "It was started as a family business, and we're trying to continue on with that for a period of time, anyway."

Langmo has a son who is employed as an engineer in Duluth and doesn't have an interest in coming back to work on the farm, so the family business may end with him when he decides to retire. It's not an unusual story these days, he notes: "We're having less and less farmers, but each farmer has to produce more and more food."

With increased consumer interest in organic food, many people would point to organic turkey farming as a way to garner interest in a future buyer, but Mike says that while organic farming may be ideal, it's simply not practical for him. "I looked into going organic. Man, that's a losing proposition. I'm brooding five times a year, and I'm brooding two flocks each time. If I were to go organic, I could raise two flocks a year," he explains.

> And you can't use any antibiotics, and your feed has to be all organic. You're going to lose more birds; the feed is three times the cost of commercial feed. And then if you get a disease, you have to treat the birds with antibiotics, and then you've put all these costs in there and you can't sell them for the premium. The organic rules state right in there that if your birds get sick, you have to treat them with antibiotics, and then you can't sell them as organic.
>
> If we could do things here on the farm through the feed or whatever [to reduce disease], I'm all for it. I want to produce the safest possible product going into that processing plant.

Langmo continues, "People think, 'Well, you're feeding them all of these antibiotics because you want to make more money and all that.' No, it's not about money. From my personal standpoint, it's about the health of every single one of these turkeys that's in my care . . . If it was about the money, I wouldn't be doing this—I'd be working a job someplace else. It's about the lifestyle and the care of these birds. I'm self-employed. I decide what I'm going to do every day. Sometimes we work long hours. It's the nature of the beast."

But despite Langmo's hesitations about going organic, other farmers have taken the plunge, often to satisfying results. Jessi Wood and Joey Stout met while working at the Whole Foods in Minneapolis and later took their passion for natural and organic foods to Madison, Minnesota, where they founded Humble Roots Heritage Farm. Here they raise a young family and two breeds of heritage turkeys, Bourbon Reds and Black Spanish, as well as heritage Mulefoot hogs. Unlike commercially raised turkeys, the heritage breeds have not had their distinguishing characteristics changed by genetic selection, and they can mate without human assistance.

"The heritage turkeys form a nice flock. They roost up on top of our trees and on top of our buildings. It's their natural defense against predators. They don't have to be locked in a barn all the time," Wood says. She adds:

> Turkeys need a 29 percent protein diet, so the more time they can spend getting bugs and worms outside, cost-wise it's better. But in order to do that, they have to be able to fly and protect themselves. That's how they naturally live, so that's important to us—to give them as real a habitat as it could be. We base a lot of our decisions on the beauty of the animals.

They're really beautiful. They're not overbred to fit into this size box so they can travel in a refrigerated truck this far. Without breeding out all of those characteristics, we're left with their natural personalities.

Heritage turkeys tend to be smaller—twelve to fourteen pounds for a hen and twenty-two to twenty-eight pounds for a tom—than conventionally grown birds, and they put on weight at a much slower rate. Wood and Stout get their birds in mid-April and butcher them right before Thanksgiving. In those seven months, Mike Langmo will have raised and sold at least four flocks of turkeys. The difference in price tends to be large as well: the heritage turkeys from Humble Roots sell for $7.50 per pound, while in 2009 the American Farm Bureau Federation estimated the cost of a sixteen-pound turkey to be $1.16 per pound. And instead of sending their birds to a processing plant, Wood and Stout sell their turkeys directly to consumers, who enjoy the birds for Thanksgiving dinner.

Turkeys raised outdoors, Peterson Turkey Farm, Cannon Falls

While raising heritage turkeys may result in fewer birds overall, Wood foresees that the other benefits of this method of turkey production will increase the number of heritage growers in Minnesota. "I think there's no way that it can't get bigger. I think every time you get a food scare, more people turn to smaller farms and places where they might know where their food comes from. It's probably not that far off that somebody's going to cook a turkey and find out there's something in it, and it will be too late for a recall. As much as I hate to see that happen, small farmers like us are a little happy because we're trying to promote the small farm and trying to get out of mass-producing food," Wood says.

The Genesis and Genius of the Minnesota State Fair

Small farmers like Wood and Stout are the reason the Minnesota State Fair exists. To the surprise of many fair-loving Minnesotans, the fair wasn't always about consuming mass quantities of food. It was originally con-

The New Turkey Holiday

Whereas the month of February is cold, and dark, and equidistant from both the warmth of the beloved December holidays and the eventual renewing goodness of spring

and whereas the only holiday in February is the execrable Valentine's Day . . .

and whereas there has never been a better time of year in which to insert a new holiday

and whereas Thanksgiving, as a celebration of camaraderie and fantastic food, is about as good a holiday to which one can possibly point

Now, therefore, it is resolved to celebrate a second Thanksgiving in the February of each year, on the Saturday on or following Valentine's Day (superseding that holiday whenever possible) . . .

Having spelled out our purpose, we therefore proclaim this new holiday "Febgiving," and invite any and all to celebrate it.

WITH THESE WORDS, the husband-and-wife team of James Norton and Becca Dilley announced their newest holiday to the world in February 2010. Deemed "Febgiving," the event combines Thanksgiving's family atmosphere and bounty of food with the often dreary and desolate month of February to create a reason to celebrate, complete with a roast turkey. "We always make a roast turkey for Febgiving because the bird is so celebratory and communal. It's food that people gather around, and share, and it also happens to look absolutely fabulous. The spectacle of a whole roast turkey being plated and carved is absolutely mesmerizing. Particularly if you happen to be hungry," Norton says.

"Febgiving is a time when you don't have to be hemmed in by family tradition because you are always creating new traditions with your friends. Don't like green bean casserole? Don't make it! Found a new recipe in a magazine? Try it! The only thing we require is turkey and laughter. And mashed potatoes," Dilley adds.

For turkey lovers—or anyone who likes a good excuse to throw a dinner party—Febgiving is a welcome addition to the holiday schedule. Visit febgiving.com for stories and photos to inspire your own version of the February feast. ○

ceived as a way to persuade new and prospective residents that, despite the cold winters, Minnesota was an amiable place to settle, offering an abundance of land and fertile soil. In fact, the first fair occurred before Minnesota was even a state. The territorial fair debuted in 1854, becoming a state fair in 1859 after Minnesota entered the Union.

The early fairs focused on education. As University of Minnesota professor emeritus Karal Ann Marling wrote in her 1990 book *Blue Ribbon: A Social and Pictorial History of the Minnesota State Fair,* "fairs served the cause of progress in frontier agriculture by exposing Minnesotans to new types and breeds." Attendees could learn about new vegetables, fruits, and animals that could become their livelihood. Marling noted that the fairs also gave residents the opportunity to showcase their cultural and artistic achievements, such as needlework and gardening. Amusements were present as well—horse racing, music, and fire engine water-throwing contests, according to the mother-daughter team of Kathryn Strand Koutsky and Linda Koutsky, whose *Minnesota State Fair: An Illustrated History* is one of the most recent and comprehensive looks at the state's summer institution.

After bouncing around the state for several years, the Minnesota State Fair settled into its permanent home in Hamline, a town that bridged Minneapolis and St. Paul, in 1885, when the Ramsey County Board of Commissioners donated its 210-acre poor farm to the State Agricultural Society, which oversees the fair. The fairgrounds began to take the shape that fairgoers would recognize today—the Main Building in the southeast corner, Machinery Hill in the northeast, the Grandstand and animal barns close to the center.

Though the general layout and many buildings remain the same, today the fairgrounds are larger, at 320 acres, and it would be an understatement to say that attendance has grown. From 74,508 people in 1885 to the record-breaking number of visitors at 1,790,497 in 2009, the Minnesota State Fair is an end-of-summer tradition for more and more attendees each year. And while the majority of them aren't coming to pick up agricultural tips, they still enjoy many of the same exhibits, attractions, and rides as did the early fairgoers. "The original fairs were there to say, 'Look, we can grow great crops. We can breed great livestock and come here and settle.' Now it's a different focus, but it still has the same components," says Linda Koutsky.

After the Koutskys' book was published in 2007, they spent twelve straight days at the Minnesota State Fair to sign books and talk with fairgoers, who were eager to share stories about the fair. Being modest Minnesotans, most of the people who spoke with the Koutskys didn't boast about any perceived superiority of their state fair compared to neighboring states' fairs or express any particular regional pride in the fair, but they still reported a deep-founded love and enthusiasm for the summertime event that has delighted families for generations. Reports Koutsky:

> We were amazed at how many countries people came from that had grown up here or had relatives here and they loved the fair and they came back at fair time, from Germany and Great Britain, and certainly from across the country. People just think it is so much fun. They loved the food. The animals were second. Where else can you see all those animals? They love to look at all the chickens and all the different kinds of rabbits. And then earlier, they used to actually do their household shopping there. They would look at stoves or refrigerators or sofas or sleepers. That's not so much true anymore. So it's certainly evolved over the years … But they just seem to love the food and the people watching. I think it's just a way to have fun. It's a totally different way to have fun.

Anyone who watched network news or read a daily newspaper during the summers of 2007 and 2008 could scarcely avoid scenes of political candidates asserting that they were "just one of the folks" at a state fair. They shook hands, kissed babies, and forked through fried food to demonstrate that they eat as poorly as many American fairgoers. Candidates from several political parties, not just Democrats and Republicans, set up booths throughout fairgrounds to rally their supporters and try to sway undecided voters to choose them come November. The Minnesota State Fair is no exception. But this isn't a modern phenomenon: politicians and orators have been courting Minnesotans for more than 150 years, beginning with the early fairs in the 1850s. "Nowhere could office seekers make contact with such huge numbers of voters over such long periods of time than at the fair," the Koutskys wrote. "Local politics took center stage, but U.S. presidents and countless other candidates saw the Minnesota State Fair as a worthwhile stop on campaign trails north."

Why do political candidates put Minnesota on their must-travel list? The state usually reports a high voter turnout—in 2008, more than 2.9 million people (78.2 percent of the eligible population) cast a vote in the presidential race, according to George Mason University professor Michael McDonald, who headed the United States Elections Project. And in this politically active state, citizens want to get as much face time as they can, not only with the candidates for local, state, and national elections but also with their fellow Minnesotans whose votes could potentially swing an election in their favor. That's why fairgoers have not only heard from the likes of Teddy Roosevelt, Rutherford B. Hayes, Calvin Coolidge, and Dwight D. Eisenhower but also come in contact with almost every state and national political candidate's most avid supporters.

The Great Minnesota Get-Together draws six-figure crowds each day

All politics aside, though, the state fair is also recognized for the effect it has on the local economy. The 2008 Minnesota State Fair Economic Impact Study examined the revenues, expenditures, and earnings generated by local and non-local concessions stands, ride and game operators, and livestock exhibitors and determined the total economic impact for the Twin Cities area to be approximately $75 million. The fair also requires a staff of about 2,700 during its twelve-day run, in addition to the seventy full-timers and 150 seasonal employees who work during the summer to finish preparations for the end-of-August event.

Food at the Minnesota State Fair

> "One hundred years ago, 80 percent of the people who came to the fair were ag-based or in the agrarian economy and were farmers, and now it's less than .08 percent, so how much it's evolved in the last hundred years is kind of incredible. We used to say tongue-in-cheek that it's always been about agriculture, it's just that it used to be for farmers and now it is about farmers, and it's about eating."
> **DENNIS LARSON**, license administration manager, Minnesota State Fair

> "It's the number-one most popular thing when they ask people what do you like about the fair. The biggest response is for the food."
> **LINDA KOUTSKY**, coauthor of *Minnesota State Fair: An Illustrated History*

Since the first fair, there has been food, of course. Attendees and exhibitors traveled to the fair from all over the state, and they needed to eat. But they didn't grab a corn dog or a cone of chocolate chip cookies from a stand along Carnes Avenue. Instead, they relied on a higher power—more specifically, churches.

Nearby churches operated dining halls on the fairgrounds so visitors could enjoy a hot meal and a seat at the counter. Breakfast, lunch, and dinner were served up by parishioners who volunteered their time and their kitchen expertise, typically providing meat-based dishes like meat loaf or a turkey roast or a stack of pancakes or waffles. With space at a premium, the dining halls often relied on food carted in from volunteers' homes rather than preparing it on-site. The off-site cooking had another benefit: donations of prepared food meant that churches could keep more of the revenue earned from sales and spend less on ingredients.

"I feel like [the dining halls are] a part of our heart and soul. That's where the fair got known for the good food because the grandmas would make it at home and the dads would haul it out here and then the volunteers would sell it," says Dennis Larson, who has managed concessions at the fair for the past sixteen years. "That was the reputation—going to the fair and having a good meal."

The early years also brought in vendors who ran tent-based restaurants and cafés, but the addition of permanent buildings, such as the Arcade and Food buildings, later drew these dining options inside. The smaller stands that popped up in place of the food tents didn't offer the broader menus of the dining halls and cafés but instead focused on a few specialty food items, such as ice cream, or more portable options, like hamburgers. And with the introduction of a certain battered hot dog on a stick in 1947, the concessions stands and booths rose to a new level of popularity and began to shift the perception of fair food from a necessity to a novelty.

"The Pronto Pup was the beginning, if you will, of the deep-fried whatever on a stick, and it's now over sixty years old. And that, I always say, is the grandpa of everything else that has come along," explains Larson.

Now, though the church dining halls and small restaurants still have a place at the fair, the food that grabs the lion's share of attention possesses an undeniable quirkiness or kitsch factor that fairgoers can't resist. Many of these offerings follow the Pronto Pup's food-on-a-stick model—recent additions include spaghetti and meatball on a stick, camel on a stick, and Fry Dogs, a French fry–covered, deep-fried hot dog on a stick. Others blend seemingly contrasting flavors, like chocolate and bacon, to create a buzzed-about new product. But year after year, the newest fads fail to make a dent in the stronghold that traditional fair favorites maintain among fairgoers. "It's interesting that many flash-in-the-pan or nov-

ON PAPER, becoming a food vendor at the Minnesota State Fair doesn't look to be a difficult task. You go to the fair's website (mnstatefair.org) and download a registration form to complete and mail back to the fair's concessions and exhibitions department. The one-page form is generally straightforward, asking for the vendor's contact information, business and banking references, the type and amount of space needed, and—oh yeah—your concept.

There's the rub: you could have what you believe to be the greatest idea since the deep-fried candy bar, but anything that doesn't have that "it" factor likely won't make it past the review stage. And no, placing the food on a stick doesn't guarantee a spot on the vendor roster. "That's probably the biggest perception that I fight—that if I get a quirky new product on a stick I'll get into the fair and make a million dollars. Well, it has to make sense to be on a stick, you have to know what you're doing, and you have to be able to produce it and sell it to a million people and keep up your quality. Otherwise, nobody would come back," concessions manager Dennis Larson says.

What does pique Larson's interest? Delicious, high-quality food that makes the fairgoer want more year after year. "With fair food, if it's not an experience, it's not special. You can go to the mall food court, go to McDonald's, go to wherever every day of the week. So out here, if it's not special, if it's not fun, if it's not a good show, even down to the customer service, if nothing else, if the person doesn't make eye contact and have a friendly greeting, then I'll just want another hamburger [elsewhere]."

But the food concept is only one part of the picture. Availability is a huge factor in determining how many entrepreneurs get their shot at fair greatness each year, and there are only two ways for that to happen: either an established vendor forfeits his or her spot or the fair decides to expand its food offerings. Considering that Larson expands only "very slowly and methodically"—and that three to four hundred registrations are kept on file each year—it may take a lot of patience to gain a gastronomic foothold on the fairgrounds. In 2009, only four new vendor registrations were accepted.

But take heart: registrations are reviewed annually, kept for three years, and can be re-filed an infinite number of times. Larson recalls a quesadilla maker who applied six times before he was accepted, and his father had tried multiple times before him. Persistence does help increase your odds of success. "It's like playing a slot machine. If you put in one quarter and leave, you're probably not going to win. I say patience is a virtue," Larson concludes. ⊙

Turkey to Go stand at the Minnesota State Fair

elty items may seem really big or huge, but they don't compare to what I call the icons of the fair," Larson says.

The top ten list of highest-grossing fair foods typically contains simple pleasures like chocolate chip cookies, ice cream and other dairy treats, cheese curds, french fries, mini donuts, roasted corn, and hot dogs. In 2010, only two foods in the top ten were stick based: the corn dog (number two) and the pork chop on a stick (number nine). The most exotic items on the list are gyros and falafel, which have overtaken pizza for number ten. Regardless of the type of food consumed, chances are it's eaten by fairgoers who are simultaneously making their way through the crowds rather than sitting down at a counter or table.

"The grandmas and grandpas will eat several of their meals at a church dining hall, and that's where they go because that's what they were raised on and that's what they want at their age in life, whereas someone in their twenties, I would challenge: have they ever been in a church dining hall? Probably not, because it's not what they want. They want something quick and fun and something they can eat on the run. They don't want to stop. Everybody's moving all the time," Larson says.

The Turkey Sandwich

Though not on a stick, the Minnesota State Fair turkey sandwich meets the portability standard for modern-day fair food. But the sandwich is part of a rich history of turkey dishes served at the state fair, and it has evolved several times in its journey to become the sandwich it is today.

When the Minnesota Turkey Growers Association first opened its res-

Assembling the Minnesota Turkey Growers Association fair sandwich

taurant, known as the Turkey House, at the Minnesota State Fair in 1958, its menu closely resembled the bills of fare at the church dining halls of the era. Fairgoers could purchase turkey roast dinners and turkey casseroles as well as barbecued turkey wings and drumsticks, turkey sandwiches, and turkey salads. In 1988, the state fair offered MTGA the opportunity to move into a new facility on the east side of Clough Street between Judson and Carnes avenues, and with the relocation the restaurant pared down its menu to focus on five items: grilled, marinated turkey tenderloin sandwich; grilled turkey burger; deep-fried turkey nugget on a stick; turkey salad; and cold deli turkey sandwich. "We were pretty smug when we got that restaurant with all that new equipment and everything," remembers Marilyn McAlpine, the retired home economist for the Minnesota Turkey Research and Promotion Council who helped develop the turkey dishes served at the fair.

Cutbacks were necessary again in the midnineties, when it became hard to maintain a good staff and the MTGA wanted its restaurant, now called Turkey to Go, to mimic other popular concessions stands by focusing on one premier item. With the growing popularity of deep-fat turkey fryers, the association decided to offer a deep-fried turkey sandwich and worked with one of its growers who had considerable catering experience to develop it. McAlpine describes the process:

> That was also the time that a Creole or Cajun or Jamaican or jerk type of flavor was so popular, and oftentimes those turkey deep-fat fryers were sold with a package of some kind of dry seasoning you could use, so we experimented a little bit and developed a flavor that would be typical of this method of preparation. Plus, it would introduce this type of seasoning with turkey—a turkey is a marvelous carrier of any kind of seasoning, really, because it's a delicate meat flavor. But here in Minnesota we had to play around with it a little bit because we weren't sure if our customers were going to accept it. But it was very well received and became wildly successful as a sandwich.

But by the mid-2000s, the turkey sandwich was ready for another makeover. Even though the deep-fried turkey sandwich required fewer staff than the original restaurant did, the MTGA was running into space constraints: it had to keep ten burners going continuously to meet the demand for the sandwiches, and soon that number wasn't enough. "We got to a point where we reached our limitations [within the restaurant], so we had to either take preparation off-site or do something different," Olson says.

Enter Drew Levin. In 2007, the Minnesota-born-and-bred entrepreneur— and turkey sandwich fanatic—approached the MTGA, which at the time

Giant turkey sandwich at the Minnesota State Fair

was weighing its options for the sandwich, with his new concept for cooking and preparation. "It just so happened that our idea and passion for the sandwich merged with [the MTGA's] timing and their desire to promote Minnesota turkey throughout the state and the country," Levin says. "As we went through the whole process and discussion, it was important to us to really be able to maintain the level of quality that that turkey sandwich delivered to everyone who loved it. It has a really interesting cult following that is growing and growing fast."

Though Levin had no previous culinary experience, he was a resourceful entrepreneur who, through a series of family connections, found local chef and caterer Tim Malloy to help him develop the sandwich. After a couple years of experimentation, the new turkey sandwich debuted at the Minnesota State Fair in 2009, and the response was overwhelmingly positive. "I don't think anyone noticed the difference, which is the best part. That was what our goal was. I think we delivered just as juicy a sandwich, just as tasty, and we did it in a healthier and probably a more responsible way," Levin adds.

Instead of deep-frying whole turkeys, Levin and his crew roast deboned turkey breasts and thighs. Not only is this cooking method healthier than deep-frying, it is safer for employees, who no longer have to deal with hot oil and the mess of carving whole birds. The cooked turkey, a 70/30 blend of white to dark meat, is shredded and then marinated for twenty-four hours in a mixture very similar to that used on the deep-fried version of the sandwich. The meat is piled onto a Minnesota-made Country Hearth bun specially cut with a thicker bottom half to absorb the meat's rich juices. "I always suggest to people they eat it naked. The sandwich walks alone better than anything else," Levin opines, but two Ken Davis barbecue sauces are offered on the side, as well as relish, mayonnaise, mustard, and Cajun seasoning blend.

The restaurant also serves roasted turkey legs, but the thirteen thousand legs sold in 2009 were dwarfed by the forty-eight thousand sandwiches fairgoers devoured. Fans include WCCO-TV's Mark Rosen and Don Shelby, Vikings owner Zygi Wilf, and CNN anchor John King, along with tens of thousands of Minnesotans who enjoy Minnesota-raised turkey. "I recently just had a friend tell me that, when he was at the booth, he had heard a police officer had the sandwich and then radioed, 'Everybody has to come down here and get this sandwich. This is incredible,' and apparently within ten minutes, there were six or seven officers there having sandwiches," Levin says.

And to the excitement of these and other turkey sandwich fans, Turkey to Go has now expanded beyond the Minnesota State Fair. The Turkey to Go mobile food cart began selling sandwiches in downtown Minneapolis in August 2010, serving hungry downtown workers and Minnesota Twins fans heading to a game at Target Field. Sandwich lovers can check the Turkey to Go Facebook fan page or Twitter account for the cart's location that day.

The MTGA keeps its recipe for the turkey sandwich under wraps, but it shared enough tips on its flavoring and cooking methods for us to create one in the spirit of the state fair version. The sandwich showcases roasted turkey breast tenderloin that is shredded and immersed overnight in a Cajun-based marinade. Nestled inside a whole-wheat bun, it requires no additional sauces or seasonings but is quite tasty with a side of home-made pickles.

Turkey Sandwich

Makes 4 servings

Adapted from Cooks.com

1 pound turkey breast tenderloin
1 cup olive oil
4 cloves garlic, crushed
1 teaspoon dried thyme
½ teaspoon cayenne pepper
½ teaspoon black pepper
½ cup white vinegar
1 teaspoon dried oregano
1 teaspoon paprika
4 whole-wheat buns, sliced

Preheat oven to 350°F. Roast tenderloin 30 minutes or until juices run clear. Immediately shred meat using two forks and place into large bowl. Combine marinade ingredients (olive oil through paprika) in a jar and shake until well blended. Pour marinade over shredded turkey and refrigerate 24 hours. Reheat turkey in large saucepan until warm. Scoop into whole-wheat buns and serve.

5 The Hot Dago
Sausage, Sauce, and Strife

JAMES NORTON / PHOTOGRAPHS BY BECCA DILLEY

𝒥n the amiable, workaday, easygoing world of sandwiches, the hot dago is a standout: it's both a Minnesota original and the only sandwich to be targeted by a government agency for its intellectual content. Dating back to St. Paul's 1930s-era Italian enclaves, the hot dago takes its name from two things: the hot peppers that once accompanied its marinara-covered sausage patty plus a well-known term—many would say slur—for Italian Americans. These days, the peppers usually sit on the side, but the simple sausage patty–marinara–Italian/Vienna bread combination continues to be the heart of the dish.

Regardless of its size (which varies widely), the dago is a hearty sandwich, an adaptation of Italian American red gravy pasta to a grab-and-go format. The spicing of the sausage, the sweetness, depth of spice, or spicy heat of the sauce, and the slight funk of provolone or milder flavor of mozzarella come together to give this particular dish a real kick-to-the-mouth impact. Depending on the hand at the tiller, the hot dago can be many things. It can sport a garlic jolt, taste of pure tomatoes, be a melted cheese bomb, crunch with vinegared veggies, soggily fall apart in your hands, be totally portable, or require the use of cutlery. Like so many sandwiches, the hot dago started as a simple spin on American-adapted comfort food and, over the years, drifted in numerous directions.

Jack, Diego, and "Dago": What's in a Name?

The endlessly simmering controversy over the hot dago is driven by the name's history as a slur directed at ethnic Italians. It's a controversy complicated by the fact that those selling (and often buying) the sandwich have overwhelmingly been of Italian American descent themselves. *Dago* itself has a tangled history, haphazardly jumping languages, continents, and meanings over its lifespan. It originated in the early nineteenth century as nautical jargon. English deckhands were commonly known as *Jack;* their Spanish or Portuguese counterparts were given the name *Diego,* later to become *Dago.*

Writing in 1890 about the term *Jack-o-nape,* Dr. Charles P. G. Scott considered the connection between *Jack* and *Dago* via a common Latin origin: "The word Jack was often used with reference to Italians. It is a curious coincidence that the American word Dago, etymologically the same as Jack, though originally applied to Portuguese (Pg. Diego, Lat. Jacobus) is now more commonly applied to the more numerous Italians." So, *Dago* comes from *Diego,* which comes from *Jacobus.* Once largely applied to Portuguese sailors, it had, by the end of the nineteenth century, come to stick to their Italian counterparts, and then more generally to Italians in America.

A collected volume of *Popular Science* monthlies from 1890–91 contains a lively back-and-forth over the name. An essay titled "What Shall We Do with the 'Dago'?" captures the mood of the era's anti-Italian hate speech: "This 'dago,' it seems, not only herds, but fights," wrote Appleton Morgan,

> The knife with which he cuts his bread he also uses to lop off another "dago's" finger or ear, or to slash another's cheek. He quarrels over his meals; and his game, whatever it is, which he plays with pennies after his meal is over, is carried on [with] knife at hand. More even than this, he sleeps in herds; and if a "dago" in his sleep rolls up against another "dago," the two whip out their knives and settle it there and then; and, except a grunt at being disturbed, perhaps, no notice is taken by the twenty or fifty other "dagoes" in the apartment. He is quite as familiar with the sight of human blood as with the sight of the food he eats.

A reader named W. H. Laerabee, writing from Plainfield, New Jersey, objected strongly: "Mr. Appleton Morgan's query in the Monthly for December, What shall we do with the 'Dago'? suggests many other questions. I presume the writer did not design that his description of the 'dago' should be regarded as typical of the Italian people, or of any considerable part of them, but only intended it to apply to a peculiar variety of the dangerous classes that happens to come from Italy; but his paper is, unfortunately, liable to the former offensive interpretation, and has, I happen to know, been taken in that sense in at least one quarter."

Laerabee goes on to defend Italians in general, explain the existence of a small Italian criminal class (particularly in the south, due mostly to foreign occupation), and add, "No European nation, excepting Greece, has done more for civilization and few for liberty than Italy." He concludes, "What shall we do with the dago? Give him a chance."

The late nineteenth century saw a high point of anti-Italian feeling. In 1891, the largest mass lynching in American history took place in New Orleans: eleven Italian Americans falsely thought to have assassinated the police chief were murdered by a mob that called out "hang the dagos" throughout the event. For many Italians newly arrived in America at the beginning of the twentieth century, *dago* could therefore be a truly hurtful and hateful word—a reference to poverty and criminality. American immigrants have always, to lesser and greater degrees, faced accusations of criminal behavior and suffered demonization as outsiders, and the word *dago* is only one example.

Though not much in use as a contemporary slur, it crops up memorably in *The Godfather* (released in 1972 and set in late 1940s New York). Lawyer Tom Hagen, the adopted son of mafia boss Don Corleone, approaches a Hollywood producer to ask a favor on the don's behalf. The producer assumes Hagen is Italian and insults him accordingly:

> Jack Woltz: Johnny Fontane will never get that movie. I don't care how many dago, wop, guinea, greaseball goombas come out of the woodwork.
>
> Tom Hagen: I'm German-Irish.
>
> Jack Woltz: Well, let me tell you something, my kraut-mick friend. I'm gonna make so much trouble for you you won't know what hit you.

The tone is hostile, but the slurs are almost conversational rather than murderous, rattled off by a speaker who, himself Jewish, has no doubt faced prejudice in America.

While Minnesota has never been a particular hotbed of anti-Italian feeling, Italian immigrants and Italian Americans here have faced challenges just as their countrymen and women have around the country. Michael Natalie, a retired stationary engineer and pipefitter in Duluth, quoted in the 2007 volume *Italian Voices: Making Minnesota Our Home* by

Mary Ellen Mancina-Batinich, recalled, "When I was a young boy, I'll never forget that I used to play with a boy that used to live right next door. His folks were American [born] and he used to have [a butterfly collection] and all that little stuff. I used to like to go over to the house and just look, but then the mother—I'll never forget the mother—one day she told me, 'You get out of here, you little—you little dago! I don't want you playing with my boy.' I went home and cried and cried."

As the fortunes of Italian Americans rose throughout the twentieth century, the word lost some of its sting; as popular perception of Italians shifted from suspicion and hostility to tolerance, assimilation, and even welcoming, the word evolved further. Thus it was ripe for reclamation at midcentury by Minnesota's Italian American community, whose members applied it to a sandwich eaten on a daily basis by many from within and eventually outside of their neighborhoods.

The sandwich's name has faced a number of challenges in the modern era of politically correct language. In 1991, Joe Soucheray, a columnist at the *Pioneer Press,* railed against the St. Paul Department of Human Rights for advising restaurants to remove the word *dago* from their menus at the request of a ticked-off New York lawyer named Dominic A. Villoni. Villoni visited St. Paul and was unpleasantly surprised by the appearance of what he regarded as an offensive racial slur on a downtown restaurant's menu.

In 2000, *Pioneer Press* columnist Nick Coleman quoted the tough-talking Ramsey County political maven Dino Guerin on the hot dago controversy: "We've got our own heritage and our own values, and we're not going to let someone from outside tell us about our own food. If hot dagos didn't offend my Italian grandfather and grandmother, they sure as hell aren't going to offend me." In 2007, the issue was reignited by another St. Paul human rights director, W. H. Tyrone Terrill, who requested removal of the term from the menu at DeGidio's in St. Paul. As of 2010, the name's still there—and on the menus of at least a dozen other establishments scattered throughout the Twin Cities area.

Thus, in a nutshell, the story of a word: from a Latin name (Jacobus) to a Spanish one (Diego) to a Portuguese nautical nickname (Dago) to a derogatory and sometimes hateful reference to Italian Americans to a Twin Cities sausage sandwich (hot dago).

The hot dago sandwich at DeGidio's, St. Paul

The Silence of the Dago

Pursuing the story of the dago, we contacted by mail and/or phone a number of different restaurants, including three of the oldest and most notable, all located in St. Paul: DeGidio's (founded in 1933), Yarusso-Bros. (also '33), and Cosetta Italian Market (founded in 1911, and now selling its dago under the house name of the Cosetta sandwich). The only one to reply was Yarusso's, and, well, what happened next perhaps most vividly reflects the ambiguity that swirls around the name of the sandwich.

Yarusso-Bros. sits in the southwestern part of Payne-Phalen, a St. Paul neighborhood obviously in flux. The hulking mass of the Hamm's Brewery dominates the skyline, its doors shut since 1997; Vang Motors sits next door to the Testa Barber Shop; a street banner printed with an image of Italy flaps in front of a Mexican restaurant; and the Taqueria Los Paisanos diplomatically speaks the language of the old along with the language of the new.

Next door to Yarusso-Bros. sits Morelli's, a liquor and meat market frequented by the neighborhood's older residents, where hot dago–style patties are sold by the half dozen or case under the name of "hot paisano" patties. Dating back to 1915, Morelli's has its own complicated history, told in part by columnist Don Boxmeyer, who wrote about Matt Morelli's road-tripping antics and St. Paul political power brokering in his book, *A Knack for Knowing Things*.

Inside Yarusso's, the mood is purely, defiantly, even aggressively Italian American. Dark wood and low lights give the place a vibe that sits somewhere in the center of a Venn diagram that includes "romantic," "nostalgic," and "menacing," and assorted Italiana including *Godfather*-inspired hand-and-puppet strings and Yarusso's shirts decorate the walls. Three televisions hung over the bar play all three *Godfather* movies—one per screen—"all day, every day," according to the waitress on duty. *The Godfather* is a complicated choice: for some it symbolizes the climb from immigrant to American in all its subtle complexity; for others it represents a gangster caricature of a country and people who have always had much more to give than an offer that can't be refused.

When contacted for an interview, Annette Yarusso, wife of owner Mike Yarusso, got in touch by e-mail, writing, "You picked the right place—[the current owners'] grandfather invented the 'hot dago.' Give me a call to set up a time to meet with one of the brothers."

Things went downhill quickly after that. A phone call yielded the exciting tidbit that an alternative explanation for the hot dago name got around the awkward "ethnic slur" aspect of the word *dago,* and an interview time was scheduled. But soon after that, Annette cancelled, explaining, "We decided to not do the interview. We would rather not bring attention to the controversy around the name hot dago."

A grouchy author, blocked from a good story, might argue that one easy way to avoid controversy would be to stop selling sandwiches called hot dagos unless you're willing to give the general public the benefit of some sort of explanation or back story. But invoking the code of silence makes a certain amount of sense when it comes to controversial sandwiches: you're spared the experience of talking to tediously self-important writers and of dustups such as the one that still swirls around the hot dago's name.

We were, however, able to talk to barber and local business owner Roberto Cocchiarella, owner of Roberto's on Grand. Cocchiarella, the youngest of six children, came from a family with grandmothers who spoke no English. This lifelong St. Paul resident's family hails from the southern Italian province of Campania, home to Naples and Mount Vesuvius. Cocchiarella's memory of the Swede Hollow neighborhood (now a park) and Payne Avenue goes back to the earlier part of the twentieth century: "My father came over in '21," he recalls, "and back then the Italians and the Swedes didn't like each other. Because Swede Hollow was along Payne Avenue, and the next group was the Italians coming in, it was a little like *West Side Story.* They used to have street fights."

Roberto Cocchiarella, lifelong Italian American resident of St. Paul

The early 1900s marked the dawning of Italian immigration into Swede Hollow, which was, according to Ralph Yekaldo's account in *A Knack for Knowing Things,* "a city within a city . . . They began to call it 'Little Italy,' and they made the most of it. If there was an empty piece of land, they had a garden planted, and it was like gold to them. I remember when the tomatoes started to get ripe, it was tomato paste time."

Time helped to tame the once rough-and-tumble, insular neighborhood, however. "Like every group that comes over from another country, once you go to school, your kids go to school, and mingle with the other kids, you become a melting pot, which we think is so wonderful," says Cocchiarella. The process of immigration and assimilation is always, however, a bumpy one. "My brother's name was Mariano, and we all called him Marve. Nobody wanted to be ethnic in the fifties—no ethnic, only American. Lots of friends had names like 'sonny,' 'Junior.' In the seventies and eighties, everybody wanted to be ethnic again."

Cocchiarella points to four main industries that drew Italian immigration to the city: the railroad, Hamm's Brewery, 3M, and Whirlpool. The St. Paul Water Department was also a major employer. "Each neighborhood was its own nationality on the east side of St. Paul. That area [near Yarusso's] was called Railroad Island. My father's family started there and was sponsored by his sisters; their husbands worked in the railroads," he recalls. "Up north it was the mining. What amazed me was that there were five separate families with bar restaurants that all did well [on Payne Avenue]. I think part of it was the industries, so people came for lunch. [Yarusso's] was basically a workingman's bar for a long time. On Payne Avenue, there were five restaurants and bars within a two-mile radius— but Yarusso's is the only one still alive."

Boxmeyer, writing about the "pipe smoke, cigar smoke, and spaghetti sauce"–scented restaurant, noted, "On Sundays, the men would gather at Yarusso's restaurant to play bocce ball and moda, a game similar to paper, rock, and scissors in which participants 'throw' fingers simultaneously and bet on the total number that will be displayed. The game was said to be illegal in Italy because it produced too many serious fights over the score."

On the sandwich, Cocchiarella's feelings are clear and heartfelt: "I love hot dagos," he says. "I've had them my whole life." His definition is straightforward: "Hot dago—basically—is a smashed meatball on bread with sauce," he says. "They don't have it anywhere else in the country. A lot of families will have hot dagos at graduation parties, make a whole electric roaster full of them. Salad on the side, Italian cookies, and stuff. A hundred twenty people at an open house, family and friends, you know." He continues, "The hot dago was probably the same kind of this, probably leftover meatballs. I talked with Freddy [Yarusso] over at Yarusso's about it: he said you just take a meatball and put it in bread. I don't know why they started calling it *dagos*; probably some restaurant started calling it that."

As for the controversy over the name, Cocchiarella takes the side that seems to prevail among many if not most local Italian Americans: let the name stand. "I don't understand it, and the people who are complaining aren't Italians," says Cocchiarella. "They think there is some ethnic slur. Originally it came from Spanish and Italian men who were hotheads during World War II—they called them 'hotheaded dagos.' We even liked being called *dagos,* with each other. I don't see the problem; I never took offense to it. The word that bothered us was *wop,* because it means without papers."

"We didn't eat out a lot when I was younger; we mostly stayed home. But when I got into high school, my friends and I would go out to Yarusso's every Saturday, almost every Saturday. Hot dagos and greasy fries," he recalls.

Cocchiarella notes the change that has slowly transformed his old stomping grounds. Many Italian Americans, he relates, moved on out to Woodbury and other more suburban settings. "[Payne Avenue] has become pretty African American. Hispanics are moving in a lot there now, too. And I have seen some of the stores open now with Hispanic names. More as you get up the avenue." He concludes, "[Payne Avenue] was a great area to grow up in. Every nonna [grandmother] knew you. And if you were doing something wrong, even if they yelled at you, you knew that they cared about you."

Talking Dagos in Nordeast

Leaving St. Paul, the story became a little easier to pursue. Dusty's Bar in Northeast Minneapolis is known citywide for its dagos, and a mural painted on its exterior proudly touts the sandwich: HOMEMADE DAGOS • BURGERS • SOUPS • COCKTAILS. The sign out front is even more direct: DUSTY'S DAGOS & LIQUOR.

The interior is dark and quiet, comfortable to its clientele and intimidating to the outsider. When my photographer and I tentatively entered the bar, the heads of seven regulars swiveled in unison to follow us in. Lacking a truly appropriate response to the mildly irritated attention of a group of strangers, we walked to the back of the room like we knew where we were going. We caught the barkeep's eye.

The barkeep turned out to be the owner, the gentle and softly spoken Pasquale "Pat" Stebe. Numerous times during our interview, Stebe excused himself to refill a beer or settle a tab, keeping his regulars happy even as they continued to cast suspicious glances at the camera- and

ABOVE: Pasquale "Pat" Stebe, owner of Dusty's Bar, Minneapolis

BELOW: Fifties food: Stebe family photo at Dusty's

mp3 recorder–wielding duo. "Don't answer no questions," advised one of the patrons, talking to Stebe. "You don't know who these people are! They could be internal revenue."

When it became clear that the interlopers' mission was gathering information about dagos rather than collecting taxes, the drinker's mood shifted from hostile to friendly. "Got the original hot dago right here!" the man at the bar laughed, pointing at himself, "And be sure you put in your little book that this is the greatest bar in the world." So noted. Talking to Stebe, we went back to the beginning of the bar, which opened more than fifty years ago. Stebe's father ("Dusty") was from Gilbert, on the Iron Range, and he married an Italian woman.

"That's how it all started," Stebe recalls, talking about the beginning of the dago sandwich at Dusty's. "My dad said to my mom—my mom's Italian—'Why don't we start making some dagos?' That was fifty years ago, since about '58." He continues, "My dad and my uncle bought it in '52. Before that they had a 3.2 joint on Twenty-ninth and Nicollet by the Nicollet ballpark. They sold it, and my dad was all set to move to California and work for Honeywell. Just before they moved, my uncle said to my dad, 'Dusty, let's go look at this bar in Northeast,' and he said, 'I'm all set up to move to California.' My dad bought my uncle out eight years later."

Stebe walks to the other side of the bar to refill a customer's Grain Belt Premium. When he returns, he's carrying a 1950s-era black-and-white photo of seven people in party hats, smiling and dancing. In the background, a sign reads, "Try Our Delicious Italian Sausage Sandwich: 40 cents." Stebe's mom, purse in hand, sports a smile and is a bit removed from the action; his dad, wearing a serious expression and black-rimmed spectacles, surveys the crowd of younger folk with a not-entirely-celebratory expression. "My ma was a great cook," Stebe recalls. "We just figured, let's start making some hamburgers and dagos, so we started doing that. It's a family deal. It's my mom's recipe. It used to be grandma's recipe—mom kind of reverse[-engineered] it. She changed it a little bit."

The dago (no "hot" in the name at Dusty's) is unlike any of the others we stumbled upon. Minus the splash of sauce and with a pepper and onion garnish, Dusty's version of the sandwich is like a hamburger reincarnated with a sausage patty in place of ground beef. "We used to get buns from Blackie's," recalls Stebe. "It was just a great bakery. It was the best. They went out of business five years ago. I keep on searching for Blackie's Bakery. It was a nice, soft, fresh bun with flavor to it. It's just good, you know? It just had a nice sweetness to it." These days, the bar's buns (still

A Dago Messiness Spectrum

THOSE WHO SEEK OUT dagos (and dagos-by-another-name, including Italianos, Paisanos, and Cosetta sandwiches) have a wide range of options to wrestle with. The sandwiches are generally priced between five and seven dollars, although DeGidio's and Roma's are eight dollars, probably to account for their Brobdingnagian size. The following is a field guide to the sandwich, with a special eye cast toward relative sloppiness: least sloppy sandwiches up top, progressing downward into cheesy, saucy messes. Note that some shops profiled below offered sloppy and non-sloppy versions: we went with whatever was recommended or highlighted on the menu.

Dusty's Dago with the Works, $4.75. There's an austerity to this sandwich that is almost un-dagolike. A geographic outlier (Dusty's is in Northeast Minneapolis; most other notable dago joints we hit were in St. Paul or points east), Dusty's is a stylistic outlier, too. The Dusty's Dago is much like a hamburger, minus the burger and plus a salty Italian sausage with sweet peppers and onions. The lack of marinara makes it the rare dago you can eat while wearing clothing you care about.

Flicker Meats' Hot Dago, $4.50. Our come-from-nowhere dark horse sandwich, discovered by chance at an Oakdale strip mall meat shop. Similar to Dusty's in that it's served on a bun (not sliced bread), the Flicker Hot Dago, while saucy, is relatively edible without creating a sauce-based clean-up challenge. A spicy and flavorful sausage patty stands up to the thickness of the bun, bringing some heat to a well-balanced package. Pickled jalapeños add more welcome heat and vinegar flavor to the mix.

Roma's Hot Dago, $8, Willernie. This ciabatta-based creation certainly has the potential to mess up a sweater, but it's a relatively coherent piece of food after all's said and done. The ciabatta holds together well, and the sauce is drizzled (not slopped or poured) on. The giardiniera is finely chopped, dispelling fears of big vinegared vegetable pieces flying out onto your fingers or lap.

Dari-Ette Drive In's Hot Italiano, $6.89, St. Paul. Dating back to the 1950s, the Dari-Ette serves a Hot Italiano that boasts an almost sloppy joe–like tangy meat sauce and a split Italian sausage rather than a patty or meatball. Robust, almost foamy bread contains the meat, cheese, and sauce within. One of the best-balanced dagos that crossed my lips. Relatively neat, but keep in mind that you'll probably be eating in your car.

Cosetta's Cossetta Sandwich, $6.79, St. Paul. Thick-cut bread does a relatively good job of containing the sauce within this classic, if somewhat bland interpretation of the dago. The patty itself was quite dense and flat, the sauce a bit dull in terms of flavor, the accompanying pepperoncini a nice touch that helped the package as a whole.

Brianno's Hot Dago with Cheese, $5.95, Eagan. Probably the messiest of "pick-upable" sandwiches out there, the huge, thick, sauce-drenched spherical meatball filling oozes out the sides of the sandwich and actually soaks and penetrates the relatively flimsy but pleasantly crusty Vienna bread. More of a trap than a sandwich, this thing essentially disintegrates between your hands as you eat. Also, absolutely delicious.

Yarusso's Hot Dago with Cheese and Sauce, $7, St. Paul. A lot of melted cheese and the liberal use of sweet sauce make this a dago that requires attention from a fork and knife. No surprises in the flavor department; this unreconstructed Italian American–style dish would be right at home in the mideighties.

DeGidio's Old Fashioned Hot Dago, $7.95, St. Paul. Like Yarusso's, this cheese- and sauce-covered behemoth is so messy that it's relatively clean: use of cutlery is not an option—it's a requirement. This version is actually more of a lasagna (with bread, rather than noodles) than a sandwich, per se. Drowning in rich, milky cheese and sweet but kicky sauce, this monster dago demands a big appetite.

Fireside's Sloppy Hot Dago, $6.99. Proudly marked as this comfy West St. Paul bar's signature item, the Fireside Sloppy Hot Dago consists of a dense, mammoth sausage patty buried in a good quart to quart and a half of sweet sauce. The cheese, unfortunately, gets lost in the mix, but the bread is toasted almost to the point of being charred, contributing a pleasant crunchy, carbon-kissed element. Like DeGidio's, the Fireside dago demands a big appetite or a doggie bag. ⬤

The Italiano sandwich at the Dari-Ette, St. Paul

quite tasty) are made by Uptown Ovens, and the pork for the sausage patties comes from Ready Meats in Northeast; the peppers that garnish the sandwich are grown on a farm especially for the bar.

The name, says Stebe, was never that big of a deal. "Here [in Minnesota], it doesn't mean so much," he says. "Once you get east of Lake Michigan, they start getting really sensitive about it. I mean, they probably had to take a lot of crap for it. Dago, wop, guinea—it doesn't mean much to me, you know? And I'm half Italian. But if someone says *Eye-talian,* that pisses me off."

Building a Better Hot Dago

John DeGidio, of DeGidio's, was quoted in an October 3, 2003, edition of the *Pioneer Press* thus: "It's all right for an Italian to use the term 'hot dago,' but if you're not Italian, you shouldn't. Now, people who aren't Italian are using it, and I don't think that's right." DeGidio may have unwittingly been talking about the future of the sandwich, which—in all its saucy, cheesy, controversy-inducing glory—may lay outside of its traditional playground and in the hands of culinary innovators like the Pilrain brothers of Willernie.

Brent and Brian Pilrain, who operate the newly opened Roma Restaurant, Bar, and Market, have taken ownership of the hot dago in a way that's assertive—particularly since the brothers don't claim Italian heritage. In fact, they take on the outsider challenge in a full-throated and direct manner on their website, writing, "Our family name is of French descent and our lineage consists of Germanic and Gaelic ancestry. From approximately 700 B.C. until 400 C.E. the Romans ruled, settled, and civilized much of Europe so it could be said that most Americans with European heritage have some form of Roman in them whether it be by genetics or culture."

"We have a love for the history of ancient civilizations and the Roman Empire—it's just fascinating history," says Brent Pilrain, whose enthusiasm for his job shines through when he enthuses about the hot dago. "We saw them as a good use for our hot Italian sausage, which is something we customized and spiced the way we wanted to," he explains. "It was kind of taking something we had seen in this area of Minnesota as kind of a signature hot sandwich. Ours has a few elements that not all of them have."

First and foremost is the bread: rather than choosing Vienna or Italian, the brothers use a buttered, toasted ciabatta. Pilrain describes the sandwich: "It goes on there with the sauce and provolone and a homemade giardiniera that we put on top, which adds a nice texture and crunch, a lot of garden vegetables—hot sport peppers, green olives—and a blend of spices that we mix in with oil and vinegar." The giardiniera is the X-factor that really sets the Roma version of the sandwich apart, bringing a garden-fresh crunch and a vinegared brightness to the overall package. The sauce, too, has a cleaner, fresher taste than some of the old stalwarts.

"It's our homemade marinara sauce—it's a clash of a classic pizza sauce and a traditional spaghetti sauce, where it's one sauce that can be used

for everything," says Pilrain. "It kind of simplifies things for us, and it's a very clean and simple sauce—probably seven ingredients total in it—and a very clean tomato flavor, not really spicy, no heavy herbs in there, no overpowering garlic. It's not too sweet, so you can really taste the tomato to it. It really kind of cuts through everything."

The sausage, too, is formulated in-house for maximum impact. "We have the benefit of having our own butcher shop here," continues Pilrain. "Hand-trimmed, hand-cut meats; we grind our own pork sausage . . . all of our fresh certified chuck.

Making the hot dago sandwich at Roman Market, Willernie

So we're mixing our beef with pork, hand trimming it all so it's a really nice blend. Adding our own spices to it, hand pattying everything . . . which I think gives us an end result that's hard to match."

The sandwich, says Pilrain, became part of Roma's offerings after its 2006 opening as a deli. "We just kind of saw them here and there—sandwiches are a big thing, and we're foodies," he explains. "I think the dago just kind of came from over-the-counter conversations with customers, with them giving ideas of new sandwiches to add to the menu. The original deli probably had like six hot specialty sandwiches, and now we have like eighteen."

As for the name, Pilrain understands the controversy, but for him, the hot dago is just part of the culinary landscape—nothing more. "I didn't create the name; it's kind of what we know it to be," he says. "In researching it, we found it's a Minnesota thing, where that name stuck to be a sandwich. That's how deep it goes with my knowledge of it. Obviously the term goes back farther, going to the East Coast and immigrants and things of that nature. It's a sticky situation when you get into what it is." But, he explains, "I think for most Minnesotans, when you hear *hot dago,* you don't think of anything derogatory. You think of Italian sausage, a bun, sauce that's going to drip down your chin . . . and deliciousness."

Roma Hot Dago Sandwich

Makes 1 serving

Contributed by Brent Pilrain, chef

6-inch ciabatta bun, lightly buttered with unsalted butter
⅓ cup fresh homemade marinara
1 (12-ounce) cooked hot Italian sausage patty (heated to 165°F)
3 slices provolone
4 tablespoons drained giardiniera (recipe follows)
Fresh chopped Italian parsley to garnish

Lightly grill buttered ciabatta bun. Place marinara sauce on cooked sausage patty in saucepan set over medium heat and steam, covered, about 3 minutes. Top with cheese, cover, and steam an additional 3 minutes. Place sauced patty on bun and top with giardiniera and parsley. Serve.

Giardiniera

4 ribs celery, finely diced
1 large onion, finely diced (about 1 cup)
½ medium green pepper, finely diced (about ½ cup)
½ medium red pepper, finely diced (about ½ cup)
1 large carrot, finely diced (about ¾ cup)
½ cup finely diced green olives
5–10 sport peppers, finely diced (about 1 cup)
2 tablespoons minced garlic
1 teaspoon dried oregano
1 teaspoon crushed red pepper
1 teaspoon black pepper
2 teaspoons salt
½ cup red wine vinegar
½ cup 80/20 oil (80 percent canola/20 percent olive)

Combine first seven ingredients (celery through sport peppers). Stir together with remaining ingredients (garlic through oil). Store covered and refrigerated.

Hot Dago

Makes 8 servings

Minneapolis-based chef Chris Olson, who created this recipe specifically for *Minnesota Lunch,* writes,

Researching the hot dago sandwich was an exhaustive process. Over the course of two weeks I ate seven of these sandwiches, in various incarnations. Although the fourteen-year-old boy in me loved the giant plate of food with more fries than one could shake a stick at, the thirty-year-old man in me soon realized that a light salad was the more responsible choice of sides.

It was difficult to pin down exactly what really makes a hot dago. Some had the sauce on top, some had the sauce inside, some had cheese that seemed to be made of plastic, but some didn't have any cheese at all. This journey through the sandwiches of east St. Paul provided a bevy of inspiration for my own version.

This recipe is a mélange of flavors and ideas from the Capitol City. The sauce, tangy and sweet, was inspired by the Dari-Ette Drive-in, where your food is served by teens who couldn't care less. The sausage is reminiscent of that found in Cosetta Italian Market, spicy and rich, although the exact Cosetta recipe seems to be more guarded than the Vatican. The construction of the sandwich is inspired by DeGidio's on West Seventh Street, where it seems that every St. Paul native will flock for their weekly hot dago fix.

Sauce

1 large onion, roughly chopped (about 1 cup)
1 tablespoon olive oil
6 cloves garlic, minced
1 cup wine, divided
1 (28-ounce) can pomodoro tomatoes with basil
3 tablespoons dried oregano
3 tablespoons dried basil
2 tablespoons maple syrup (or sugar, if preferred)

4 tablespoons sherry vinegar
1 teaspoon salt
1 teaspoon black pepper

In a large saucepan over low heat, cook onions in olive oil until trans-lucent, about 5 minutes. Stir in garlic until fragrant, about 30 seconds. Increase heat, add ½ cup wine, and reduce by half. Set aside remaining wine. Add remaining ingredients (tomatoes through pepper), and cook, stirring occasionally, about 45 minutes. Pour remaining wine into glass and drink. Remove sauce from heat and blend with an immersion blender until smooth (alternatively, transfer sauce to container of electric blender; cover and blend until smooth). Set aside.

Sausage

2 pounds ground pork
2 teaspoons red pepper flakes
2 teaspoons hot pepper sauce (Tabasco)
1 teaspoon fennel seeds
2 eggs
¼ cup bread crumbs
1 teaspoon salt
1 teaspoon black pepper

Preheat oven to 350°F. Combine all ingredients (pork through pepper) in a bowl; mix well, then form into 8 equal portions, flattening into patties. Place patties on a baking sheet. Bake 20 minutes; remove from oven and set aside.

Assembly

16 (¾-inch-wide) slices Italian Vienna bread (from Cosetta)
2 cups shredded mozzarella

Preheat broiler. Place 8 slices bread on greased baking sheet. Top each slice with one patty, ½ cup sauce, and another slice of bread. Top sandwiches with remaining sauce and mozzarella. Pop that bad boy in the broiler until the cheese has melted and is starting to brown, about 2 minutes. Remove from oven, cool slightly, and enjoy.

6 The Mexican Torta
Meet Me at the Intersection of Taco and Sandwich

SUSAN PAGANI / PHOTOGRAPHS BY KATIE CANNON

𝓘𝓽 𝓽𝓪𝓴𝓮𝓼 𝓪𝓽 𝓵𝓮𝓪𝓼𝓽 𝓯𝓲𝓿𝓮 𝓷𝓪𝓹𝓴𝓲𝓷𝓼 to eat a torta. From the first bite, the juices—meat mingled with chipotle mayonnaise and pickled peppers—escape the sandwich's wax paper wrappings to roll down the diner's wrists and pool on the paper plate. It's part of the experience, no matter where you eat it.

In the Twin Cities, many Mexican restaurant menus offer at least one torta, which can be loosely described as a grilled sandwich that combines meat, beans, cheese, pickled peppers, and a modicum of vegetables and mayonnaise. Yet, without a doubt, the sandwich's most famous proponent is Manuel Gonzalez, owner and chef of the eponymous Manny's Tortas in Minneapolis, which serves only sandwiches, a dedication that has paid off in enthusiastic followers that keep two shops in Lake Street's Mercado Central and Global Market hopping day and night.

From Mexico City to the Twin Cities

Gonzalez is a native of Mexico City. In the early eighties, he finished up administration and cooking at the Escuela de San Ángel culinary school and decided to move to the United States. Ask him how he chose Minnesota, of all the cold, snowy places, and he'll answer without hesitation that he wanted to learn English. "I went to the American Embassy to ask for English courses in the United States," he says. "They showed me this brochure of ten thousand lakes. It looked very beautiful and I wanted to go somewhere where I would have to speak English. Texas, California, and Chicago are very popular, but you can get away—there are people who speak Spanish there. So that's how I picked Minnesota, because at that time, nobody spoke Spanish. And I love it; it's a beautiful state."

Six months of winter aside, people come to Minnesota for many reasons: economics, family, health, political asylum, and just plain serendipity not the least of them. According to Dionicio Valdés, writing in *Mexicans in Minnesota,* the first recorded Mexican immigrant arrived in Minnesota in 1886. Luis Garzon, a nineteen-year-old oboe player in the traveling Mexico City Orchestra, likely had no intention of settling in the Midwest. When the orchestra came to Minneapolis to perform at an industrial exposition, Garzon fell ill, and when the group moved on, he had to stay behind to recover.

By the turn of the twentieth century, the permanent Mexican population in Minnesota as a whole had reached twenty-four, and it continued to grow at a trickle until the mid-1940s, despite the fact that many Mexican workers were coming into the state to toil in the railroad, meatpacking, and sugar beet industries. With huge factories in the Red River Valley, Fargo, and Moorhead, the last was particularly successful in wooing Mexican workers from Texas with the promise of train fare, housing, and wages: by 1928, there were seven thousand Mexicans working in the valley picking beets.

At the end of the season, those jobs would dry up, and especially during the Depression, smaller communities did not allow Mexican workers—now gaining a reputation as migrants—to stay through the winter. Many left the state or wintered in the Twin Cities: if not a job, they might at least have family or friends in the small communities established in the Seward neighborhood or in the railroad district of Sixth Avenue North in Minneapolis and in St. Paul's Swede Hollow, where the railroad provided boxcars for its workers. During World War II, urban factories offered steady, year-round jobs for Mexican workers, and that period seems to be when the state's Mexican population started to take seed, growing to three thousand, with only six hundred of that number living outside the Twin Cities. Census figures in 1980, nearly forty years later, show that the vaguely defined Hispanic/any origin population had grown to 32,115.

At this point you may be asking yourself: what do these numbers tell us about a sandwich? In theory, they shed some light on how an immigrant community—and the infrastructure that supports it, such as small businesses like Manny's Tortas—forms over time. For example, when Gonzalez arrived here in 1983, there were few Latino businesses: "I think the only place I knew of was the El Burrito Mercado [in St. Paul]," he says. "That's where the Mexican community was—it was very small. Now it's a nice, big store, but at the time, it was tiny, like—how do you call it?—a hole in the wall. In those times, a lot of people didn't even know what cilantro was, so that's where I could find my Mexican products, and it was the only connection that I had with the culture."

Like all cooks, culinary school graduate or no, newly arrived Gonzalez had to work his way up through the kitchen ranks. "And, like any other immigrant," he adds, "in the beginning, I was just learning the language, so I started working as a dishwasher at Ol' Mexico. Within a year, I was on the line as cook, and then I moved on and started working in other restaurants in the Twin Cities." Among them Prom Catering, where he stayed for ten years, honing his cooking skills on large weddings, conventions, and international golf tournaments featuring a variety of cuisines, including French, Italian, Chinese, and Mexican.

A torta at Manny's Tortas, Minneapolis

Gonzalez's favorite? His own sandwiches. "I used to make sandwiches in all the places that I worked," he says. "I missed the sandwiches; there was nowhere that made them here. You know, they're very popular in Mexico City—it's how you grow up."

The Torta: A Tale of Forbidden Love and Warring Grains

If Jeffrey Pilcher, author and history professor at the University of Minnesota, has it right, the torta has been a part of life in Mexico City since the turn of the last century and is the happy side effect of a centuries-old battle between conquering wheat and native corn. This detail is particularly fascinating to writers of sandwich books, who continuously stumble on the question of how a culture that is not wheat focused came to have something like a sandwich—e.g., the torta or the Vietnamese bánh mì.

Generally, this culinary development can be attributed to European invaders, but it is challenging to find a source that so thoroughly recounts how something like wheat is absorbed into a culture.

In his book, *¡Que Vivan Los Tamales!*, Pilcher does just that, presenting a vivid cultural history of food in Mexico, one that is in large part dominated by the rather epic yet ultimately failed effort—beginning pretty much with the landing of Fernando Cortés in 1519—of the incoming European intellectuals, political leaders, and social elite to convince the Native American population to set aside corn and adopt a wheat-based diet. By the seventeenth century, this ideal was fairly entrenched, and in a time when social status had evolved to become more a function of culture and wealth than of race, wheat eating provided a leading indicator of both. It's simultaneously tragic and hilarious when Pilcher writes of the gentlemen of Chiapas standing in their doorways to shake bread crumbs—real or manufactured—from their clothes and thereby solidify their social standing.

In a cautionary tale, Pilcher recounts *The Flight of the Chimera,* a 1915 novel by Carlos González Peña, in which the protagonist—a young, impressionable wife—is led to an adulterous affair and a precipitous death by her mischievous husband, who introduces her not to drugs and alcohol but to the gluttonous pleasures of street food, specifically tamales!

Around the late 1800s, this cautionary tale nearly became science when Francisco Bulnes, a senator and member of the intellectual elite, wrote "The Future of the Hispanic-American Nations," a treatise on "Mexican backwardness" that attempted to use the very new concept of nutritional science to attribute corn with having rendered the indigenous population passive, disinterested, uneducated, uncivilized, and a host of other weak traits. Pilcher explains, "He asserted that the great civilizations of antiquity—Egypt, Greece, Rome, and Vedic India—all grew out of wheat fields. The corn-fed Aztec and Inca empires 'appeared all powerful, but [were] in fact so weak as to fall victim to insignificant bands of Spanish bandoleros.'" By feeding them wheat, Pilcher writes, the *científicos* hoped to "ignite vigor in the Indian masses."

This summary is an oversimplification of history and Pilcher's engaging retelling of it, but suffice it to say that, though persistent, wheat never completely overcame corn. In later years, they were proven to be nutritional equivalents, and in fact, corn eventually regained its status as the basis of the nation's cuisine. Along the way, however, new dishes were created using wheat and traditional indigenous ingredients—in the torta's case, perhaps to overcome the double stigma of corn and street food.

"It may have been some unknown Porfirian taco vendor who created the most popular use of bread in modern Mexico, the *torta compuesta*," writes Pilcher. "The typical recipe . . . hints at the substitution of bread for tortillas in urban street food. The origin . . . has passed into legend, but it is possible that the Mexican sandwich became common as wheat consumption spread about the turn of the century."

Pilcher notes the appearance of a tortero in the 1899 play *Las Luces de Los Angeles,* and the sandwich itself turns up on the menu of a student party of the time, a quirky sort of torta featuring the unlikely (today, at least) combination of chicken and sardines. And a bit later, in 1902, it flits across a health board notice bringing public attention to the "possible hazards of unsanitary ingredients used in the torta compuesta. Scientists stated that 'for some time and increasing every day,' street vendors had been constructing stands to sell these sandwiches to workers and poor families."

According to Gonzalez, the contemporary torta is ubiquitous in Mexico, eaten by everyone and found on the streets and in restaurants variously. "It's like the hamburger," he says. "You can find a really nice hamburger on the street or in a nice luxury place. Tortas are as popular as tacos in Mexico, but here in the United States people tend to think only of tacos. They didn't know tortas until ten years ago." He remembers going to the movies as a child with his father, who also loved tortas and often punctuated their outings with a sandwich. Later in life, he and his high school friends would skip out on classes in the late afternoon to go eat tortas.

A Local Favorite: Manny's Tortas

In talking, Gonzalez can make the sandwich sound like a national pastime, but one suspects it was somewhat of a personal obsession. Lucky for him, in 1999 an opportunity to make tortas a full-time gig presented itself in the form of a new, cooperative Latino business: Mercado Central on East Lake Street in Minneapolis.

The nineties were a time of extraordinary growth in the Latino community. According to a 2000 census, the Twin Cities' Latino population—which is nearly 70 percent Mexican and, in that year, nearly 50 percent American—grew from 53,885 to 143,382 over the preceding decade, not including an estimated undocumented fifty thousand people. These numbers were especially significant because that decade saw the population of Minnesota grow by thirty thousand, yet without the influx of Mexicans, the Cities would have lost population due to suburban flight.

A study looking at why Hispanic immigrants choose Minnesota cited a variety of reasons but concluded that, overwhelmingly, the two keenest motivations were family and a strong perception that there were jobs. "Everyone told me that in Miami it was better because there were many Latin people there," said one person, "but in Miami there is almost no work, and that is why I came here." In 1999, Mexicans comprised 30 percent of the state's work force in roofing; 25 percent in nurseries, landscaping, raising fruits and vegetables, the hotel and lodging industry, and janitorial services; and 15 percent in meat- and poultry-processing plants, bars, and restaurants.

In order to support this new and established population—statistical data at the time reveals that nearly 60 percent of the state's Latinos were born here—a host of new businesses opened. In fact, from 1990 to 2000, the number of Latino-owned businesses tripled to three thousand. A review of Twin Cities dailies from 1999 to 2005 supports this fact, documenting not only the emergence of new Mexican restaurants and businesses in the established District del Sol in St. Paul but also a focal shift to East Lake Street in Minneapolis. In fact, the sudden, dramatic growth of the Mexican food scene prompted the *St. Paul Pioneer Press* to publish a list of food terms, which defines a torta as a "Mexican sandwich on a French roll, typically slathered with beans and avocado."

Manny's Tortas, Minneapolis

Manny's Tortas was there from the start. In 1998, Gonzalez was working at Prom Catering when an article in *La Prensa* caught his attention. "They were looking for restaurants to open in a new project, Mercado Central in South Minneapolis," he says. "I remember going to ask for information. They told me there was only space for five restaurants, and each space has to have the unique food, you know, it has to be specialized. I thought, 'Oh well! I can do my tortas.' There were probably twenty-five restaurants that applied; they chose me, I was very lucky."

Was it luck, or did the Mercado Central simply recognize a very tasty sandwich? For the original Manny's Tortas, Gonzalez came up with a menu of eleven tortas. "That's not very extensive," he says, "but basically I wanted to put, you know, a sandwich for every kind of taste; some people like pork, the steak, vegetarian—and that's the basics, what we used to eat down in Mexico all the time." According to Gonzalez, what differentiates his tortas is that, unlike many in town, they come on a pan Frances, a long French roll, not a telera or bolillo roll. This element, he says, is not only very authentic, it's also very important: "We were dominated by the French; we have an invasion, you know: that's why we celebrate Cinco de Mayo," he says. "This bread is key; it's the crunch."

"My tortas are from Mexico City," Gonzalez continues. "You know, that bread and the ingredients, but it's a little bit more upper class, and that's what I wanted to do. Yeah, there's other tortas that have like a round bread, but it doesn't have the same consistency as French bread; it's like a hamburger bun." Gonzalez explains that tortas vary by region. Cooks in Guadalajara, for example, make a *torta ahogado,* which literally means "drowned" and refers to the fact that the sandwich is served with soft bread, stewed meat, and sauce. We were fascinated by the idea but could not find a single torta ahogado anywhere in the Twin Cities.

As outlined in the sidebar on pages 127–28, Gonzalez begins his torta by slicing open a French roll, spreading a thin layer of refried beans on each side, and placing it face down on the grill. Once the beans are toasted, he piles on a moderate amount of meat—diners have a choice of everything from breaded steak to ham, pork loin, turkey, and combinations thereof—grilled vegetables, pickled jalapeño peppers, avocado, cheese, and chipotle mayonnaise. Although the sandwiches won't set your mouth on fire, they are spicy. Still, a little bit of heat hasn't been a hard sell, contrary to what the rest of the country might think about Minnesotans. "You know, it's funny: I think Americans used to be afraid, but then slowly they started to enjoy the flavor," Gonzalez comments. "Of course, I tell people about the peppers, and

The Entrepreneurial Perez Brothers

WE VISITED DON PANCHO'S BAKERY in St. Paul's District del Sol to speak with owner Efrain Perez about telera, the soft, round bread used in tortas. He gave us a lot of good information about bread, but along the way the entrepreneur revealed a complex relationship with baking, bread, tortas—and life balance.

Perez and his nine brothers learned to bake from their father, a panadero, who acquired the skill of turning flour into a variety of tasty goods—from decorative tres leches to flaky croissants and crusty bolillos—from his grandfather. Yet, when Perez left his home in Morelia, Mexico, and moved to the United States to work with his brothers, he thought he would give up ovens and flour. "When I came here, I didn't want to work in the bakery," he says, "because in Mexico, I work all my life in bakery. But once I was here, I work in construction, landscaping, restaurants, and factory work—and all the work was boring, you know, so I started working in the bakery."

Perez and one of his brothers started out in Chicago, where they met a woman from Guatemala who owned both a beauty parlor and a bakery half a block from one another. "This is not a good combination," he notes. "It doesn't work: every day, she goes from one business to the other; she never goes home." So Perez and his brother first rented and then eventually bought both her bakery space and a second store. In Chicago, they met other bakers and picked up new recipes. In particular, they connected with an older baker who had traveled and worked extensively in Italy; his breads would influence not only the Perez brothers' taste for crunchier breads but also their recipes and baking methods.

Perez also told us of a friend, a successful baker, who delivered goods to 240 different stores seven days a week. Meeting those pro-

Bolillos at Don Pancho's Bakery, District del Sol, St. Paul

duction levels required him to work around the clock and caused him endless worry as he connected with so many people. For Perez, this man's experience provided a cautionary tale: "He never goes home," says Perez. "Too much pressure: they call, and they say they need this, this, and this delivered. He works, works, and works, and then he had a heart attack on the bakery floor—and he dies. He never goes home, just to the hospital."

In 1998, when nearly all of his family had settled in the Twin Cities, Perez and his brother decided to move to Minnesota. Initially, the Don Pancho's space was a restaurant, which the brothers rented. However, as soon as they were able to buy it, they cleared out all of the restaurant equipment to open the bakery. "I don't like to work in a restaurant," he explains. "When the previous owner opened the store, all that equipment was new, but by the time we bought it, it's not, so we give it away—grills and everything—to the church and to   ◗

friends." And then they brought in an oven and tables for the bakery, a tiny, efficient space.

Today he and his brothers are doing well: in addition to Don Pancho's—which employs two bakers and two cashiers—the family owns Marissa's Bakery on Nicollet and Durango Bakery in Northeast, both Minneapolis locations, and La Concha Bakery and Café in Richfield. And one brother still operates a bakery in Morelia. This success, Perez says, is due in part to his combination of entrepreneurial spirit and hardworking baker. "Sometimes, if you don't know how to make the bread, it's not good," he says. "Those guys come into work and say, 'I don't want to work tomorrow.' People will push you, and what are you going to do? Not only do I have to take the cashier at times, but sometimes my wife comes in to be the cashier so I can do the work in the back. We have to be able to do everything."

If you go in the early morning, Don Pancho's is steamy with the smell of fresh baked goods, yeasty and sweet. Racks of croissants—chocolate, jalapeño, feta!—fill proofing racks set at the center of the shop, which is lined with cases of doughnuts, cakes, pastry, and cookies. And, of course, the breads used to make tortas: bolillo and telera.

According to Perez, the rounder telera, with its thin, soft crust and fluffy crumb, is the official bread of tortas. Not at all chewy, it melds with the other sandwich components; it is one of many elements, a vehicle rather than an outstanding flavor—and we mean that in the best way. Bread should never overwhelm the other ingredients. Part of that softness comes from the baking process: telera are set on a regular baking sheet, like sweet breads and certain pastries.

However, for his sandwiches, Perez prefers the oval-shaped bolillo, which has a crunchy, thick crust and a soft inside. "The bolillo is more crispy," he says. "And when we make tortas, we don't use the others." Perez cooks his bolillo on a special aerated tray with wide channels for the bread—not unlike pans used to create baguettes—that help the crust thicken up nicely.

Perez loves tortas. In Morelia, his favorite torta spot was an hour's drive, there and back, taking up his entire lunch hour—yet he would go every week, several times. "Some places in Mexico, they have only tortas and waters, you know, like a horchata," he recalls. "My favorite, it takes one hour and fifteen minutes to go there, and we went every week—you would go that far. Those sandwiches, they make everything fresh—fresh meat—and when they put on the telera, with some butter, and put it on the grill, they make like crispy and small, not big. So that way when you eat it, it's very crispy. Some place here, it's not crispy; it's soft, and then it's not good. I don't like it." Sadly, he can't find a torta in the Twin Cities that tastes as he remembers them. Instead, he makes his own in the back of the shop, piling tomatoes, ham, cheese, and mayonnaise on a bolillo toasted extra crispy. It's tasty, but he and his wife still hold out hope for a restaurant that will make tortas that match their treasured recollections.

In the meantime, he sells about 120 telera a day to torta lovers—and more than three hundred loaves of bolillo. The latter, like white bread everywhere, are used with other sandwiches and soups and eaten plain or buttered. Soon, Perez plans to build an addition onto the bakery—a simple café, so people can have a cup of coffee and sit with their pastries. He does not, however, plan to expand his business and deliver telera and bolillo to Twin Cities markets and restaurants. "We don't sell too much here," he says, "but we've got a good business for us. Not too busy like before—we work in the [early] morning and then we have the afternoon to relax." ○

if they can't take it—some people have health issues—then we take them out, but basically, I wanted to introduce it as is, for authenticity."

Gonzalez's ingredients are simple; it's really the careful layering, the proportion of the beans, cheese, peppers, and vegetables to the meats—and yes, all those soft, juicy ingredients against the crust of the French bread—that makes his tortas so excellent. "Mine is the best, and I'll tell you, I try other places," Gonzalez says. "A lot of people have tried to copy me because when I opened, nobody has it. You know Masa, Chino Latino—they try to put the torta on their menus, but they're not the same. People tell me, 'Manny, this restaurant, they have tortas; we tried them, but they are not the same as yours!' That makes me happy."

El Mercado Central and the Rebirth of East Lake Street

As obviously delighted as he is with the overall success of his tortas, Gonzalez is also extremely proud of the changes he has seen on East Lake Street in the last decade. Prior to Mercado Central, Gonzalez says, that strip of East Lake had a reputation: "When the Mall of America opened, Sears moved. So that building was empty for more than ten years, and this avenue was very dangerous, a lot of drugs and prostitution. So when Mercado Central opened, it was a challenge, but it was kind of—how do you say—it was an adventure." He continues, "At that time, the Latino community in the neighborhood had really started to grow. Right now it's bigger than St. Paul. So that's why I was so excited to open Mercado Central: the people were already here! So we opened, and it was very successful; two years later, a lot of owners opened another business."

Among them was Gonzalez, who staked out a location on East Lake and Twenty-seventh Street South, near Minnehaha Avenue. It did not do as well, primarily because of the economic downturn and construction on Lake, which reduced traffic through the area. "And let me tell you something," he says. "Two years ago, we saw a decrease in the Latin population because of jobs. A lot of the growth, that population explosion, had been people who work in roofing or some other kind of housing construction. When the economy collapsed, they didn't have a lot of jobs, and a lot of people went back to Mexico." Even though it ultimately closed, the store had a lasting impact on Gonzalez's business: "When I opened [in] Mercado Central, basically it was all Mexicans, probably 80 percent Latino and 20 percent Americans that like to go and see a different market," he says. "The second location was the other way around. I think because it was more like a neighborhood with middle-class Americans. You know, sometimes people weren't sure about the mercado, whether they should go there or not. Today, it's different. We have schools that take their kids there to practice Spanish—that's one of the programs we implemented—and it used to be all white: we painted it and now it is beautiful and colorful."

In 2007, Gonzalez opened a third location in the Midtown Global Market, a kind of glorified mall of markets and food counters that is also located along East Lake Street, in the aforementioned Sears building, but focused on a variety of foods and cultures, from sushi to sambusi and French pastry to farm-fresh eggs. "They were going to bring Avanca, a big, national, Spanish supermarket," he says. "But since the mercado opened, a lot of small businesses had opened, Latino businesses, and we thought, 'Well, if this huge supermarket is going to come in here, it's going to destroy all the small businesses.' So we talked to the city and the politicians and blah, blah, blah—that's how this concept came to be: like the mercado, but more global."

According to Gonzalez, who was president of the cooperative Mercado Central for two years, as a community gathering place it has helped improve the political dialogue between the Latino community and politicians. "It has been very influential politically, because the mayors and other politicians, when they want the Latino vote," he explains, "they go to the mercado and they talk to the people, talk to the community. Jesse Ventura and R. T. Rybak have both been there."

And, as successful business ventures, both Mercado Central and Midtown Global Market have helped pave the way for new Latino businesses, improving the neighborhood at the same time. "All this has changed: before it was just car dealerships and American businesses; it was not like this," he says. "But it's huge, you know; other communities have started growing outside of South Minneapolis, and they have their own grocery stores and restaurants. So, yeah, I think that it opened the doors for a lot of entrepreneurs to go out there and try. The mercado was a huge help. It was a stepping-stone."

The super-sized torta at
El Taco Riendo, Minneapolis

You Gotta Have a (Tasty!) Gimmick

MIGUEL CRUZ-GOMEZ, owner of El Taco Riendo, has lived in the Twin Cities for twenty-six years, and, like many people, he can remember when the Latin community was much smaller. "When I got here, there was nothing," he says. "I used to live at Hennepin Avenue and Thirty-third South—there were no Latinos. Sometimes, I would go over to Robert Street [in St. Paul] to buy peppers and tortillas; we'd go to Morgan's Mexican-Lebanese Deli, Boca Chica—oh, and El Burrito because they had a variety of Mexican food."

Today, the Latino community has grown, along with the number of restaurants to serve it. Cruz-Gomez, and indeed the whole of the Twin Cities, can have his pick from tableside guacamole in Uptown to fish tacos at the midtown farmer's market to tamales on Robert Street—and tortas everywhere in between. So how is he to distinguish his Northeast Minneapolis establishment from the crowd? The restaurateur found the answer in a giant telera.

Every Tuesday and Thursday, DJs on the Spanish radio station La Invasora 1400 evangelize the Torta Riendo, a veritable raft of a torta—filled with roasted pork leg, guaca-mole, lettuce, queso fresco, chipotle mayo, sour cream, tomato, onion, peppers, and beans—and well able to feed four people. "When they see, people start laughing: 'Oh my God, who is going to eat that?'" Cruz-Gomez says. "We are the only restaurant in the Twin Cities that came out with that sandwich, with the roasted pork leg and giant telera. It's a very popular item these days."

If asked, Cruz-Gomez will tell you that he never acquired any cooking skills; his superpower is customer service, a motif that ran through the many jobs that preceded owning his own restaurant. In Mexico City, Cruz-Gomez was a car salesman for Volvo of Mexico. As a young man, he often visited Minnesota with his father, who worked for 3M and attended seminars at the company's headquarters in St. Paul. Eventually, his brother and a couple cousins moved to the Twin Cities, and he followed.

He spent the past twenty-two years working his way from the fast-food counters of Wendy's and Burger King to banquet captain at Hyatt Regency and a la carte waiter at Oceanaire.

❍

After all that time in the front of the house, he decided he wanted his own spot. "I went to Chicago in 1992," he explains. "And I noticed that all the Mexican restaurants there were a big success; they were pretty busy all the time." In style, Cruz-Gomez found the Chipotle model inspiring: "I thought, this is what you need to have, a place where you can see how all the food is made, where you can choose what you want—but the food is more authentic. Some places you sit down and are served, but for me, being able to see the food is more exciting."

He also liked the fast pace of Mexico City restaurants. "There, you go into little restaurants where all the food is precooked and they are serving quick lunches," he recalls. "In Mexico City, life is always very active; you are always in a rush: I only have time for one taco. And that's when I came up with the idea of El Taco Riendo. That has a couple of different meanings: If you run the words together, it's *corriendo*—you have running, and that's what we have: fast food—you get in and you get out. And the word *riendo* means "to smile." Customers walk out of here smiling because we have good service and good food."

On the service side, "That's what I've always been good at: being friendly," he says. "And, along with having good food, that's the main ingredient. And cleanliness, that's one of my main goals: keep the restaurant clean because when I worked at the Oceanaire, that place was immaculate . . . really clean."

Cruz-Gomez had strong ideas about the food, too. He partnered with Jose Velasquez, an experienced chef familiar with the style of cooking Cruz-Gomez favored. "His cuisine has a great flavor," he says. "He's originally from Oaxaca, Mexico, where he learned to cook from his family. I told him what I wanted to put on the menu. He said, 'I can do this, I can do that'—and that's how we came to the menu." Said menu is pretty standard in fare: tacos, burritos, chimichangas, tostadas, and, yes, tortas. However, it distinguishes itself in the richly spiced stewed and roasted meats offered in those dishes. For example, unlike at Manny's, the cooks at El Taco Riendo will ladle stewed chicken or pork over a telera and what Cruz-Gomez calls the classic ingredients, lettuce, beans, guacamole, and peppers. "Eventually, we came up with the idea of using queso fresco, a white Mexican cheese," he explains. "It has a particular flavor that can mix or match with a lot of items we have here."

The Torta Riendo may be the most popular item on the menu, but we have, in the course of researching these sandwiches, developed something of an obsession for barbacoa, roasted pork with a flavor reminiscent of the delicate spices in Indian foods. Although he would tell us that the pork is marinated in a variety of savory and sweet spices, including cinnamon, cumin, marjoram, paprika, and chili guajillo sauce, Cruz-Gomez would not give us the recipe. It falls into the trade secrets that have made the affable entrepreneur a success. "That's something that . . . no, because that particular recipe is very unique. Many people would like to have that one!" ●

Miguel Cruz-Gomez, owner of El Taco Riendo. "How do I like [being a restaurateur]? It's interesting, it's tiring—it's been a little bit sacrificing having this restaurant. I put a lot of hours in here."

More of a Tutorial Than a Recipe

Although he welcomed us, camera and all, into his kitchen, Manuel Gonzalez would not divulge the exact recipes—especially the chipotle mayonnaise and a piquant spice blend—that make his tortas stand out in a city where all sorts of restaurants, from Asian fusion to mainstream American diner, are starting to spin out versions of the sandwich. He instead provided us with a kind of primer, a loosely defined step-by-step guide to compiling the sandwich, which the beginner will likely find edifying and the aficionado, we hope, a great place to start. To it, we have added our own mayo recipe and some likely local spice blend candidates.

Manny's Special Torta

Makes 1 serving

Manuel Gonzalez serves up a torta

1 telera or bolillo roll
Butter, melted
Refried beans
3 slices steak or beef tenderloin
Spice blend (tips follow)
Olive oil
Chopped onion, tomato, carrot, and mushroom
San Marcos pickled jalapeños
2 slices ham
2–3 slices Swiss cheese
¼ avocado, peeled and mashed
Chipotle mayonnaise (recipe follows)

1. Halve the roll and apply butter to the inside of one half and a layer of refried beans to the other. Place both sides face down on pan or griddle.
2. Grill steak slices, adding a sprinkling of spice blend. Add olive oil to pan and grill chopped vegetables and pickled jalapeños. Add spice blend,

chopping it in with the side of spatula. Next, grill ham and organize it in a sandwich shape. Stack steak and grilled vegetables on top of ham. Add Swiss cheese: "Mexico City is very cosmopolitan, so we use French bread and Swiss cheese!"

3. By now, the buttered and bean-smeared sides of the bread should be crispy. Spread avocado on the butter side, then place meat and veggie pile on top. Spread a dollop of mayonnaise across the top of the meat. Place the bean side on top and close up your sandwich. Slice and eat!

Chipotle Mayonnaise

2 San Marcos chipotle chilies en adobo
1 tablespoon adobo sauce
½ cup mayonnaise, preferably with a little lemon

Place ingredients (chilies through mayonnaise) in bowl of food processor or blender and blend until completely combined and smooth. Taste and adjust mayonnaise and chilies: remember, it's going to be buried in all that meat and cheese!

Spice Blend

For the spice blend, we had great luck with the following combinations from Penzeys Spices:

Northwoods Fire: Heat and smoke balanced with a nice herby mixture of garlic, thyme, and rosemary.
Spicy 4/S Seasoned Salt: A peppery kick—no smoke, but the added benefit of salt.
Hot Chili: The most straightforward, this one offers a lot of depth and flavor—with fewer herbs, it gets all its complexity from the chilies.

The Cubano

A Torta of a Different Sort. Seems like everywhere there's tortas, there's the Cubano. It looks like a torta, it kinda tastes like a torta—some folks even call it a torta. So what's the difference?

For the answer, we made our way to the corner of Grand and Thirty-eighth in Minneapolis, where Victor's 1959 Café has been serving up authentic Cuban food for ten years. The Cubano was available from the very beginning. "I'm not sure how it got on the menu," says Victor (Vic) Valens, Jr., chef and son of the eponymous Victor. "It wasn't popular here then, but it was all the craze in Miami. I think the idea was that, like the rest of the menu, it was for the Cuban exile community that maybe would have liked to go home but were forbidden, but they could come here and enjoy that sandwich."

Once Victor's planted the seed, the Cubano spread like wildfire, turning up in restaurants—sit down and curbside—across the city. "Now it's even in the fast-food restaurants," Valens notes, "but I think it's funny when I see, like even Panera has the Cuban chicken panini with ham and Swiss. As far as I know that's chicken cordon bleu!"

According to Valens, an authentic Cubano consists of ham, pickle, and Swiss cheese layered in proportion so they don't upstage the main attraction: shredded pork. "The ingredients are pretty simple," he says, "but the key is that traditional pork and then the layering so you can taste the garlic and lime in the pork—too much pork or too little can make or break it." In Florida, the sandwich is served on Cuban bread, but Victor's doesn't have a reliable source or the facilities to bake its own bread, so its cooks use a telera, piling the ingredients on and then toasting it in a grooved sandwich press called a *plancha*—perhaps the most striking difference from the torta.

The Cubana at Victor's 1959 Café, Minneapolis

Google "Cubano" and watch the Internet light up. Like anything people have a passion for, there are blogs and wikis galore obsessively detailing the sandwich's ingredients and origins. On the latter, history is dim: everyone seems to agree the sandwich was a staple in cigar factories of the early 1900s, both in Florida and Cuba. However, at that time it was com-

mon and relatively easy for folks to sail back and forth, so it's difficult to say whether it originated in Cuba or in Ybor City (Tampa), Miami, or Key West. "I can't really comment on Cuba; I've never been," says Valens, "but I grew up in Miami, which is like Little Havana. It's a street food, really. We ate it a lot when I was growing up. You'd go to a window café and either stand and eat it at the counter or get it wrapped up to go. There, I'd say it's kind of working class, but here it has really crossed those borders. It's on the dinner menu, and we have people pulling up in Mercedes, BMWs, you know, even kids—five or six of them will run in and grab a bunch to go."

But if you had to venture a guess, is it a Cuban sandwich or a Floridian sandwich? "You know, my dad was communist and my mom was anti-Castro," says Valens. "So I learned pretty early on you don't get involved in who did what first and why."

Victor's 1959 Café Cubano

Makes 4–6 servings

Contributed by Victor Valens, chef

The key to enjoying a Cuban sandwich is evenly distributing the ingredients. Telera breads vary in size, so you may want to add a little more or a little less of the components to your sandwich—but add them evenly! You should be able to taste a great combination of flavors; too much of any of the ingredients will overpower the sandwich and ruin that balance.

1 (1–1¼ pound) pork tenderloin
1 small head garlic, minced
Salt and pepper to taste
Juice of 4–6 limes
½ cup fresh oregano
6 telera rolls, halved
Yellow mustard to taste
24 ounces ham, sliced
Swiss cheese, sliced
Dill pickles, planked

Roasted Pork Tenderloin

The start of every great Cuban sandwich is the roasted pork. Traditionally a pork shoulder is used, but unless you're feeding an army, Victor recommends a smaller pork loin or pork tenderloin.

1. Puncture loin with a fork, creating several small holes. Place loin in pan and rub with minced garlic, salt, and pepper, working the ingredients into the holes. Pour lime juice over loin to partially submerge it. Refrigerate loin for 1 hour, turning once.

2. Preheat oven to 350°F. Place loin in roasting pan and pour lime-garlic marinade over it. Coat top of loin with oregano. Roast loin, covered, until internal temperature reaches 160°F (about 1 hour per pound). About twenty minutes before loin is done, remove cover to brown loin and allow it to absorb juices.

3. Shred cooked pork inside roasting pan to capture additional juices. Using a slotted spoon, transfer pork to plate. (If the pork is too juicy, the bread will be soggy and difficult to toast well.) Set aside.

Assembly

Victor's uses telera bread, found fresh in every Mexican bakery and a great substitute for Cuban bread.

For each sandwich, slice telera bread in half and spread mustard evenly on both sides. (If you are tempted to stray from the recipe, Victor is quite adamant about the type of mustard: "We always use a basic yellow mustard, never a Dijon.") Place about 4 to 6 ounces of ham on one slice of bread and top with a slice of Swiss cheese. Portion shredded pork evenly over cheese and top with two pickle planks. Add second slice of bread and press down firmly to bring ingredients together.

The Hot Press

Now it's time to press the sandwich. Victor explains: "At Victor's, we lay our sandwich on a flat-top grill and use weights to press it down. At home, I have used a panini press and even a George Foreman grill!" If you don't have a sandwich press, a large skillet set over a medium flame will do: place each sandwich in the preheated skillet and use a few heavy plates as your weight. Brown sandwich for a few minutes on each side, remove from heat, cut diagonally, and enjoy.

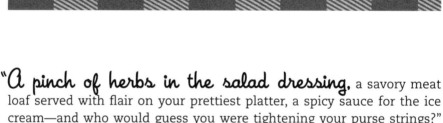

7 The Meat Loaf Sandwich
Leftovers in the Land of Comfort Food and Cattle

SUSAN PAGANI/PHOTOGRAPHS BY KATIE CANNON

"A pinch of herbs in the salad dressing, a savory meat loaf served with flair on your prettiest platter, a spicy sauce for the ice cream—and who would guess you were tightening your purse strings?" So begins the "Frankly Thrifty" chapter of the 1964 Betty Crocker cookbook *New Dinners for Two*. Ironically, no matter how fancy the serving dish, for anyone born and raised eating beef in the midwestern United States, humble meat loaf will always be instantly recognizable as an economical supper. Just as surely, meat loaf promises a comforting, satisfying, and tasty meal—or two, should you decide to use the leftovers in a meat loaf sandwich the next day.

And there's the culinary rub: the meat loaf sandwich, unlike many of the others in this book, does not truly exist as its own entity: it's a by-product of another meal. However a chef may embellish it, this sandwich's story is not about condiments or bread. It's about meat—specifically, beef.

If you were to use Google to search for "history of meat loaf," you would discover a Lynne Olver's foodtimeline.org entry. It offers a great many recipes for meat loaf's evolutionary predecessor, the meatball, touches lightly on the early mistrust of industrialized ground beef, and proffers a theory explaining why the dish doesn't turn up in American cookbooks before the late 1800s—it was simply too unrefined and homely. It does not, however, provide any evidence that the dish sprang from the oven, the product of some individual's genius, on a certain date in history. At first glance,

Olver's thoughtful attempt may read like a loose gathering of food facts related to but not actually about meat loaf, yet it might in fact be the only existing scholarship on the topic.

Many established food experts, from the Minnesota Beef Council to Betty Crocker archivists, kindly forwarded us this link when queried for information, a sign of how truly little has been written about the origins of meat loaf. "It's not something that was invented, like cherries jubilee," says Mary Gunderson, Minnesota food writer, journalist, and culinary historian. "It's a practical dish, and it's probably in every culture." She points to lumpia, the Filipino wrap; the Scandinavian tradition of meatballs; Middle Eastern kofta; Cornish pasties; Somali sambusa; Slavic pierogi; and on it goes. "Wherever you go in the world," Gunderson says, "there's meat, chopped into little pieces."

This idea supports Olver's theory that meat loaf descended from these other dishes. However, in chatting with Gunderson and other local food experts, we became convinced that meat loaf was the product of a perfect storm of culinary events: industrialized beef, refrigerated train cars, and tabletop meat grinders. Perhaps it didn't appear in early American cookbooks because it didn't yet exist.

In Minnesota, recipes for meat loaf started turning up by 1877, when Estelle Woods Wilcox published *Buckeye Cookery and Practical Housekeeping: Compiled from Original Recipes.*

The previous year, Wilcox and the ladies of the First Congregational Church in Marysville, Ohio, conceived *Buckeye Cookery* as a means to raise money for a new parsonage, a fairly common practice at the time. According to the Historic Cookbook Project at Michigan State University, soon after the recipes were collected, Wilcox moved to Minneapolis, where her husband took a job at the *Minneapolis Daily Tribune*. Wilcox continued to edit the recipes, penning

Gourmet meat loaf sandwich at Cheeky Monkey Deli, St. Paul

introductions to each of the chapters, which also provided advice on how to run a household. The book was published with a dedication to those "Plucky housewives, who master their work instead of allowing it to master them," adding that "bad dinners go hand in hand with total depravity, while a properly fed man is already half saved." That attitude must have struck a chord with spirited midwestern women: when the first printing of the cookbook went out, the ladies earned two thousand dollars for the parsonage.

Realizing the book's potential, the Wilcoxes bought the copyright and continued to publish it for nearly thirty years under the Buckeye Publishing Company, creating several editions to broaden their audience—including one in German and one for southern cooks called *The Dixie Cookbook*—and updating them each year to stay current with new foods, equipment, and recipe trends. According to Carol Fisher's *The American Cookbook,* "the book put forward such fantastic advice as how to rid your clothes of foul odors by burying them in the yard, make a toaster out of a piece of sheet metal, and get a wild goose drunk on alcohol-soaked wheat—all the better to catch it, you see."

And in the "Meats" section is a recipe for a veal loaf credited, as was the habit in cookbooks of the era, to Governor Tilden of New York. This connection does rather diminish the idea that the recipe was too homely to print. Tilden's instructions are minimal, telling readers to combine three pounds of chopped veal with three-quarter pound of salt pork, a half dozen crackers, two eggs, and salt and pepper, cover it in another half dozen crackers, and bake it for one hour. But wait a minute: New York? Could it be that meat loaf was invented on the East Coast?

Prior to the mid- to late 1800s, as mentioned above, one sees quite a few recipes for meat loaf precursors using beef, veal, pork, and lamb, such as beef balls, veal cake, forcemeat, and pâté, but nothing in loaf form, perhaps because, according to cookbook scholar Eric Quayle, many of the first American cookbooks—from the very earliest in 1796—simply recast European recipes using new-world ingredients, such as molasses, cornmeal, pumpkin, and wild turkey. Yet meat loaf, as sketched out in *Buckeye Cookery,* seems to be fairly and rather suddenly ubiquitous by the 1890s. This evidence makes one think that if not exactly an invention of the Midwest, meat loaf was certainly an American concoction, albeit one iterative of earlier dishes.

According to Gunderson and local food maven Mary Bartz, meat loaf's popular association with the Midwest may well have more to do with our long history with beef—and meat-centered meals in general—than our reputation for loving comfort food. "I think it could go back to our food heritage," says Bartz, formerly both director of the Betty Crocker Kitchens and communication director for the National Cattlemen's Association. "Most of the cattle is raised in the center of the country—from Minnesota and down through the South to Texas. You can get beef from the coast, obviously, but the climate and the water make a big difference in agriculture. I'd speculate that the diversity of agriculture out here and the fact that all of the packing plants really started out here, in Chicago and in the central portion of the country—a lot of the cropland is here; this is the bread basket, and our culture is different than out West."

"In California, there are all those fresh fruits and vegetables; it's really about fresh food," Bartz adds, "but in the days before transportation, we were really stuck out here, so we did a lot of putting up and freezing. We froze meat, of course, but we put up our fruits and vegetables, peaches, pears, all our veggies, except maybe beans. I think we've retained that tradition and economy—in fact, we are so grounded in that tradition, it is hard to really change it. It's what we eat still." Indeed, Gunderson posits, "I think meat loaf tradition really gave way to the hot dish tradition. You know, people thought, 'This is good, and if I mix it up with milk and potatoes, it gets creamy—even better!'"

James J. Hill and the Cows

So, how did the cow work its way into the center of our collective heart and plate? According to Gunderson, from the time of early European settlement until well into the 1800s, pork was the Minnesota farmer's choice of meat for various reasons, primarily because pigs were smaller, required little management, were easy to slaughter—and were cheap to feed, fattening on leftovers and harvest waste. "Everybody had a pig, everybody had a smokehouse, everybody butchered," says Gunderson. "You know what they say about a pig: you can use everything but the squeal—and that was certainly true 100 to 150 years ago, when people made headcheese and blood sausage and all those things. They used all the fat, all the protein, even the bones—well, the dogs probably got some of the bones."

Cows were much more expensive to feed and house. Unlike pigs, which could be processed at home and cured in a brine of salt, saltpeter, molasses, or sugar or dry-cured in smoke, cows were too large to slaughter and process at home, and their tough, fibrous meat did not lend itself as easily to curing. People who lived outside urban centers often paid to have their cows slaughtered by itinerant butchers, who traveled along established routes. In towns, local meat markets and butchers sold meat by the pound and also provided custom processing for farmers. However, without refrigeration, storing large quantities of meat was difficult, so most people ate fresh beef, when they ate it, and often as a celebratory community.

However, the situation changed in the mid- to late 1800s. "First of all, you had the population expansion," explains Ron Eustice, executive director for the Minnesota Beef Council, "and then you began to see more economic stability, so beef became a more important part of the diet. And . . . there was also the expansion of the railroad and, with it, the cattle industry in the state." According to Eustice, it was around this time that people in the state began to look at breeding cattle for meat. "Early cattle were draft animals—oxen were the primary source of movement—and producers of milk, so meat was secondary," he says. "Initially, we didn't have many cattle here; all you saw were Texas longhorn. Then, in the 1880s and '90s, you start to see the import of European shorthorn, which were much more suitable for milk and meat production, and that became the predominant breed."

For example, James J. Hill, founder of the Great Northern Railroad, was somewhat obsessed, as many were at the time, with creating the ideal dual-purpose cow. In the late 1800s, he brought shorthorn bulls, Ayrshires, and fancy Polled Angus from Scotland and Great Britain, hoping that by breeding beef cattle with good dairy qualities, he could create a cow suitable to the Upper Midwest winters but also able to efficiently produce good beef and greater quantities of milk than the lean longhorn. In fact, he gave away some 250 purebred bulls to farmers living along his railway, hoping that improved production would inspire them to diversify their crops and livestock—and, perhaps, to ship cattle on his railway line, thereby increasing his profits. Unfortunately, the entrepreneurial Hill found that ungrateful farmers tended to use the cows he gave them to feed their families rather than to breed livestock.

In 1886, the St. Paul Union Stockyard opened, and with it came the Anglo-American Packing & Provision Company, a Chicago-based firm. In ten years, they went from processing 31,514 head of cattle to 92,062. According to Eustice, the economies of scale this centralized production and processing allowed dramatically reduced the cost—and therefore increased the consumption—of beef. At the same time, says Eustice, the late 1800s saw the expansion of the railways and the invention of ice-cooled train cars, which made it possible for stockyards to ship fresh beef into small, rural towns and farming communities, where local butchers could sell it. Add to that factor the invention of the tabletop meat grinder in the mid-1800s, and you have every compelling reason not only to eat more beef but also to embrace recipes that allow you to grind up less desirable pieces of meat—recipes such as meat loaf.

Documenting Meat Loaf Down Through the Ages

The first meat loaf recipes seem to be more about using fresh beef than economy, as illustrated by a Pillsbury version that features a ratio of 3.5 pounds of meat to three soda crackers. More than a century later, efficient use of protein is a theme in recipes that combine several cups of cheese and starchy filler, be it a cracker, rice, bread, or cereal, with a more modest amount of beef, pork, lamb, and sometimes fish. In Minnesota, the tradition of meat loaf is carried from generation to generation quite methodically through the very same medium employed more than a hundred years ago—the church cookbook. And though it may seem as if meat loaf varies only slightly from recipe to recipe, this impression is not supported. In fact, meat loaf recipes are so specialized and prized that a cookbook—even a hand-typed one—will more often than not contain several meat loaf entries.

Such is the case with the 1904 *Ladies Aid Cookbook,* published in Annandale. It features three recipes so similar that one has to read them several times to note the small onion, extra egg, and slightly shorter cooking time that differentiate them. However, it has nothing on the 1974 cookbook of the Crippled Children, Inc., Worthington, which boasts no fewer than thirteen recipes. Thinking about how they all made the editor's cut does make one yearn to hear the catty politics that must have preceded these recipes to the page. The *Preston Cookbook 1855 to 2005,* published by the southern Minnesota town's sesquicentennial cookbook committee, also features three meat loaf recipes, but these have only beef and cereal in common. "Winning Meat Loaf" balances equal parts beef and pork sausage with a quantity of oats, tomato sauce, and rather exotic red pepper, while "My Grandmother's Meatloaf" is more old school with its Wheaties, onions, salt, and pepper. "Mini Meat Loaf" throws in a little cheddar cheese and then swathes the whole thing in a classic sauce of ketchup, brown sugar, and mustard.

Speaking of Wheaties, it is fascinating to see how age-old meat loaf adapts to meet the culinary trends of the time. *Our Best to You,* coming from Guild No. 3 of Our Lady of Lourdes Church in Virginia, Minnesota, features recipes perfectly suited to its 1967 publishing date, laden, for example, with cans of hearty beef vegetable stew or, for the Lenten supper, salmon. Written in that same year, a recipe from the Union Congregation Church's Centennial Society cookbook features monosodium glutamate—a harmless ingredient, yet a rarity in American home cooking these days.

All of those trends were likely national, but locally inspired recipes pop up, too. In the late seventies, it was not unusual to find Minnesota meat loaf recipes that replaced cereal, crackers, and bread crumbs with nutty, long-grain wild rice. "Before that time, wild rice was a precious commodity, a delicacy, and you only got it if you sort of knew somebody who hung around in northern Wisconsin or Minnesota," says Gunderson. "As it became more available, people figured out different ways to use it—meat loaf and wild rice soup—and it became sort of a Minnesota thing."

Undoubtedly, a whole library of church cookbooks will be printed this year: what will their meat loaf recipes tell us about today's food trends? Probably they will cast more than a passing glance toward recipes of old. Today's cooks seek out fresh, local, and, where possible, organic meats and produce and seem to be celebrating a return to cooking from scratch, from

The Big Stretch

IT'S NO SECRET: the economic beauty of meat loaf is that it not only makes good use of less expensive cuts of meat but also stretches that meat by expanding it with primarily bread, cereal, and other starchy ingredients. Consider this list of fillers Minnesota's cooks have employed as meat-stretchers over the years. **⊙**

BISCUITS	OATS
BREAD	POTATO
BREAD CRUMBS	QUICK OATMEAL
CHEESE	SODA CRACKERS
CORN FLAKES	WHEATIES
CORN MEAL	WHITE RICE
LENTILS	WILD RICE

cream sauces and home-ground beef to condiments such as ketchup, mustard, and pickles. Certainly these attributes hold true of the meat loaf served in restaurants around the Twin Cities today.

Meat Loaf: Efficient, Comforting, and Tasty

Historically, it is hard to say when meat loaf began turning up at restaurants, but it was definitely a popular item on Depression-era menus, in which, according to *Minnesota Eats Out* authors Kathryn Strand Koutsky and Linda Koutsky, restaurants made the most of meat loaf, pancakes, and chili, all of which efficiently utilized readily available ingredients. That tendency continued well into the thirties and forties, when Minnesota cafés flourished by providing home-cooked meals and community. "They thrived on local patronage," write the Koutskys, "Businessmen meeting over breakfast, family and friends gathering for lunch, students hanging out after school. Customers often knew the waitress—maybe even the cook—and they could depend on good service and eager conversation with every visit. Old-fashioned home cooking was as important as the friendly camaraderie." What is more old-fashioned and homey than meat loaf? The Koutskys include an Eleanor Ostman recipe that, true to the era it illustrates, features about half the meat and twice the crackers of recipes published at the turn of the twentieth century.

In the last few years, Minnesota restaurants, like many around the country, have been hard hit by the economic decline. Perhaps that's why meat loaf has such a strong foothold: some love it for the fact that they can use lesser cuts of meat and still produce a richly flavored, center-of-the-plate dish; others like that they can stretch that less-expensive meat even further with the addition of bread crumbs and cheese. Either way, meat loaf resonates with Minnesotans as real, home-cooked, comfort food. Local chefs have emphasized that aspect of the dish by not only buying locally produced meats but also grinding and curing the cuts themselves. In keeping with those aforementioned trends, they are putting up their own pickles—peppers, cucumbers, and lovely, light slaws of all kinds—and blending aioli, ketchup, and mustard to create a lively take on tradition that is fresh yet familiar. It's exciting—and somehow comforting—to think that these recipes, too, will one day find their way into a church cookbook as diners take them home and make them their own.

LOCATED IN NORTHEAST MINNEAPOLIS, the Modern Café is a classic. Some neighborhood folks still remember the restaurant in its original incarnation as Rabatin's Northeast Café, a soda shop and ice cream parlor that opened in the 1940s. Jim Grell bought the café in 1994, and though he's changed the name and menu, he's left the retro malt shop décor mainly intact and fostered a philosophy toward food that complements the comfortable deco booths and padded vinyl bar.

Meat loaf is not only on the menu; it's painted on the window, a gold-leaf promise of comforting midwestern fare. Indeed, critics regularly laud the restaurant for producing simple yet beautifully executed meals (among them, my favorite meat loaf in town) out of what must be one of the region's tiniest kitchens.

Here, the restaurant's chef, Philip Becht, talks about the role the Modern Café plays in the community and how making meat loaf—which he does without an actual recipe—is one of the more creative parts of his day.

What's behind this "simple yet beautiful" food?

I still come across people in the neighborhood, older people, who remember [the café] as a soda shop, and it was really a part of the neighborhood. So Jim's idea is to stay a part of the neighborhood as opposed to maybe going a different direction and making it less accessible. That's why we have breakfast on the weekends.

For families in the neighborhood?

Yeah, so I do get to mess around with odd ingredients, but I think Jim believes that this should be a simple, community-oriented place, where you can bring the kids, and where it's not so expensive to eat. Jim established these

principles before I came, but I have a great affinity for that idea. I have a six-year-old now, so I understand what that means to a community, and it's been a good fit for me.

That community philosophy plays out in how the restaurant is run, something you've talked about a fair bit.

Jim is a sweet man. We have health insurance, and he pays us as well as he can, so I'm able to have a home and a good life for my family—and that means a lot. So, he does things that are different but, man, what a payoff! There's a fair amount of salt and pepper walking around this place—people stick around and get invested in the business and in the people coming in the door.

What does *simple* mean to you?

Simple: we work very hard to make the food good. We make our own sausages, and I've been curing my own hams. There's actually a lot of effort and work that goes into what we do. We don't open a lot of cans here; we get in raw foods and go from there with it.

Where does that food come from?

We try to spend the money on food that is as close as possible to the Modern Café. In the summer, a lot of our food is grown in Delano, Minnesota, at Riverbend Farm and at Garden Farme out in Ramsey, Minnesota. We use only Berkshire pigs now, and we grind all of our hamburger from whole chuck.

Tell me about that.

We have this immense, black-painted grinder that Jim got at this little sausage place here—it's just beautiful. It squeaks and doesn't like to work all the time and it's just terrific: I love it. The breakfast sausage is so much better than we used to buy it. Jim makes the sausage usually—he uses fresh coriander and orange peel—and, man, it is so much better than the mystery meat we were using before.

That's fascinating because ground meat is so important to the history of meat loaf.
Yeah, I never thought about that: at some point, someone thought this was a cool idea, and we take it for granted. When we first started grinding, Jim had his grandmother's old Universal No. 2 meat grinder, the kind that attaches to the table. I started making sausages out of a pastry bag; it took me hours, just squeezing the meat out of a little tube, but it was so fun. I imagine ground beef got started that way—in small restaurants and farmhouses across America and the world—once we figured out how to make a small grinder like that.

How do you do all that prep in such a small kitchen?
Well, upstairs it's just two of us cooking the food, and then my job is to figure out how we can plate the food that comes out of the window. But downstairs we have two kind of nice walk-ins and two giant prep tables, so four or five people can be down there prepping during the day to get us where we need to be.

The question is: since we can't have one guy making pizza and another making soufflés, etc., where do we insert integrity? Where do we work our craft, and where do we get to have fun and grow as cooks? That's downstairs in the prep, where we grind the meat and make sausage and cured meats.

I'm forty-three years old. I've learned a lot, I've read a lot, and I'm not very good at leaving the office at the office. I've had some very important people in my life—Doug Flicker, Steven Brown, and Lenny Russo—who taught me to enjoy this, to want to know more and figure

Grinding hamburger at the Modern Café, Minneapolis

out the next puzzle. Being curious is helpful in this racket.

Well, this comes back to what you were talking about before, the investment.
I feel very lucky that I've gotten to work in places where people come in together to work, to cook food together, and to talk and raise their families, and have a beautiful connection to the food. This is the ancient art of cooking, and that's pretty hip, that's fun to be a part of . . . Even though my knees are a lot more sore than they used to be, I still get to be a kid and be a part of this long line, you know.

How did meat loaf get on the menu? And in such an important role—it's on your window!
Well, I think, it came with the place—you see this place, and even from a mile away, you think, "They must have good meat loaf." ◗

I didn't take to it right away. Before the recession, we only served it at lunch, but we got hit pretty hard in the first part of the recession. I thought, "What are we going to do?" Meat's expensive, and prices were getting really high. That was when Jim started saying, "Sorry, man. Meat loaf is going to have to be on the night menu. We've got to figure out other ways to make money, to survive." And that was when I really got serious about it. I tried pretty hard, not to gussy it up, necessarily, but to just make it honestly, to approach it not as an afterthought but as a dish.

How did that change of heart manifest in the meat loaf?

Well, around that time, the grinder came along, and I got a charcuterie book and started learning about *paté grandmère*, which is essentially a French meat loaf. The French patés use a panade as a binder—it's eggs, cream, and bread. The fat from the cream has a nice mouthfeel, and where the plain bread crumbs seem to just take moisture, the panade seems to give back moisture. So, now we make a panade for our meat loaf.

Now I'm eating less meat—I'm going through a middle-aged thing, I think—and I've kind of decided that I like little bits of things in there: a little more mirepoix, chili flakes, sweet pepper, garlic, onion, and then the beef and pork. Who knows: next week I'll start using lamb in there, but that's where I've got to now.

Condiments are a very hot topic these days. What's on yours?

A garlic aioli with ginger and cilantro. Sometimes canola doesn't taste good because it

becomes fishy. The garlic was a way to kind of step up the flavor and get away from that, and then someone thought of cilantro . . . and it just sort of grew out of the basement here.

Why do you think people associate meat loaf with the Midwest?

I don't know, but given that it is [a strong regional connection], it's appropriate for the Modern to have it, in some form or another. We didn't have the sandwich on 'til recently—I just kind of figured that out.

It may not have been once a week, but my mom definitely made meat loaf, and I always remember frying it the next day. I loved to get out the number ten [skillet] and fry the meat loaf in butter and eat it on white bread. That was what I really liked, even more than regular meat loaf dinner. So, the meat loaf sandwich reminded me of that, and it seemed like something other midwesterners would remember. ○

Modern Café's meat loaf sandwich

Beef Loaf

A 1911 RECIPE FROM PILLSBURY FLOUR MILLS COMPANY. From the Doughboy to the Jolly Green Giant, Pillsbury Company is one of the oldest, best-known companies in America, much less Minnesota. It began in 1869 when twenty-seven-year-old entrepreneur Charles A. Pillsbury—previously employed at his uncle's hardware store—purchased one-third of the Minneapolis Flour Mill, which was capable of producing 150 barrels of flour a day. By the time the company published the recipe below, the Pillsbury Flour Mills Company had been purchased by an English financial syndicate and had not only bought several competing mills but also updated them with state-of-the-art milling equipment, enabling Pillsbury-Washburn Flour Mills Company Ltd. to produce more than ten thousand barrels of flour a day.

According to Carol Fisher, author of *The American Cookbook*, manufacturing companies of the time were rapidly introducing new packaged and processed foods as well as cooking gadgets. Advertising for food products increased from one percent to 15 percent between 1887 and 1901—making them the most advertised commodity class in America until the automobile came along. Promotional cookbooks demonstrating the convenience and variety a food product offered were fairly commonplace, especially in the flour industry. The cookbooks worked in tandem with print advertisements, helping to create not only a need for but also an understanding of new products.

This recipe for Beef Loaf first appeared in the 1905 hardcover Pillsbury cookbook *A Book for a Cook* but was subsequently reprinted in a series of slim but attractive "cookbooklets" published starting in 1911. *A Book for a Cook* sold for ten cents, but it was also available for free through coupons printed in popular women's magazines. Fisher explains that, in order to manage that expense, promotional cookbooks were typically bound as leaflets or illustrated pamphlets, though as printing capabilities improved, so did cookbooklet covers. The recipes were often submitted by women's magazine food writers and cooking instructors. In this case, the recipes were compiled and adapted for home use by Nellie Duling Gans, director of the Chicago Cooking College from 1887 to 1915. Gans also provided recipes for pamphlets published by Jell-O and Northwestern Yeast Company.

Authors like Gans lent the books and the products they featured credibility, as demonstrated in this introduction to the 1911 "Pillsbury Cook Book": "Three hundred practical recipes, compiled by the distinguished authority Mrs. Nellie Duling Gans, who won the Medal of Honor for Perfect Bread at the St. Louis World's Fair, form the main feature of this new edition of the Pillsbury Cook Book. They have been selected more particularly for their value to the busy housewife, who must have substantial, nourishing and attractive dishes at a reasonable cost and effort, than for their demands on mere culinary deftness. This is but a further application of the Principle of Selection, which governs the manufacture of Pillsbury's Best Flour."

It's interesting to note that Gans's recipe features a whopping three pounds of ground beef and only three soda crackers, as opposed to later economy-conscious recipes that balance a relatively meager pound of beef with more substantial fillers.

BEEF LOAF
From the "Pillsbury Cook Book," 1911
This will serve 10 persons

Materials:

3 lbs. lean beef	1 teaspoonful salt
.5 lb. raw ham	1 teaspoonful pepper
3 eggs, well beaten	3 tablespoonfuls cream
3 soda crackers, rolled fine	6 hardboiled eggs

Way of preparing:

Chop the beef and ham very fine and then add the salt and pepper, the cracker crumbs, the well beaten eggs, and the cream. Mix all these together perfectly, grease a breadpan thoroughly, and press half the mixture into it firmly. Trim each end of your hard boiled eggs so as to make a flat surface, then put them on top of the mixture in the breadpan, placing them in a row end to end. Now pack on top the balance of your meat, pressing it down firmly. Cover and bake in a moderate oven [350°F] one hour. Uncover and bake half an hour longer. Serve either hot or cold in slices.

The 1911 "Pillsbury Cook Book" featured an image of the Pillsbury "A" Mill and the company's logo. The four Xs on the logo were a bold advertising ploy: in the flour industry, Xs were used to convey the flour's quality, with one being the poorest and three being the highest. By putting four Xs on its logo, Pillsbury claimed to have a higher quality of wheat than its competitors.

Wheat washers that immerse and agitate the wheat in running water until it is absolutely clean

Materials:
BEEF LOAF.

3 lbs. lean beef.
½ lb. raw ham.
3 eggs, well beaten.
3 soda crackers, rolled fine.

1 teaspoonful salt.
1 teaspoonful pepper.
3 tablespoonfuls cream.
6 hard boiled eggs.

Way of Preparing:
Chop the beef and ham very fine and then add the salt and pepper, the cracker crumbs, the well beaten eggs, and the cream. Mix all these together perfectly, grease it breadpan thoroughly, and press half the mixture into it firmly. Trim each end of your hard boiled eggs so as to make a flat surface, then put them on in a row end to end. Now pack on top the balance of your meat, pressing it down firmly. Cover and bake in a moderate oven one hour or cold in slices. Uncover and bake half an hour longer. Serve either hot

Quantity:
This will serve ten persons.

BEEF TONGUE PIQUANT.

Materials:
1 fresh tongue.
1 carrot.
1 red pepper.

1 onion.
1 stalk celery.
1 teaspoonful salt.

Way of Preparing:
Place the tongue in a kettle and cover with boiling water, adding the vegetables and seasoning. Cover and cook until tender. Take the tongue from the kettle and remove the skin and root. Put back into the kettle and reheat. Serve it sliced into half-inch slices accompanied by a made of the following:

SAUCE

Materials:
4 tablespoonfuls of flour.
¼ cup brown stock.
½ teaspoonful paprika.
1 cucumber pickle, chopped.

2 tablespoonfuls butter.
1 teaspoonful salt.
2 tablespoonfuls lemon-juice.
1 tablespoonful seeded raisins.

72

The interior of the "Pillsbury Cook Book," like many other cookbooklets, featured an illustrated tour of the flour mill. The 1911 printing even featured a free pass for a tour of the Pillsbury flour mills.

Meat Loaf Sandwich at Roman Market Meats and Deli

NOBODY LEAVES HUNGRY. If you ask Brent Pilrain, co-owner and chef of Roman Market Meats and Deli in Willernie, why meat loaf is so strongly associated with the Midwest, he'll venture that it has something to do with cold weather and comfort food. "But I feel like people eat it all over the place," he says. "As far as I understand, its origins go back to something like the beginning of time, with the Romans. I believe there's something like it in *Apicius*—the ancient Roman cookbook and one of the first recipe collections—where they chopped up tougher cuts of meat, molded it back into a shape, and cooked it to be more tender."

As far back as he can remember—not quite the fourth century BC—his family ate meat loaf. "Most people remember having it growing up," he says, "and many recipes get passed down through families as well, but even though my mother and both grandmothers were excellent cooks, I kind of concocted mine along the way."

As a thirteen-year-old boy in Stillwater, Pilrain's first job was washing dishes at the Main Café. He worked his way up through the kitchen and developed an affinity for food and the pace of restaurant life. Eventually, he progressed to culinary school and jobs at restaurants such as the Lake Elmo Inn and the Indian Hills Country Club. On a similar path, his brother Brian became a butcher's assistant as a teenager, working at Len's Family Foods, a neighborhood corner store with a substantial meat and deli department—a job that parlayed into a career as head butcher. "After working for several other people, my brother and I decided we wanted to try something

Meat loaf sandwich at Roman Market Meats and Deli, Willernie

on our own," says Brent, "taking my cooking and putting it together with his butchering skills, and open our own little deli."

Roman Market Premium Meats and European Deli opened in 2006, and a year later the brothers renovated the laundromat next door to add Roma Restaurant, a wine bar and eatery featuring pastas, wood-fired pizzas, and twenty deli sandwiches. "One of the first was meat loaf," says Pilrain. "It's a staple of butcher shops, so we have the sandwich and then we do a take and bake for people looking for something quick. I created it myself, taking ideas from different recipes that I had gathered over the years and tweaking them into something that I enjoy."

Pilrain's meat loaf is all beef, which allows him to cook the loaf a bit less than might be possible with pork, thereby retaining more moisture. However, we love it for the barbecue sauce it's slathered in, a rarified combination of seventeen ingredients—including chipotle peppers, bourbon, root beer, cider vinegar, and honey—that delivers a sweet, smoky, well-nigh addictive kick.

Don't take our word for it: the Pilrains sell something along the order of fifty pounds of meat loaf a week. In the end, the number of customers may not be as substantial as it sounds: the sandwiches are huge! "We started as a butcher shop," says Pilrain. "Butcher shops are known for making large sandwiches. If you go to a butcher shop and you leave hungry, something is wrong."

Contributed by Brent Pilrain, chef

Meat Loaf

2½ pounds ground beef
½ medium onion, finely diced (about ¼ cup)
2 tablespoons milk
2 eggs
¾ cup bread crumbs
¼ cup tomato juice
¼ cup root beer–bourbon barbecue sauce (recipe follows)
2 teaspoons minced garlic
2 teaspoons salt
1 teaspoon black pepper

Roman Market Meat Loaf Sandwich

Makes 6–8 servings

Preheat oven to 425°F. Combine all ingredients (beef through pepper) in large bowl and mix well. Pack tightly into ungreased loaf pans or form into

bread-loaf shape and place on ungreased baking sheet. Bake 40 minutes or until internal temperature reaches 140°F. Remove from oven and let stand at least 5 minutes before serving, or, preferably, refrigerate overnight and then slice into 6 to 8 equal portions for sandwiches.

Root Beer–Bourbon Barbecue Sauce

2 tablespoons butter
1 small red onion, minced (about ¼ cup)
1 tablespoon minced garlic
¾ cup bourbon
3 cups root beer
2 tablespoons pureed chipotle peppers in adobo sauce
⅔ cup honey
⅓ cup mild molasses
1 (28-ounce) can tomato puree
2 teaspoons Worcestershire sauce
1 teaspoon liquid smoke
⅔ cup dark brown sugar
3 tablespoons cider vinegar
1 teaspoon bitters
2 teaspoons hot chili sauce (Sriracha)
1½ teaspoons salt
1 teaspoon black pepper

In large saucepan over medium heat, melt butter and sweat onion and garlic until soft, 3 to 4 minutes. Remove from heat. Add bourbon; return to heat and cook for 1 minute. Add root beer and reduce by half, about 15 to 20 minutes. Add remaining ingredients (chipotle through pepper) and reduce heat to medium low. Cook 10 to 15 minutes to allow flavors to meld or until sauce reaches desired consistency. Remove from heat and set aside until ready to use. Sauce can be stored in the refrigerator.

Assembly

3 thick slices meat loaf
¼ cup root beer–bourbon barbecue sauce
8-inch French hoagie roll, halved and buttered
2 slices smoked mozzarella cheese

2 slices applewood-smoked bacon, fried
Mayonnaise (optional)

Preheat broiler. In an oven-safe skillet over medium heat, fry meat loaf slices with a splash of water until warmed through and lightly browned. Flip slices and cover with barbecue sauce. In a separate pan set over medium heat, lightly grill roll, buttered sides down. Layer meat loaf in a hoagie shape; top with mozzarella and bacon. Broil meat stack until cheese melts. Place on toasted roll, top with mayo if desired, and serve.

Meat Loaf Sandwich at Cheeky Monkey

BURY ME WITH A SIDE OF PICKLES. How does one successfully debut a restaurant in the middle of an economic downturn? With considerable attention to prices, a diverse menu, and a neighborhood atmosphere, says Matt McArthur, chef and owner of Cheeky Monkey on Selby Avenue in St. Paul. McArthur opened his deli in February 2009, just as restaurants all over the Twin Cities, and, indeed, the country, were shuttering their windows and closing up shop. "Obviously, we wanted to focus on things that were still going to sell," he says. "But we also wanted to do something that was both comfort food and real food, and at prices where people could come more than once a week, not just on special occasions. And it had to be family friendly, but a place where adults could come and enjoy wine and beer."

It turns out that family friendly, real food, and comfort all intersect at three long boards listing sandwiches, salads, and homey entrées such as potpie, pot roast—and meat loaf. "We didn't want to put beef tenderloin or strip on the menu," McArthur says. "We wanted to use cheaper cuts of meat, and meat loaf was just one of those things." McArthur's recipe uses grass-fed beef and stockyard veal from Thousand Hills Cattle Company of Cannon Falls. "I like the flavor of pork, too," he says, "but I wanted to limit the product we were using, and this gives [the meat loaf] a nice consistency and rich flavor." The recipe is styled somewhat after the Italian meatball and features not only more bread crumbs and cheese than many recipes but also lemon, parsley, red chilies, and extra-virgin olive oil. This combination gives the meat loaf a rich flavor but a moist, light texture.

However, it's the condiments McArthur layers on top of the meat loaf that make his sandwich especially well balanced and delicious. As with the rest of the Cheeky Monkey menu, McArthur and his crew of newly

minted culinary school graduates make the sweet-spicy Asian-style mustard, pickled chili relish, and bacon from scratch. "My background is that you always need spicy, fat, tangy, and sweet," says McArthur. "So, you put the food in your mouth, and the flavors go all different directions. Hopefully, the toast is crispy, you've got the sweet mustard, the vinegar and the spice in the chilies, with the rich cheese and smoky bacon—all these textures and flavors are hitting parts of your mouth."

The crunchy toast is made from English muffin bread, a choice McArthur did not make lightly. "It's crisp and it has crunch, but it also has enough body that it doesn't squish: it's something that a meat loaf can sit on for a minute, and it will still have a nice shape to it," he says. "I did not want something as chewy as ciabatta; I wanted something you could put your teeth in and go right through. You know, we thought, 'What's the best thing we can get and still use a white flour?' Well, the English muffin is a sourdough, so it's probiotic—it's real food."

Apparently, McArthur's thoughtful approach is working. The restaurant has weathered the economy so far, and it's packing in the diners, selling more than four hundred sandwiches a day, not including catering.

Matt McArthur, chef and owner of Cheeky Monkey, St. Paul

Contributed by Matt McArthur, chef

Meat Loaf

1 pound ground beef
1 pound ground veal
1 pinch red pepper flakes
5 cups grated Parmesan cheese
3 cups chopped parsley
1 pinch thyme
1 clove garlic, chopped
1 egg
1 egg yolk
4½ cups fine bread crumbs
Pinch salt
Pinch black pepper
1 tablespoon extra-virgin olive oil
¼ cup lemon juice
2 tablespoons half-and-half

Cheeky Monkey Meat Loaf Sandwich

Makes 6–8 servings

Preheat oven to 325°F. In a large bowl, mix together all ingredients (beef through half-and-half). Transfer mixture to ungreased loaf pan and bake 50 minutes, or until internal temperature reaches 160°F. Remove from oven and allow to cool. Refrigerate until ready to use.

Pickled Chilies

3 jalapeños, sliced thin
3 Fresno chilies, sliced thin
1 cup unseasoned rice wine vinegar
¼ cup sugar
1 tablespoon pickling spice

Place chilies in a medium bowl; set aside. In a nonreactive saucepan over medium heat, combine vinegar, sugar, and pickling spice and bring to a simmer. Remove from heat and strain mixture over chilies. Cool before serving.

Hot Mustard

½ cup dry mustard
1 cup all-purpose flour
½ cup sugar
1 teaspoon salt
1½ cups white vinegar
2 tablespoons vegetable oil

Combine first five ingredients (mustard through vinegar) in container of electric blender or food processor. Cover bowl and, with blade running, slowly drizzle in vegetable oil. Transfer to airtight container and allow mustard to rest, refrigerated, for at least 24 hours before serving.

Assembly

2 tablespoons butter, divided
2 slices English muffin bread
2 slices applewood bacon, fried (optional)
1–2 slices sharp cheddar cheese

Preheat broiler. In a skillet over medium heat, melt 1 tablespoon butter and fry meat loaf slices until lightly brown and warmed through. Brush bread with remaining butter and toast in a separate pan over medium heat until crispy. On a baking sheet, layer meat loaf with bacon (if using) and cheese and lightly broil until cheese is melted. Remove from oven. Apply mustard and chilies to 1 slice of bread, top with meat loaf stack and remaining slice of bread, and enjoy!

8 The Sambusa
Breaking the Somali Ramadan Fast

LORI WRITER / PHOTOGRAPHS BY KATIE CANNON

"*Ramadan is when sambusa* becomes really important," says Dr. Saeed Fahia, director of the Confederation of Somali Communities of Minnesota. "You find it in every *iftar,* which translates to breaking the fast."

After each day of fasting during the Muslim holy month of Ramadan, "usually, what will happen is this. They start with dates, some porridge, and sambusa. It's like breaking the fast, and that's just the beginning. Then the people will pray, and probably wait a little, and have a supper or something—it depends on the family—within two hours or one hour or something like that."

Sambusa—triangular pastries stuffed with ground meat or vegetables, spiced with onions, fragrant cilantro, and chilies, and then deep-fried—are celebration food for So-

"Food candy": the sambusa at Safari Express Restaurant, Minneapolis

malis. "Served," says Jamal Hashi, chef and co-owner of Safari Express Restaurant in Minneapolis's Midtown Global Market, "at weddings, large gatherings, family reunions, special occasions." Hashi grins broadly, "Like

153

The Holiest Month in the Islamic Calendar

AS PRACTICING MUSLIMS, most Somalis above the age of puberty fast from dawn to dusk during the holy month of Ramadan, the ninth month of the Islamic lunar calendar, during which Muslims believe the Prophet Mohammed, the last messenger of Allah, received the first revelation of the Qur'an. Ramadan is meant to be a time of reflection, prayer, and charity. Jamal Hashi, chef and co-owner of Safari Express Restaurant in Minneapolis, says, "Ramadan closes the gap between the rich and the poor. It teaches self-discipline as you abstain from food, sex, saying bad things. It makes you a humble person."

According to Dr. Saeed Fahia, director of the Confederation of Somali Communities of Minnesota, "Ramadan is celebrated as it is back home. For a lot of people it demonstrates you can change. Ramadan is very popular with Muslims, [even] with people who are not that observant during the year. It gives them a mission for one month, and they are in the good books again." He continues, "You get ready for Ramadan all year. You save for it. You try to be clean. People want to do something special: maybe help people, volunteer, clean other people's homes. Many elders here are isolated, so you find many women helping them. You will try to be kinder, laughing, out of character, in that one month. A lot of good can be done during Ramadan time. The most important is that people try to change. That's the purpose in it."

Each day during Ramadan, many Somalis break their fast after sunset with a small meal, *iftar*, comprised of dates, sambusa, porridge, and water, juice, or tea. Says Fahia,

Then I would go to the mosque, then I would pray. There's lot of bending. You don't have to go to if you don't want to: it's not an obligation. But you want to be good. So the person would go there and pray. It's a faster rhythm; you get a lot of exercise. The Qur'an is read in those prayers. All 114 chapters of the Qur'an have to be read within the month.

Each night [during Ramadan] you have to say your intention that you are fasting the next day, something like: "Oh my God, your humble servant, I'll be fasting tomorrow." Or you could state your intention the first day: "I'll be fasting the whole month." Or, people like to say it together [at the mosque] and repeat it after the imam. It helps people come together. But you could be sitting at home and just say it in your mind. You want to keep to your promise.

Id-al-Fitr (literally, "to break the fast"), at the end of Ramadan, is a three-day festival during which Muslims might excuse their children from school, visit relatives, and eat delicious food. On the last day of Id-al-Fitr, Muslims wear their finest new clothes and gather to pray. In Minneapolis, many assemble for prayers in the Minneapolis Convention Center.

Also on Id-al-Fitr, every Muslim, young or old, must pay charity to the poor, a sum that is approximately the price of a lunch, around eight dollars. Says Fahia, "That day you have to feed one person. Each member of your family has to feed one other person. In my family we are four: my wife and two sons. I used to also pay for my mother when she was alive. So, I had to feed five, not necessarily food, but could give them money. The money is collected [and sent to] people back home so they could buy food for that day. You have to be exact so the money [arrives] to feed them before [Eid]." Otherwise, Fahia explains, "It doesn't count." He laughs: "It expires."

food candy." Sambusa are daily Ramadan fare for Somalis, eaten to break fast at dusk. "Right after fasting, you don't want to eat too heavy," says Hashi. "Your stomach is pretty tight. So, you start with sambusa, prayers, water. About an hour after that, then you can eat heavy food."

In Somalia, says Hashi, sambusa are sold on the streets of Mogadishu "everywhere. Every block that you turn." He continues, "There's a saying: 'Tea for men; talk for women.'" Safari Express serves milky, sweet Somali tea, steaming with the aromas of cardamom, clove, and cinnamon, as well as spicy beef sambusa.

Elsewhere in Minneapolis, sambusa are served at tea shops located in bustling Somali shopping centers—such as Karmel Square on Pillsbury Avenue or Global Business Center on Lake Street. Small groups of Somali men, and sometimes Somali women, gather in the shops, sipping hot tea from paper cups. The malls are lined with stores selling telephone cards, tax services, barber and salon services, and women's clothing—flowing scarves in a rainbow's array of colors and long billowing skirts, some plain, some patterned, some glittery. All shops empty when the melodic chanting call to prayer sounds, echoing through the hallways. Shopkeepers lock up, then rush to the mosque, where they remove their shoes and wash their feet before entering to pray.

Freelance photographer and founder of the Somali Documentary Project Abdi Roble, who was born in Mogadishu and immigrated to the United States in 1989, says, "Tea is important to the Somali household and community. If you visit someone, they will host you with tea." Serving tea sig-

An estimated thirty thousand Somalis gather at the Mall of America in Bloomington to celebrate Eid. Fahia describes the scene: "Children and the whole family go to the Mall of America. It's mainly for the children. They take over the whole place. They take the rides and buy things. The mall asks that each child be accompanied by a parent, so you have a lot of hustling, with each child trying to get away from parents. A lot of stuff like that. Or you can [go to] the park and take the children to play. It's a festive mood more than anything. Eid itself is supposed to be festive." ○

Hamdi Café, Karmel Square, Minneapolis

nals "no rush," says Roble. "People will sit down and talk while preparing tea." They will pour "another cup, another cup, everyone enjoying one another's company." In the Somali community, "News travels orally and travels fast." And, concludes Roble, "Tea is the center of conversation."

A Fusion of Global Influences

The sharp point of land that forms the rhinoceros horn on the east coast of Africa, Somalia juts out into the sea, claiming more coastline than any other African country. Yemen lies across the Gulf of Aden to the north, and the Indian Ocean stretches out to the east. Somalia shares its western border with Djibouti, Ethiopia, and Kenya.

Hashi, who was born in the capital city of Mogadishu and immigrated to the United States with his family as a teenager, says that Somali cuisine has been shaped by diverse influences over the centuries. Fusion makes the cuisine unique: "Somalia was divided into three parts: the north was French, the middle was the UK 'red coats,' and the south, Italian." He continues, "You can't say there's Somali this or that, but each region is special. The south is known for sweets, pasta, and marinara. The north gets influences from Djibouti. The way we use spice is different, from the north to the south."

Bananas from the trees planted and then abandoned by the Italians have become a staple of the Somali diet. "The banana," says Hashi, "is the number-one fruit of all. J&J Distributing, which owns the Produce Exchange [in Minneapolis], provides more bananas to Somali restaurants in the Twin Cities than to all other businesses combined."

Somalia's location on the Indian Ocean and the Gulf of Aden historically enabled active trading with India, Pakistan, and the Middle East, particularly Yemen. "We get mixed fusion, the cultures blended into one," explains Hashi. "So, we have curry with pasta and beef marinara. We use both potatoes and pasta. Crepes with sesame oil and brown sugar are very common. In Ethiopia, their *injera* [flatbread] is soft and spongy, made from *teff* [a grass seed ground into flour]. Somali injera [called *canjeero*] also includes butter and milk."

Nearly all Somalis—including the estimated forty thousand who reside in Minnesota today, the overwhelming majority of whom have arrived in the United States as refugees since civil war erupted in 1990—are Muslim. Says Hashi, "Most Somalis observe [Muslim] halal dietary guidelines," rules governing "mostly how the meat is prepped." Consumption of pork or alcohol is strictly prohibited.

Dur Dur Bakery and Grocery Store, which operates a halal meat counter and bakery, has occupied, for the past ten years, the northwest corner of Lake Street where it intersects Sixteenth Avenue in Minneapolis. Ingebretsen's Scandinavian Gifts and Foods stands on the southeast corner, where it has been since 1921. Cooperativa Mercado Central Authentic Latin American Marketplace is located one block north, while a Mexican restaurant, butcher, and tortilleria occupy the block to the south. According to Nur Hamed, shift manager at Dur Dur, "We get a lot of different people, but the majority of people are Somali." Dur Dur sells direct to the public but also to restaurants and groceries around town.

Hamed continues,

We get some of our halal meats from Australia. And the beef side more often we get it out of local companies. Green Bay, Wisconsin, or American Foods Group in Alexandria: they make halal meats, halal beef. Halal is mainly the animal that has been slaughtered according to Muslim religion. It has to be slaughtered with the name of Allah, the name of God, with somebody saying the name of God. And that's what makes it halal. Muslim people always eat halal if it comes on the meat side. If it's being slaughtered in a different way, if it's being shot, it's prohibited by religion. That's haram. Halal and haram are opposite sides. Halal is allowed and haram is not allowed.

Hamed explains, "Companies when they are making the halal product, they contact the Islamic centers nearby them. They have a certification and show their process. A Muslim person has to do the slaughtering for them. And they process it at a different time as other products; they can't share time. No pork in the facility at all. That's what we ask all the time: 'What kind of animal do you process in your plant?' We don't want any leftover pork to contaminate the meat. They can't have any haram meats there."

As far as the beef that customers buy for making sambusa, Hamed says, "We grind the meat, and the cookers go from there." Dur Dur also sells chicken, provided by a plant in Georgia, goat meat, and camel meat out of Australia. However, Hamed reports, "Not a whole lot of people buy the camel. Elderly people out of back home still remember it. The younger generation is not used to it. Goat meat is the most popular meat."

Indeed, Hashi considers goat meat to be the national dish of Somalia. But, he comments, "It's a very sensitive meat. It takes some loving and caring; you have to nurture it, like a baby." However, it is not typical to include goat meat in a sambusa. Says Hashi, "Goats are small, and there wouldn't be enough meat. People would get upset." Similar with chicken: "It's not a big item. Not enough meat. You'd rather keep them for the eggs."

Hamed has lived in the United States for eighteen years, since 1993. He was eighteen when he arrived. He says, "Some of my family is back home, but a lot of family is here. I make my own family here now: kids and wife." Hamed learned butchering here. He recalls, "When I first got here, it was difficult to have access to halal meats. People became vegetarians. People would stay away from all kind of beef, fish. They'd tell stories: 'Oh, I tried to buy some beef, and all of a sudden I get a bunch of pork meat.'"

He continues, "A gentleman who works for us, he was ahead of us. People welcome him. People fill [a refrigerator] with American beverage; lots of pork chops: 'This is your food. This is your freezer.' He was scared." Hamed says, "Now the people who come, they have an easier time. People

That Which Is Permissible under Islamic Law

ISLAMIC LAW REQUIRES Muslims to follow that which is permissible, halal, and avoid that which is forbidden, haram. Halal dietary laws explicitly prohibit consuming, among other things, pork and pork by-products, including lard and gelatin, and alcohol and food ingredients containing alcohol such as vanilla extract and Dijon mustard.

Halal prescribes a ritual slaughter of all animals, excluding fish and most sea life. The method calls for a swift, deep incision with a sharp knife on the neck, cutting the jugular veins and carotid arteries of both sides but leaving the spinal cord intact.

Vegetarian and vegan food is considered to be inherently halal. Animals for food may not be killed by being shot, boiled, or electrocuted. The carcass should be hung upside down long enough to be blood free.

The Qur'an allows an exception in the case of hardship or lack of alternatives. **O** can communicate in their own language. And [non-Somali] people are better informed about halal rules."

Zahra Dirir, a Somali who lives in Burnsville with her husband and children, says, "I don't remember anything from back home because I was a child when I left there. I was thirteen." Born in Mogadishu, Dirir was less than a year old when her mother died. Her grandmother took all of the kids to live in northeastern Somalia. When Dirir was kindergarten age, she moved in with her sister, who, at nineteen, was recently married. When Dirir was in the eighth grade, the family relocated back to Mogadishu. As war erupted, Dirir and several other teenage girls fled to Kenya, which borders Somalia to the northwest. Her family eventually joined them.

Zahra Dirir cooks sambusa filling at home

Dirir moved to the United States, initially to Brooklyn Center, in October 1998, after her husband had been living in Texas for a year. "Minnesota was my choice," she says, "because I have family—my sister's own family—here." Family connections are important because, Dirir explains, "Somalis identify by tribe." She belongs to the Darot, a northwest tribe.

Dirir started cooking at age seven by preparing the family's breakfast before school. She learned to make sambusa when she was older. She says, "Recipe instructions are just in our mind. It's hard for daughters to learn." For Ramadan, Dirir cooks only for her family. In comparison, she says, "My aunt cooks for forty men."

Making Minnesota Home

Dr. Fahia believes that finding shelter is the most urgent task for Somali refugees entering the United States. He explains: "It's likely your whole family will stay in one room or two rooms during that whole time. If I have five kids and my sister with three will be coming, twelve of us will be staying." Social welfare agencies such as Lutheran Social Services assist refugees in finding housing. Fahia says, "Most people are from civil war and then refugee camps. There is a lot of trauma associated with that. They want a quiet place most of the time: a place where they kind of think through. They experience cultural shock initially. For a long time."

"I think for Somalis—and it's different from one person to another—usually they want to be in a place where other Somalis are," Fahia continues. "That's why there is a premium on [Minneapolis neighborhood] Cedar-Riverside. You have the largest concentration of Somalis anywhere in the world, even in Somalia, within those two high-rise buildings."

"Cedar Riverside Plaza [Apartments] has eighteen hundred units. Then across the street is another thousand units. There can be seventy-five hundred Somalis in there. Nowhere in the world in that kind of small area are there that much Somalis," says Fahia. "Usually you find there are two kinds of housing here: subsidized housing—Section Eight or low income or whatever—and market rate." The advantage for those who pay market rate, according to Fahia, is that "kids can go to playrooms or Qur'anic religious classes." There are "mosques, two or three small centers where you can buy Somali food. There is East African, Arabian, and Indian stuff in those stores." He continues, "This neighborhood has been very helpful. Some people move to suburbs later on. In some cases you can't get a Section Eight here now. Every position for Section Eight has been taken. So you have to move to a suburb to get a low-income housing. That is happening now," Fahia explains.

Finding schooling for children and securing employment are the next challenges. "The

Dr. Saeed Fahia, director of the Confederation of Somali Communities of Minnesota

Sambusa in Other Culinary Traditions

THE SOMALI SAMBUSA, its name derived from the Persian sanbosag, belongs to a family of triangular or half moon–shaped pastries— savory or sweet, baked or fried—common throughout the Middle East and South and Central Asia. The Somali sambusa in Minnesota is most commonly stuffed with spiced ground beef, less often with chicken, tuna, or vegetables, and might also be labeled *sambus, samosa, sambosa,* or *sambuusi.*

Da Afghan Restaurant in Bloomington offers both savory and sweet sambosa. The savory version is a baked puff pastry filled with a mixture of seasoned ground beef and onion, served with a garlic-yogurt sauce. The dessert apple sambosa is puff pastry stuffed with diced apples and served warm alongside a scoop of vanilla ice cream.

Blue Nile [Ethiopian] Restaurant & Lounge in Minneapolis presents crispy, fried sambusa missira, stuffed with lentils and spiced with onion, jalapeño, garlic, and herbs. T's Place in Minneapolis also serves Ethiopian-style samosas.

CurryUp [Indian] Restaurant and Grocery in Maple Grove offers spiced potato and pea samosa with various chutneys. And Kabobs Restaurant, with locations in Bloomington and Maple Grove, serves traditional Indian and Pakistani cuisine, including vegetable, chicken, or beef samosas.

Saffron Restaurant & Lounge in Minneapolis specializes in Mediterranean and Middle Eastern cuisine. Happy hour guests can indulge in mini deep-fried spiced-potato samosas, fragrant with garam masala and served with a cool cucumber yogurt.

For Tibetan- or Nepali-style samosas, try Everest on Grand in St. Paul or Himalayan Restaurant in Minneapolis, both of which serve up fried potato-and-green-pea samosas.

Forepaugh's Restaurant in St. Paul, on its hipper, cheaper downstairs menu, offers fried Malaysian chicken samosas stuffed with curried chicken and served with a tangy and sweet green mango dipping sauce. Sapor Café and Bar in Minneapolis has devised a parsnip samosa with dal, pomegranate yogurt, and cilantro, though it claims no culinary heritage. ○

government demands it [that] they try to find work quickly. If you ask the resettlement office program in Minnesota, which is part of the Department of Human Services, if you ask them, 'How does a refugee integrate?' they will tell you 'housing and employment.' Employment is important to the program, so they have to find work quickly." Additionally, says Fahia,

> Learning some English, ESL [English as a second language], is important too. Some people learn faster than others. It depends on the education you have in your own country. If you are fluent or a writer in your own language, then it is easier to learn at another age. Age is another thing. I've worked with a lot of people who are doctors in Somalia, who have been students in other places, maybe the Soviet Union, who try to get a job in their field. It's hard when you're fifty, sixty years old to try [to] take the exams. In English. So they take jobs as medical advocates or nurses.

"The work process is difficult for people in the beginning," continues Fahia. "In Somalia in particular and in Africa people used to work for themselves. They owned animals, had a farm, or worked in a family-owned store or business. Or they fished. This big corporation where you have a boss and you are expected to do something, and the pace of the work, your pay comes from that—it takes a while for people to understand. There is a language barrier."

Fahia estimates that in parts of Somalia today 35 percent of Somalis are nomadic, compared with 60 percent in the 1960s. "People help each other a lot in Somali culture," he says. "When someone moves. [When] you have a famine. When there's a drought or, for example, [when] you lose all your animals." He continues, "I'll tell you why hospitality is important. Many Somalis are nomadic. So, you travel in the desert, and you want to feel welcome wherever you go. You can't carry enough food, can't carry enough water. So welcome and hospitality means that everybody is treated fairly and everyone is helped out. In all nomadic, desertlike countries you find that often."

Fahia grew up in a fishing village, "an old one. The houses were mainly palm. And we didn't use mud or anything to plaster." He remembers, "Every five years, the palm gets old and the persons would want to replace it—cut the palm and put it together and replace it. And people would help for four or five days. And the person would give them tea or feed them. People helped each other out of necessity." He continues, "You can't do everything yourself. It's really important for us. For example, here someone will come from village or from Somalia and would ask me, 'Who can find me a job?' If you know someone who owns a restaurant or something to hire him."

Fahia recalls passing through the airport in Rome, Italy, on his second trip to the United States, in 1987:

> I had a hundred bucks U.S. money. I had to stay in Rome one night. I needed to eat something, so I had to change it. I needed maybe two, three dollars. But, when I tried to change it back at the airport, they said, "It can't be done." I thought, "What do I do with this useless lire? I'm in a fix. I need to call someone. I don't have a quarter or anything like that."
>
> There was this Somali coming back to the U.S. ahead of me. I [had] never met him. I asked him where he came from. He says that he lives in the U.S. and came to Italy to be part of the Olympic team, a long-distance runner.
>
> So, I said, "You must have some U.S. money."
>
> And he said, "Yes."
>
> So I said, "How much does it take to make a call [in the United States]?"
>
> He said, "One dollar."
>
> So I said, "I need at least one dollar." He gave me a hundred dollars.
>
> I said, "Where do I find you?"
>
> I've never seen the guy again.

Roble expands on this concept of hospitality: "You're insured wherever you go. The first Somali person you see, it's their responsibility to take care of you. The importance of being part of a group is where being a Muslim and being Somali comes together. It's imbedded deeply in the culture. It has been the tradition. Everyone needs you; you need them. You're insured. If you lose your job, you don't have that fear of being homeless."

Says Roble, "You have to be part of community. And the community is part of you." And where there is community, there are sambusa.

Sambusa

*Makes enough for
30+ large sambusa*

Contributed by Zahra Dirir

Allow yourself about three hours to make the wrappers and filling and to form and fry the sambusa.

Zahra's Sambusa Wrappers

Chef Jamal Hashi says, "Some people use premade eggroll wraps or tortillas instead of making the wrapper from scratch, but there is nothing like handmade if you want the best results." Dirir pats balls of dough into thin pancakes, brushes them with oil, and stacks them two high. After flattening them with a rolling pin, she slices them into four wedges and then heats them briefly in a nonstick pan to dry them out. Alternatively, Hashi stacks his pancakes four high for rolling out and dries them briefly on a lefse griddle set to 450°F.

Hashi notes that "olives are scarce in Somalia, so sesame oil is common" as an ingredient. This recipe yields a tender sambusa wrapper. For a crispier wrapper, add up to ½ cup olive oil when mixing the dough.

5 cups all-purpose flour
2 teaspoons salt
Up to ½ cup olive oil (optional)
2 cups hot (but not boiling) water

Paste (for "gluing" sambusa together during assembly)
4 tablespoons all-purpose flour
3 tablespoons water

For rolling dough into wrappers
Olive oil
Flour

1. Mix 5 cups flour, salt, and olive oil (if using) with a wooden spoon in a handled large bowl or stockpot. Gradually add water, and continue to mix with your hands. You may not need all of the water: the dough should not be so sticky that it comes off on your fingers.

2. Knead dough inside bowl until smooth. Alternate using a kneading motion and pushing down and twisting with your fist. Cover bowl with plastic wrap and allow dough to rest 30 minutes. Make sambusa filling (recipe follows).

3. Gently mix together 4 tablespoons flour and 3 tablespoons water with your fingers in a small bowl, trying not to create any bubbles. Set aside.

4. To shape and roll wrappers, knead dough for 2 minutes, and then divide into 14 pieces by twisting off palm-sized segments and rolling them into balls the size of a small apple. On an unfloured surface, press each ball into a pancake approximately 3 inches in diameter. Brush each pancake with olive oil. Stack pancakes 2 high so that you have 7 stacks.

5. Sprinkle top pancake lightly with flour, then use a rolling pin to flatten each stack to 10 inches in diameter. Try to achieve a perfect circle. (If the dough cracks, it is too dry.) Slice each stack into 4 wedges with a sharp knife.

6. In a nonstick pan over low heat, toast each wedge (still stacked 2 pancakes high) for 20 seconds. Flip and toast another 20 seconds. You are trying to dry out the wedge, not cook it. Repeat with remaining wedges. With a knife, trim the outer edge of each wedge so that it forms a smooth arc. Stack wedges; cover with plastic wrap until ready to use.

Zahra's Beef Sambusa Filling

This recipe is mildly spiced. Dirir likes to add finely diced bell peppers, but "the kids won't eat them," she says. In Somalia, according to Chef Jamal Hashi, "every family's sambusa is different, so you know whose is whose when you bite into it. My neighbors used to add ginger to the meat. Another family had basil taste." Hashi's cousin makes his favorite sambusa. "She won't tell you her secret," he says. "She always surprises you with something different."

Another typical flavor combination is cumin, black pepper, crushed red chilies, salt, garlic, cilantro, diced yellow or white onions, and sliced green onions. Hashi says, "You want fine diced, as tiny as possible. You don't want anything big jumping out at you."

2 pounds halal ground beef (very lean)

½ teaspoon chicken bouillon (Dirir uses Maggi brand)

1 teaspoon ground garam masala (Dirir uses Rajah brand)

5 medium yellow onions, finely diced

½ bunch fresh cilantro, leaves thoroughly dried and finely chopped, stems discarded

1 large bunch green onions, thoroughly dried, greens quartered length-
    wise and finely chopped, root ends and whites discarded
3–4 green Serrano chilies, seeds and veins included, finely chopped
    (wear gloves)

1. Cook ground beef in a large, uncovered stockpot over high heat until
all liquid has disappeared and meat is crumbly, about 20 minutes. Stir
frequently with a wooden spoon to break up any lumps.
2. Stir in chicken bouillon and then garam masala. Cook and stir 2 minutes. Add remaining ingredients (yellow onions through chilies) and cook,
stirring, 5 minutes. Remove from heat. When meat is cool enough to handle, proceed with assembly directions.

Assembly

Canola oil

1. Take a wedge from the stack and separate the two wrappers by peeling
one sheet from the other with a slow, steady movement. Hold one wrapper with the bottom point of the wedge toward you and the rounded edge
away from you. Fold the right point of the wrapper toward the center. Dip
your index finger in the flour paste and paint the outside of the portion of
the wrapper that you just folded over.

Folding and Filling a Sambusa Wrapper

2. Fold the left point toward the center of the wrapper. The underside of the left portion should stick to the paste, but ensure a tight seal by using your index finger to press along the seam, adding paste as necessary. Take special care to pinch and seal the point at the bottom: leaky seams and unsealed corners will cause the sambusa to take on oil during frying.

3. Open the wrapper to form a cone, holding it so that the seam faces away from you. Fill cone with 2 tablespoons meat mixture. Pull the front (seamed) portion of the wrapper toward you and tuck it over so that the filling is completely contained inside the triangular pocket. Use a little paste to seal along the top of the triangle, taking care to pinch and seal the pointy corners at the left and the right.

4. Paint the inside top flap with paste and fold it over the front of the sambusa, pinching and sealing the corners. Set aside and repeat with remaining sambusa.

5. In a large, uncovered frying pot or wok, preheat 2 inches oil over medium-high heat. Working in batches, lower sambusa into oil. Check frequently and turn with a slotted spoon when the underside is golden brown. When both sides are golden brown, approximately 10 minutes total, use a slotted spoon to transfer sambusa to paper towel–lined plate to cool. Dirir says, "Don't forget to serve yourself, too."

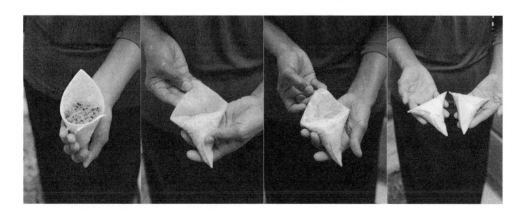

Tuna Sambusa

*Makes enough for
56 large sambusa*

*Adapted from a recipe provided
by Garad Mah Mahamed of Chicago
Food and Deli's Chicago Catering,
Minneapolis*

These sambusa are boldly spiced but not overpoweringly so. Chicago Food and Deli sells their sambusa to restaurants and tea shops throughout Minneapolis. They use no oil during cooking, but we adapted the recipe to add a little at the beginning of the process to prevent the spices from sticking to the bottom of the pan. "Fish," says Mahamed, "is always halal."

Deep-frying the assembled sambusa is the traditional preparation, but you may bake them on an ungreased baking sheet in a preheated oven at 350°F for 20 minutes. Rotate the baking sheet after 10 minutes.

Filling

1½ tablespoons canola or other neutral oil
1½ medium white onions (about 6 ounces), finely diced
4 green Serrano chilies, seeds and veins included, finely chopped (wear
  gloves)
6 (5-ounce) cans chunk light tuna in water, drained
2 teaspoons chicken bouillon
2 teaspoons cumin
2 teaspoons garlic powder
1 teaspoon curry powder
1 bunch fresh cilantro, leaves thoroughly dried and finely chopped,
  stems discarded

Heat oil in a large, uncovered stockpot over medium heat. Add onions and cook until soft. Add chilies and cook, stirring, 2 minutes. Stir in remaining ingredients (tuna through cilantro) and cook, stirring frequently with a wooden spoon, 7 or 8 minutes, until the tuna is heated through and the spices are evenly distributed. Remove from heat. When mixture is cool enough to handle, proceed with assembly directions (page 166–67).

*Sambusa are often eaten
to break the Ramadan fast*

Jamal Hashi, chef and co-owner of Safari Express Restaurant, Minneapolis

The Hashi Family's Bizbaz (Hot Pepper) Sauce

Contributed by Jamal Hashi, chef, Safari Express Restaurant, Minneapolis

This quick and easy spicy dipping sauce is the Hashi family secret. It pairs well with sambusa but can be drizzled or dollopped onto any dish for added zing.

4 whole jalapeño peppers, seeds and veins intact
6 cloves garlic, peeled
¼ cup cilantro
¼ cup diced yellow onion
¼ cup lime (or lemon) juice
2 tablespoons extra-virgin olive oil
Salt, to taste

Place all ingredients (peppers through salt) in container of an electric blender. Cover and blend until smooth, occasionally stopping to scrape the sides. Serve alongside sambusa as a dipping sauce.

Contributed by Raghavan Iyer

Educator, hospitality consultant, and author of acclaimed Indian cookbooks including *660 Curries, The Turmeric Trail,* and *Betty Crocker's Indian Home Cooking,* Raghavan Iyer is a native of Mumbai, India, and a longtime Twin Citian. Iyer says, "Every country has its samosa: some kind of pastry shell stuffed with anything and everything. These samosas are the most popular of snacks, not only in India but also in other parts of the world. The crust is very similar to the European flaky pie crust and tradi-

Traditional Samosas

Makes 10 servings

tionally houses coarsely smashed potatoes perked with chilies and plump peas. From the northwestern state of Punjab, the wheat-growing capital of India, these samosas are slightly labor-heavy, but once you get into that rolling, shaping, and frying rhythm, the results are highly addictive. Serve them with any sweet-tart dipping sauce."

Iyer also offers this advice: Keep the remaining dough chilled while working with individual rounds. Even though more difficult to roll, a chilled dough will be easier to shape into cones. Freeze leftover fried samosas for up to a month. Thaw overnight in the refrigerator and then place on a baking sheet and warm in a 300°F oven 10 to 12 minutes or until centers are hot.

Pastry Dough

2 cups unbleached all-purpose flour
¼ teaspoon coarse kosher or sea salt
½ cup chilled unsalted butter, thinly sliced
½ cup cold water

Mix flour and salt in medium bowl. Cut in butter using pastry blender or by rubbing between palms of hands, until mixture resembles coarse bread crumbs. Add water, 2 tablespoons at a time, mixing by hand or with a wooden spoon. Continue adding water to bring dough together into a ball that is neither sticky nor dry. Knead in bowl or on lightly floured surface 2 to 3 minutes or until dough is smooth. Roll dough into 2-inch-thick log. Cover with plastic wrap and refrigerate at least 30 minutes or up to 2 days.

Filling

2 tablespoons canola oil
1 teaspoon cumin seeds
1 medium onion, finely chopped
1 tablespoon finely chopped fresh ginger
3 medium red potatoes (1 pound), peeled, cooked, and cut into ¼-inch
    cubes
1 cup frozen green peas, thawed
¼ cup finely chopped fresh cilantro leaves and tender stems
¼ cup finely chopped fresh mint leaves

2 or 3 fresh Serrano chilies, stems removed, seeds intact, finely chopped
2 teaspoons garam masala
1 teaspoon coarse kosher or sea salt

Heat oil in wok or deep 12-inch skillet over medium-high heat. Add cumin seeds; sizzle 30 seconds. Stir in onion and ginger. Cook 2 to 3 minutes, stirring constantly, until onion is golden brown. Stir in remaining ingredients (potatoes through salt); remove from heat. Cool completely, 20 to 30 minutes.

Assembly

Flour
water
Vegetable oil

1. Cut dough log into 10 slices. Working with one slice at a time (cover and refrigerate remaining dough), roll on lightly floured surface into 6-inch circle. Cut each dough circle in half. Lay one half across the fingers of one hand (the best position is when your four fingers are together and your thumb is pointing skyward) with its straight edge in line with your forefinger. Dab a little water over the dough, leaving a ¼-inch border. Lift the edge closest to your thumb and twist it, laying the flipped side against the wet side, fashioning a cone. Spoon a heaping tablespoon or two of filling into the cone, pushing it down. Wet the top round edge of the cone, and press it together to seal tightly. Place triangular-shaped samosa on a floured plate. Repeat with remaining dough rounds and filling.
2. Place 2 to 3 inches oil in wok or deep 10-inch skillet and heat over medium-high heat until temperature reaches 350°F. Gently place samosas in hot oil without overcrowding and fry 4 to 6 minutes, turning occasionally, until golden brown. Remove with slotted spoon; drain on paper towels. Repeat with remaining samosas. Serve.

Saffron Restaurant's Spiced Potato Samosas

Makes approximately 3 dozen samosas

Contributed by Sameh Wadi, chef and owner

Chef Sameh Wadi, a native of Palestine, describes Saffron's samosas as "a hybrid: a cross between an Indian samosa and a Middle Eastern sambusek. The Indian version is the inspiration." Saffron uses special handmade dough for the wrappers, but for ease of preparation, this recipe calls for wonton wrappers. Wadi explains, "When we first moved to the U.S., we went crazy over wonton wrappers. It makes it so easy." Wadi says his mom will make samosas "using wonton wrappers and all kinds of fillings—beef, lamb, and other things as well—except for big-deal events, when the whole family is over," when she'll make the dough by hand. Wadi adds, "At the restaurant, we sell these in huge amounts. They are cheap [on the happy hour menu], only $3.50 for an entire order. I devote an entire day every other week, making them in batches of a thousand."

"*Garam masala*," according to Wadi, "literally means 'hot mixture' or 'warming spice.' [It is] an all-purpose blend called for in many northern Indian dishes. This is a rather aromatic spice that can take [the] place of a 'yellow curry' in a stew or sauce. [It's] made from eleven ingredients, including cardamom, fenugreek, mace, and Tellicherry pepper." Saffron's house-blended Spice Trail Garam Masala is available for purchase at Saffron Restaurant and Lounge in Minneapolis or at www.SaffronMpls.com.

Soybean, canola, or peanut oil
1 pound Yukon gold potatoes, skin on, diced into ½-inch cubes
Salt, to taste
3 tablespoons ghee (or substitute clarified butter)
½ yellow onion, diced (about ½ cup)
3 cloves garlic, thinly sliced (about 2 tablespoons)
1 tablespoon grated fresh ginger
½ Serrano chili, stem removed, seeds and veins intact, chopped
    (about 1 tablespoon)

1 teaspoon anise seeds, toasted
½ teaspoon turmeric
1 teaspoon Spice Trail Garam Masala
1 tablespoon water, if needed
1 cup frozen peas
2 tablespoons roughly chopped cilantro leaves and stems
1 package small square wonton wrappers

1. Fill deep fryer with oil, enough to fully submerge samosas. Preheat oil to 350°F. Deep-fry potatoes for about 4 to 7 minutes, until golden brown. Remove with slotted spoon and season with salt. Drain on paper towel and set aside.

2. In medium saucepan, warm ghee over low heat. Add onion and garlic and sweat 3 minutes. Add ginger, chili, anise seed, turmeric, and garam masala and cook an additional 2 minutes. If ingredients stick to pan, add up to a tablespoon of water to deglaze. Add peas and fried potatoes and cook 2 minutes. Stir in cilantro. Remove from heat and cool completely.

3. Place a tablespoon or so of filling on top of wonton wrapper. Brush edges of wrapper with water, and fold wrapper to form a triangular shape. Gently press edges to make a tight seal. Set aside on a floured plate. Repeat with remaining filling and wrappers.

4. In deep fryer with oil at 350°F, fry samosas in small batches 2 to 3 minutes, until golden brown and crisp. Repeat with remaining samosas. Serve with cucumber yogurt salad (recipe follows).

Cucumber Yogurt Salad

Chef Wadi likes the color and texture that the delicate skin of the cucumber provides, so there is no need to peel the cucumber before dicing it.

½ English cucumber, finely diced
2 cloves garlic, grated
1 cup thick and tangy homemade yogurt (or substitute Greek yogurt)
1 tablespoon fresh mint, thinly sliced
1 teaspoon lemon juice
Salt, to taste

In medium bowl, mix first five ingredients (cucumber through lemon juice), adding salt to taste. Refrigerate until ready to serve.

9 The Ju(i)cy Lucy
The Molten Cheese Core of South Minneapolis

JAMES NORTON / PHOTOGRAPHS BY BECCA DILLEY

𝒟efining the appeal of a food that's actually a bit physically dangerous to eat is easier than it may seem. Consider the roller coaster: the overwhelmingly illusionary danger provides a cheap but very real thrill. Thus the jucy lucy: a cheese-stuffed hamburger that presents the possible but not totally terrifying threat of spewing molten American cheese all over your arm, face, clothing, or dining companion. Along with particularly devilish hot wings, it's one of the few midwestern bar snacks that's routinely served with a verbal warning.

While stuffed hamburgers pop up here and there throughout the country, they are unique to Minnesota as a seriously established local dining culture. They have their roots in the 3.2 bars of Minneapolis, neighborhood joints that were legally allowed to serve nothing stronger than beer with an alcohol content of 3.2 percent. These taverns dotted the neighborhoods of South Minneapolis in particular, and their presence is still felt between Lake Street and Highway 62 from north to south and between 35W and Hiawatha Avenue from west to east. Some of these old neighborhood standbys are still operating under their fifty- or sixty-year-old original names; some have gone through numerous changes of ownership and title; most have faded away entirely. But their cheese-stuffed legacy looms large—larger every year, it seems, as the jucy lucy enjoys a renaissance that goes far beyond its home turf.

Long after its development in the fifties, the jucy lucy made serious

The jucy lucy sandwich at the 5-8 Club, South Minneapolis

inroads in St. Paul, where its DNA mutated, producing gourmet and exotic versions of the once straightforward classic, traditionally stuffed with American cheese and topped with grilled onions. It has also begun popping up in restaurants as far out as Duluth and into northwestern Wisconsin.

"To me, at its best, it's corner bar–type food—it's something you'd have with fries and a pitcher of [Grain Belt] Premium," says Ed Kohler. Kohler, a prodigious blogger and community activist, has made cataloging the burger part of his lifestyle: he's the curator of jucylucyrestaurants.com, the definitive online resource for the dedicated jucy hound. According to Kohler, there's a practical reason the tradition has, until recent years, been largely contained to its South Minneapolis roots. "It's something you do in the neighborhood," he says. "It's easier to do if you only do it [and no other food], because it's a very different way of cooking a burger."

Poorly executed lucys can be undercooked, or rubbery, or—worst of all—suffer a cheese blowout on the grill. "You don't want to have a blowout," says Kohler. "I had problems with that at Bar Abilene in Uptown, where they were doing a Mexican-style lucy: the cheese leaked out of it while it was cooking, and they still served it, which is just amateur." His disdain, expressed through a sorrowful shake of the head, registers clearly even in the dark and noisy confines of Matt's Bar on Cedar Avenue in Minneapolis.

A number of different schools of thought on the best way to prepare the burger exist: one specifies an inner burger and cheese ball wrapped by a second layer of hamburger, another calls for crimping together two patties, and some have even suggested that pre-freezing the cheese can aid in the cooking process. The America's Test Kitchen *Cook's Country Cookbook* version, which will likely represent the nation's go-to jucy recipe for the ages, specifies using a panade (a milk and bread mixture) to make for a moister, more meatball-like burger that can stand up to the slower cooking required for a good jucy.

The craft of making this sandwich is a subtle one: there's a lot you can screw up. "It's an art form to get it done," says Penny Jernberg, general manager of the 5-8 Club in Minneapolis, one of the burger's original homes. "People would call us after the show *Man v. Food* [which featured the legendary sandwich] and say, 'I just can't get it done right.' The cheese will leak out and it won't get totally done . . . you can burn the outside if it's thick."

The reward of a perfect jucy is substantial, however. The juicy (but not undercooked) burger oozes hot cheese that actually, over the course of cooking, partially fuses with the beef—rather than tearing away at one large, partially melted sheet of cheese, the diner enjoys a dairy product

A Brief Note on the Spelling of the Ju(i)cy Lucy

MATT'S BAR HOLDS FAST to *jucy lucy* as its spelling of choice. The 5-8 Club calls 'em *juicy lucys* and produces a sassy stock response to interview questions: "We say if it's spelled right, it's done right." Adrian's does a *juicy lucy* as well. Along with interpreting the burger, restaurants have a tendency to interpret the name: the Nook has a *juicy nookie*; the Blue Door does a variety of *blucys*.

Minnesota Lunch went with a default of *jucy lucy* for three reasons:

1. The jucy constitutes a unique regional eating tradition. An unusual name that has to be taught to outsiders helps hammer that point home.

2. Matt's has the most solid (and aggressively asserted) claim to being the originator of the burger and captures the 3.2 vintage ambiance as well as any other bar in the Cities.

3. The site jucylucyrestaurants.com doesn't use an "i," and curator Ed Kohler has cataloged more versions of the burger at more places (nearly thirty) than anyone else. **O**

that is almost elementally incorporated into (and flowing out of) the meat. As a bonus, any excess cheese generally drips onto your plate, creating instant cheese fries in the process. Unless, of course, it shoots onto your arm and burns you. But that's just part of the charm.

Let There Be Stuffed Cheeseburgers

Very little is agreed upon when it comes to the origins of the burger. The 5-8 Club, one of the two oldest locations, is willing to concede that, while it was early in the game, it wasn't the first. "There's a story that somebody started it [at] Matt's and then immediately had a falling out with them and brought it down here," says Jernberg. "But we don't know for sure."

Penny Jernberg, 5-8 Club, South Minneapolis

Twenty-three blocks to the north on Cedar Avenue, Matt's Bar agreeably grasps the title of jucy lucy originator for its own. Owner Scott Nelson passed along the lore of the bar's burger as he heard it from the establishment's namesake, Matt Bristol. Nelson places the invention of the burger in 1954, the year Matt's became Matt's. "As Matt tells it, it was actually invented by customers who wanted their burgers cooked a little different, so they started stuffing cheese in them," says Nelson. "The term *jucy lucy* came from when one guy bit into one and said, 'Wow, that's one juicy Lucy!' And the reason they're misspelled is that, when the name was first put through the printer for the menu, it was misspelled. It's kind of our trademark." Food writer Dara Moskowitz Grumdahl, telling the story of the burger in a 1998 *City Pages* article, tracked the misspelling to a menu board, rather than a printed menu, but it's the little wrinkles and inconsistencies that make oral history so irritatingly charming.

Interestingly, however, some of the 5-8 Club's veteran customers—who began eating the bar's distinctive burgers not long after the end of World War II—suggest that Adrian's Tavern might be the jucy's actual point of origin. "I don't think they started here. They started at Forty-eighth and Chicago, I think," says longtime 5-8 customer George Town, giving the address of an establishment called Adrian's since 1963, another former 3.2 bar that is locally infamous for serving a gargantuan jucy.

Old School: Matt's Bar

When you walk into Matt's Bar, it's hard not to notice that very little has changed over the past five-plus decades. That's the way the owners, Scott Nelson and his wife, Cathleen, like it. "I've got pictures from '56, and this is the same wallpaper—it looks kind of cruddy now—but I told Matt, you started this, and I'm just kind of carrying it on," says Nelson. "I think it's kind of a cool thing. Not everything's supposed to look like a chain restaurant. I think people appreciate the nostalgia of coming to an old fifties dive-y bar and getting good food."

Nelson hails from a background of managing chain restaurants, so he's vividly aware of what Matt's, as he sees it, is not supposed to become. "I grew up going to [famous Eden Prairie burger bar] Lions Tap, and I used to go here [to Matt's] in high school as well. And I just wanted to stay in that field. [Matt's is] the kind of place I like to work in. I worked so much in chains where you don't know anybody, and here you get so many regulars. I want to perpetuate that."

Nelson is content to let his competitors talk about sourcing gourmet ingredients or novel flavor combinations. His thing is simplicity, and if you've ever had a Matt's Jucy, you'll grant it that: it's a humble,

Scott Nelson, owner of Matt's Bar, Minneapolis

old-fashioned hamburger stuffed with easy-melting, free-running, unpretentious American cheese. "Apparently they're doing some at the stadium?" asks Nelson, referring to the newly opened Target Field, home to the Minnesota Twins, a ballpark brimming with food vendors. "Twelve-dollar jucy lucys, apparently? Fine. They're not going to do it as well, and people are going to end up coming here."

The relatively modest size and ambitions of the burgers are part of the point. "Here's the deal," says Nelson. "We keep it really simple. They're not giant: the patties are relatively thin, which allows the cheese to get really hot and get absorbed into the burgers. So it tastes actually different than a double cheeseburger, because the cheese is actually absorbed into the meat. I think we just do it well. We only do a couple of things. They're not giant; they just taste really good. We use fresh meat, never frozen."

The burgers sell. A typical day, according to Nelson, sees 450 to 800 jucys going out to customers packed into the restaurant's booths, tables, and bar stools. "You've seen the little grill," he continues, referring to Matt's limited "kitchen." "One fryer and one little grill. After the [TV] shows [exploring the sandwich's history], we were very busy. I'd come in the morning and make two thousand patties, starting at three in the morning. We'd have to have the production to make the jucys, which are hand squeezed all day." He shakes his head at his exhausting good fortune. "We're busy, but there are worse problems to have."

The burgers are more than the calling card at Matt's Bar—they're key to the place's history. "In the old days, there were tons of these 3.2 beer joints all over Minneapolis," explains Nelson. "In the fifties, you got off work and you didn't go home; you went to the local tavern. These were more beer joints in the old days. Matt used to sell—I'm a restaurant that serves beer; he was a beer place that served burgers. I'm probably 75 to 80 percent food; he was probably not quite the other way, but close." The stuffed burger became this neighborhood bar's lifeline. "The development of the jucy lucy made us a local hangout, and we became known for our food, and as 3.2 joints dissipated all over town, we stayed rockin,'" he says.

Nelson points with pride to the multigenerational nature of his clientele: grandparents, parents, and grandkids often eat at Matt's together. "It's not just the old folks; it's everyone," he says. "After a funeral, you know, maybe the grandpa went here, and the whole family will come in and take over the place." Younger people who don't necessarily live in the neighborhood or have long-standing family ties to Matt's still are drawn to the bar by its reputation and increasing fame.

For Ed Kohler, it's a unique facet of Minneapolis that he enjoys sharing. "I meet a lot of people from companies I work with, and I'll bring them here," he says. "Yeah, we could go to another steak house and have the exact same meal, and it's expensable, but why don't we do something interesting, something unique to Minneapolis? We'll have people from Montreal, or Vancouver, or Michigan—and they love it." The beauty, according to Kohler, is that the experience isn't merely a meal; it's a story. "It's a totally different experience, and something they never would have found on their own," he says. They try a burger they've never had before, and they leave with a story. They come here, and they'll tell me a story about a place they need to take me next time I'm in their town. So, there's this connection that's made."

The Evolution of the 5-8 Club and Its Neighborhood

Once upon a time during Prohibition, the 5-8 Club was a couple of bunga-lows on the edge of town, across the street from a dump. A speakeasy and the residence of the owners, respectively, the two little houses have long since merged into a big, comfortable, casual modern restaurant. At that point, the name was different: "It was the 58th Street Club," notes general manager Penny Jernberg. "It was based on Fifty-eighth Street and Cedar Avenue. Over time people just shortened it, and it became the 5-8 Club. And now people just say 'the 5-8.'"

After Prohibition, tough liquor laws meant that the 5-8, like so many other neighborhood taverns, could only serve 3.2 beer. "There was no hard liquor past Lake Street, as the horse patrols didn't go further south," says Pat Lindquist, a veteran PR professional who works with the 5-8. "Lake Street was thirty blocks out of the city, and you go much further south, and you're basically in the country." Even today, liquor laws are daunting, and the 5-8 is still not a hard drinker's paradise. "Most of the bars in South Minneapolis only serve strong beer and wine to this day. The city of Min-neapolis has a lot of regulations," notes Jernberg. "Because we're across the street from a church, we can never have more than that. We had to petition for the strong beer and wine license, and that was contingent upon selling a high enough percentage of food."

Jernberg recalls a classic juicy lucy incident from the midnineties: "Be-fore we remodeled, there was a little corner table here. A customer came in with a nice bomber jacket on, and he took a bite of a juicy lucy, and it got ALL over him. It just shot all over him. He said, 'I've had a million juicy lucys. What was I thinking?'"

According to Jernberg, the quality of ingredients in the 5-8 juicy lucy distinguishes it over many of its competitors—including the one that's twenty-three blocks ("and fourteen feet!" adds Lindquist) to the north. "We use 100 percent USDA choice ground beef, and it's fresh, never fro-zen," she says. "For our quarter-pound burgers, it's a ball of meat that we hand flatten. For the juicy lucy, it's two patties we seal together. We get our buns from Denny's [Fifth Avenue Bakery of Bloomington]. They're sweet, soft, bakery fresh, delivered six days a week." Even the handling of the bun merits a mention: "[Some competitors] get kind of your run-of-the-mill bun, and they're presliced. We slice them here so they maintain that freshness and softness inside."

To get a sense of perspective on the club's history, we talked to George

Ridge, George Town, and Don Sovell, three customers who have been coming to the restaurant on and off since the end of World War II. "Before I was born, during Prohibition, there were bootleggers on every corner," Sovell relates. "My uncle, my dad's younger brother, was making the booze in a bathtub, and my dad, he was selling it. And so then, [my uncle] got busted . . . so he took off, and they didn't see him for fifteen years. And he became an itinerant farmworker."

Post-Prohibition, as the 5-8 transitioned into one of the dozens of 3.2 bars that studded South Minneapolis, the club occupied a relatively remote patch of land far from the relative glamour of downtown Minneapolis or St. Paul. "The owners were Al and Edna," says Town. "Actually, his name was Elmer Brumm, but they called him Al. They owned the joint. Al was down on Lake Street talking to a guy, and he said he owned a saloon. 'I own a bar down on Fifty-eighth and

Left to right: George Ridge, Don Sovell, and George Town at the 5-8 Club

Cedar,' he said. 'You mean the dump out there on Cedar Avenue?' said the other guy. 'No, we're across the street from the dump!'"

"There wasn't much out here," adds Ridge. "Most of the homes . . . were G.I. homes. It was originally a speakeasy: it just sat out here by itself; there was nothing around, just a gas station across the street." Town continues, "When we first started coming here, it was just a beer joint. They couldn't get a liquor license . . . so we'd come here and drink beer. And this wasn't a place to pick up girls—it was just guys. The girls wouldn't come into this hole." The birth of the 5-8's grill came in the late forties. "The only thing I remember about it is we'd be sitting at the bar, and we'd want some food, and we'd have to leave," says Town. "And we asked, 'How do we get some food in this joint?' So Al decided to feed us."

The old neighborhood truly was a different place: overwhelmingly white, modern concerns about diversity and racial sensitivity were still decades away. Sovell tells a story of one of his childhood games. It involved a sort of tennis ball tag where the kid who was hit with the ball—or the kid who threw the ball and missed—would get a stone. "If you got five stones, you went against the garage, and everyone would go back about twenty-five feet or so and throw that tennis ball at you and hit you as hard as they could. We just loved that. We called that game the n-word." There's a moment of silence after he finishes the anecdote. "We didn't even have any blacks in our schools," recalls Ridge. Times change, of course. "One of my daughters married an Ethiopian that she met at the university," says Sovell. "He came from the intelligentsia. His father was an ambassador for Haile Selassie."

In the decades after World War II, South Minneapolis was less diverse and more working class, a heritage still reflected by the plumbing and hardware stores that dot Minnehaha and Hiawatha Avenues and East Lake Street. "There used to be a lot more factories on Hiawatha Avenue," says Kohler. "Way back in the day, Powderhorn Park used to be a very Swedish neighborhood. A lot of Olympic speed skaters came out of this neighborhood. There was a speed skating oval down in Powderhorn Park, and basically the park was a stadium, and people would come and watch that. They'd do barrel-jumping, too."

As for the area's modern diversity, which includes whites, blacks, Latinos, and African immigrants, Kohler continues, "Today there are enclaves that are starting to rejuvenate. There are hipster groups who wanted to buy a home in an affordable neighborhood, and this certainly qualifies as that. Now probably the biggest immigrant population is the Mexican population, but you don't see that at Matt's . . . It's not that anybody is not welcome at Matt's, but they just haven't found it yet."

To St. Paul and Beyond

If it took the 3.2 taverns of South Minneapolis to give birth to the jucy lucy, it took the culinary innovation of St. Paulites to bring it fully and truly into the twenty-first century. According to Jeremy Woerner, co-owner of the Blue Door Pub on Selby Avenue, the focus on jucys at the bar, which calls its stuffed hamburgers "blucys," was semiaccidental. "We were literally typing out our menu the day we opened," he says, referring to the late fall of 2008. "We were thinking about doing a Philly [cheesesteak]; we were going to do a Coney [Michigan-style hot dog] . . . but we didn't really have those where we wanted them."

Woerner and partner Patrick McDonough are both veterans of the Groveland Tap in St. Paul, which features a jucy lucy. It was one dish that made the jump to the newly opened neighborhood pub/restaurant. "We always thought we were going to feature the jucy but that people would be ordering other burgers," says Woerner. "But after day four, it was clear that everybody was ordering them."

The Blue Door's approach to its burgers has been collaborative from the get-go. "We had a competition with our cooks where they could make whatever they wanted, and they could each enter up to two burgers," recalls McDonough. "We had people coming in on their days off with bags from Whole Foods [market], saying, 'You mind if I use the kitchen to work on my burgers?' Then we had the staff vote on what they liked best." One of the burgers to emerge from the contest was the Bangkok Blucy. "That was mozzarella cheese soaked in coconut milk, with pickled vegetables— ginger, cucumber, and red onion—and then we do a side of curry that you can dip the whole thing into. It's pretty spectacular. It's a hamburger, but it's a lot of flavors you wouldn't typically get from a hamburger."

The Bangkok Blucy is just the tip of the iceberg with the restaurant's jucy experimentation. "Blucy of the Moment" contests solicit new ideas from customers ("there's a guy who will send in a list of fifteen every time," says McDonough), and the owners have a stable of about fifty different burgers from which to draw at any given time. A fried egg–topped Breakfast Blucy is a perennial favorite, and the Lumberjack Blucy is a good example of some of the more far-out creations the Blue Door has featured. Stuffed with smoked Gouda and served with salty thick-cut bacon and spicy cayenne pepper, it's accompanied by a maple syrup glaze that pools at the bottom of the paper-lined basket and acts as a dipping sauce. Salty, hot, sweet, meaty—all in one delectable, ridiculous package.

Left to right: Patrick McDonough and Jeremy Woerner, co-owners, Blue Door Pub, St. Paul

But why did the jucy light such a fire not only with the Blue Door Pub's clientele but with Twin Cities residents in general? "I think the burger's kind of a blue-collar food," says McDonough. "I think of Minnesota as a blue-collar state. It's a cultural thing. I think Minnesotans really want an identity—we're not New York, we're not California, and we want something to embrace and define us." Adds Woerner, "I think people are fiercely proud of their state, and their city, and even their neighborhoods. I think the competition between the [Twin] Cities may have helped forge this. It's a uniquely Minnesota thing, and people are always bringing people from out of town to try them—you know, 'That's what we do.'"

Upstarts though they may be, the Blue Door has won plaudits from at least one old school rival. "I think the Blue Door Pub has done some really interesting things with the jucy," says the 5-8's Jernberg. "They have something on their menu that's very respectful about how they're inspired by a tradition that started over in South Minneapolis." The owners of the Blue Door Pub, as the newest kids on the block, had to contend not only with their alma mater of Groveland Tap but with the St. Paul jucy lucy powerhouse known as Casper and Runyon's Nook. "People are so supportive of their burger joints," reports Woerner. "We had people come in, and before they even ordered, they'd say, 'Your burger's not going to be as good as the Nook's.' It was funny."

Lori Writer, in a review for the *Heavy Table,* described the Nook as a sports memorabilia–studded neighborhood institution with an emphasis on high-quality bar food–style eats: "The Nook serves up burgers from a tiny grill, frequently manned by Casper or Runyon. French fries are hand-cut and buns are bakery-fresh from P. J. Murphy's down the street on Randolph Ave . . . [The Nook's] burgers achieve char without tasting thoroughly burned." Comparing the Nook to Matt's, the yardstick for the jucy, Ed Kohler says, "I think the biggest thing they have there is a little bit higher-quality ingredients. The buns are a little bit nicer, the burgers are a little bit bigger, and overall, they cook a little higher-quality food, which isn't knocking Matt's. They're just taking a slightly different spin." It's hard to fault any aspect of the Nook's food, but the wait can be a deal breaker, particularly in the depths of February. Should you get caught in a line stretching out the door, just remember not to hold it open as you wait: pick a side and commit. And know that the burger within is well worth your time.

MATT'S BAR Come for the atmosphere. Order a pitcher of Grain Belt Premium and a jucy, hunker down at a booth if you can, and enjoy the cheerfully raucous ebb and flow of a real old-fashioned neighborhood joint. If you're looking to impress an out-of-towner with a slice of South Minneapolis charm, Matt's is the place—assuming there's not a line out the door, spurred by yet another mention in the national media. Matt's notoriety keeps the grill humming and the room packed, which is a blessing and a curse.

THE 5-8 CLUB Less of a bar and more of a restaurant, Minneapolis's 5-8 sports clean, modern décor with some vintage touches; it's an easier place to bring your family (particularly if kids are part of the expedition), and its onion straws are really second to none. A more varied menu than Matt's (including some novel twists on the jucy lucy) means that it's more likely to please a picky or diverse group, and like its competitor to the north, it's got neighborhood charm and a multigenerational clientele, minus the grunge.

THE BLUE DOOR The crusading gourmet is most likely to be satisfied by the ever-changing, often wild combinations of stuffed burgers at this St. Paul restaurant and bar. A strong local beer collection and great wings make the Blue Door a fine place to decompress after work, but the relatively small restaurant fills up quickly and easily, a sad situation that started very soon after its successful and much buzzed-about opening. Whether this upstart establishment can stand the test of time like its South Minneapolis rivals (and the Nook) is yet to be seen, but it's off to a roaring start.

CASPER AND RUNYON'S NOOK Home to what is likely the best all-around traditional jucy lucy experience in the universe, the Nook's high-quality ingredients and attention to gastronomic detail—plus its stellar hand-cut fries—make it the burger lover's destination bar. This sports-focused bar near Cretin-Derham Hall high school in St. Paul really fills up (particularly on weekends or game nights), so getting a table can be a patience-trying affair. The Nook's sister restaurant, Shamrock's on West Seventh, also in St. Paul, has notably less consistent food: you're best off waiting it out or trying the Blue Door. **O**

Blucy sandwich, Blue Door Pub, St. Paul

Uncooked patties stacked with cheese for juicy lucys at the 5-8 Club

The Heavy Table's "Local Lucy"

Makes 6 servings

2 pounds ground beef (80–85
    percent lean)
6 slices American cheese
Steak seasoning or salt and pepper
Pickle slices (optional)
Fried onions (optional)
6 hamburger buns, sliced

1. Preheat grill to 400°F. Divide beef into 6 portions. Roll one portion of meat between hands, creating a tightly formed ball (the beef should not be crumbly). Divide ball into two, forming one half into another ball and then flattening it into a circle (larger than a bun) on a cutting board.

2. Fold 1 slice American cheese into quarters and arrange in the center of the beef patty, overlapping slices to leave beef edges exposed. Roll the other half of the beef into a ball and flatten into a circle the same size as the first, then lay it atop cheese. Pinch edges of beef patties together, sealing all holes. A lump in the top of the patty will show where the cheese lies inside. Repeat with remaining beef and cheese. (Patties can be made in advance; refrigerate until ready for grilling.)

3. Place burger patties on grill, pocket of cheese up. Sprinkle each patty with steak seasoning or salt and pepper. Grill, covered, 8 to 9 minutes, then flip burgers. Pierce each patty once with a sharp knife to release steam from the melting cheese. Continue cooking, covered, 7 to 8 minutes longer. Move patties to low heat until ready to serve.

4. To assemble: layer pickle slices (if using) and fried onions (if using) on bottom half of each bun. Add jucy lucy patty and top of bun. WARNING: The cheese inside a jucy lucy is extremely hot. Let burgers rest a couple minutes before eating.

10 The Scandinavian Open-faced Sandwich

Old-world Grace for a Busy New Country

JAMES NORTON / PHOTOGRAPHS BY BECCA DILLEY

How do you make a Scandinavian open-faced sandwich, and what does it have to do with Minnesota? Quick answer number one: there are several hundred legitimate ways to go about it. Quick answer number two: on one hand, it doesn't have much to do with Minnesota, and on the other, it has quite a lot. First things first: the food.

Like American barbecue, the open-faced sandwich has regional variations, dedicated condiments, and attendant controversies. Danish renditions emphasize ham and other pork products; the Swedish version may tend toward sweeter flavors; Norwegian variations might make use of the seafood the country is so rightfully known for. In the most general terms, the open-faced sandwich tends to start with small pieces of rye bread with butter. "The Danes butter their bread," says Kirsten Larsen. Larsen is a native Dane, a longtime Minnesota resident, and the author of the authoritative *Danish Sandwiches: Only One Slice*. "The butter acts as a seal on your bread, so it doesn't get soggy," she notes. "And if it's soggy, it can't carry all the stuff we put on it."

That stuff is mind-bogglingly diverse, including fish, roe, meat of all sorts, cured and not, cream cheese, lettuce, radishes, chives, eggs, shellfish, and far, far more. The result: a gorgeous-looking stack of edibles including bread, butter, veggies, protein, and sometimes garnishes and/or sauce, eaten with knife and fork.

Though a fading presence in Minnesota, the open-faced sandwich pops

up throughout Scandinavia, where it's a gastronomic way of life. In Denmark, it's smørrebrød ("butter and bread"); in Norway, smørbrød (ditto); in Sweden, smörgås ("butter goose," the "goose" referring to bits of butter that float to the surface of churned cream like fat little geese); and in Finland, you can find open-faced sandwiches on the voileipapoyta ("sandwich table"). Writing of the Finnish style of eating, Duluth-based author Beatrice Ojakangas notes, "When Pekka [a neighbor in Helsinki] has his morning coffee before going to work, he usually has a couple of open-faced sandwiches, too. Sometime between eleven o'clock and one he has a dish of puuroa (cooked cereal such as oatmeal, rice, or farine). Later on, Pekka and his associates have coffee and perhaps another open-faced sandwich."

The food, thus, is the material of everyday life—but it can also be part of a Scandinavian tradition of feasting. Writing of the Swedish smorgasbord, in which open-faced sandwiches play an important role, Dale Brown noted in the magisterial 1968 The Cooking of Scandinavia,

> Anyone with a serious intention of eating his way through or around it, as the case may be, will find himself in fairly short order defeated by its parade of dishes. I remember my own misgivings during my first encounter with a homemade smorgasbord in Sweden many years ago. I was naive enough to think—after putting away several kinds of bread with butter, herring (both pickled and smoked), shrimp, pickles, meatballs, smoked reindeer, boiled potatoes, asparagus souffle, mushroom souffle, beer, and aquavit—that I had come to the end of the meal. But, no: my plate was whisked away, another was put in its place, and I was invited to begin the meal proper.

In the fifties, the Viking Room at the Minneapolis Radisson had a dedicated Smorrebrods Seddel menu that would, when unfurled, stretch for about five feet. Each sandwich was listed by category (fish, fresh meats, cured meats, etc.) and could be had on white bread or toast, whole-wheat bread or toast, rye bread or toast, or pumpernickel bread. Prices ranged from 45 cents (for a caviar and smoked salmon or cream cheese and chives sandwich, for example) all the way up to $1.95 (lobster with asparagus in mayonnaise) or $2.50 (tenderloin steak with cold béarnaise sauce). In total: two hundred sandwich choices, fourteen hundred if you multiply the toppings by the available bread selections. Where have they gone? These days, you can pick from small arrays of sandwiches at places like Café Finspang at Midtown Global Market in Minneapolis or at Takk for Maten in Duluth. But the Viking Room's feast of plenty is a thing of the past.

OPPOSITE: *Kirsten Larsen teaching a class on open-faced sandwiches at Ingebretsen's, Minneapolis*

Smorrebrods Seddel menu (partial) from the Viking Room, Minneapolis, 1950s

The Open-faced Slowdown

Curt Pederson is curator of collections and exhibitions at the American Swedish Institute, a castlelike structure on Park Avenue in Minneapolis. The historic Turnblad mansion that houses the ASI is one of the most conspicuous outposts of Scandinavian culture in the state. Entering the building is like stepping into an embassy; the art, carved stone and woodwork, murals, and overall vibe mark the place as northern Europe, not South Minneapolis. Beyond hosting cultural activities and preserving Swedish culture, the ASI also serves open-faced sandwiches to groups of visitors and as part of its monthly smorgasbords.

From Pederson's perspective, the relative scarcity of the open-faced sandwich is a commentary on the disconnect between the Scandinavian pace of life and the American way of doing things. "A lot of it is the evolution of fast food in America," he says. "McDonald's . . . It's the pace we see. A sandwich, you eat quickly. It's something you can eat quickly. In the Scandinavian countries, the open-faced sandwich, it's still a little more formal." The use of cutlery means that eating an open-faced sandwich requires a table, a chair, and some patience. "You take time," Pederson explains. "That break for lunch in midday, it's relaxing, it's spiritually and physically a time they take a breather before going back to work. That's in my mind part of it."

"I was just saying to one of my friends the other day [that in Sweden], people don't eat in their cars," says Sibbon Johnson, a native of Finspang, Sweden, who runs a boutique named for her home town. Operating in South Minneapolis's Midtown Global Market, Café Finspang sells all manner of Scandinavian goods, including baked items and open-faced sandwiches. "People in Sweden, you eat breakfast . . . that's almost like a ritual for us," she says. "We have our yogurt and an open-faced sandwich and a boiled egg . . . We actually eat dinner for lunch: we eat the biggest meal of the day in the middle of day. And when we come home in the evening, we do something lighter and smaller, like an open-faced sandwich. For different occasions, we do them fancy or less fancy. Sometimes it's just a slice of bread with a skinny layer of butter and a thin layer of cheese or salami or something like that—it doesn't look fancy at all."

Open-faced sandwiches at the American Swedish Institute, Minneapolis

Despite difference in lifestyles, Johnson says that making the jump to Minneapolis was a surprisingly easy one. Although Johnson runs a shop, she trained as a performance artist, and her new home city has no shortage of outlets for the artistically inclined. "For me, I love South Minneapolis," she says. "You can feel like you're living in a small town in the country, just like the place where I grew up, in some ways, but you can still have the thrills of a big city because it's very easy to just take Park Avenue downtown . . . or go to the Guthrie, or any other theater . . . or a concert . . . so you can have both right here. And there are lots of artists. I'm an artist even if I'm not supporting myself being an artist."

Scandinavian Modern Meets Minnesota Casual

Although the open-faced sandwich ranges from humble to edible master-piece, it always calls to mind the slower, more civilized pace of life that Pederson celebrates. He points to Aquavit, the renowned Scandinavian restaurant operated by Swedish chef Marcus Samuelsson. The restaurant garnered rave reviews but closed its doors in 2003 after a more than four-year run. "It wasn't Victorian in formality; it was Scandinavian modern," recalls Pederson. "A meal had an appetizer, a salad, and [an] entrée, and it was artfully presented. But I heard locals say, 'Well, you sure didn't get much for your money.' I visited Aquavit only twice, once was a three-hour meal . . . the other time, it was with four Swedes, and I can't remember how long the meal was because the Swedes led the way through an alcoholic . . ." He trails off, smiling, looking for the right word. "Honestly, I lost track of more than just time," he says. And then he continues,

> It's our pace. The Scandinavian way of eating, it's a period of time, and it involves conversation, and someone might tell a story . . . you'd have conversations with other people at the table . . . It's just a pattern of re-laxation. Formality might not be the predominant aspect. It seems to be formal, because there's a white tablecloth and silver, but it's really about a slower pace. Enjoying the flavors, enjoying the mouthful you might have taken, and with a wine . . . or beer . . . maybe some schnapps . . . It's really that slower pace. I think it all comes down to that.

While the open-faced sandwich can be taken to sushi-like heights of visual impact and artistry, Pederson traces its roots to day-to-day eating. "My guess is that it evolved as a staple—as so much folk food, like lutefisk, did. It was a simple answer to daily needs," he explains. "You could prepare the sandwiches en masse, rather than an individual creation like an entrée. The sandwich evolved to a bit of an art form, so the sandwich has become elevated. If you go to Stockholm or Gothenburg, which are the two metropolitan areas which really have a cosmopolitan feel, the open-faced sandwiches you would see there really are an art form. Yet that sandwich can be—today it is as visually appealing as it is sustenance."

Larsen, talking about the joy of the open-faced sandwich, invoked the slower pace of her Danish homeland. "I feel sorry for people who don't learn that you need to sit down and have conversations and sit together—all that is very important," she says. "It takes time, and people tend to get rushed. American children have so much going on—they have their

Sibbon Johnson, owner of Finnspang, Minneapolis

sports, they have music, they have arts, but they're always running to get to the next thing."

The sandwiches, often built on small pieces of rye bread, also reflect a different sense of scale than their American counterparts. "When I first came [to the United States] in the sixties, I went [to] a restaurant alone for lunch, and it was kind of a drugstore that had counters," recalls Larsen.

> And they had signs that had all the kinds of sandwiches they had, what kind of food they had. So I had just been in the country for maybe a week, so I went to this lunch counter, and I sat there thinking, "Well, what should I have . . . ?"
>
> In Denmark, it's polite to order a couple sandwiches; you never order just one. You order at least three. So I say, "Oh, I'll have the sausage sandwich, and I'll have the salami sandwich, and then I'll have that one there with ham." And the girl behind the counter looks me up and down and says, "Okeydoke!" So everybody else was there with, you know, a grilled cheese sandwich, and I was there with three! And a knife and fork . . . You live and learn!"

Those discrepancies in both scale and pace of eating may reflect why Minnesota, a strikingly Scandinavian state, offers relatively few opportunities to would-be smorrebrod snackers.

In some way, shape, or form, at least a third of the state's residents trace their ancestry back to Swedish, Norwegian, Finnish, or Danish stock. Scandinavians flocked to Minnesota in the latter half of the nineteenth century, mostly becoming settlers and mill, factory, and railroad workers. Between 1850 and 1930, more than 1.3 million Swedes alone arrived, and by 1910 they were the largest ethnic group in Minneapolis, second-largest in St. Paul. Churches, mutual aid societies, restaurants, and bars reflected the heritage of this new population, which put a heavy mark on the look and even sound of the state: the stereotypical "Minnewegian" accent, using a sing-song intonation and elongated o vowel sounds, reflects the impact of Scandinavian languages. In the Twin Cities in 1910, 75 percent of the population was of Scandinavian or German extraction, a high-water mark that would decline through the years. As it is, Vietnamese, Mexican, and Japanese restaurants are nearly everywhere, but Scandinavian restaurants are very few and far between.

Johnson notes that part of the disconnect between the sandwich and the population of Minnesota has to do with the tough economic conditions that brought families to America. "Most people came here during the famished time in Sweden, about 110 or 120 years ago," she says.

> People here in Minnesota still want to do the food they inherited from their grandparents and great-grandparents. I understand that. But growing up in Sweden, where food is constantly evolving, [I also know that] the famished times have been long gone. I had no idea what some of the food were that Ingebretsen's [Scandinavian gift store] was selling: what's "Swedish sausage"? Oh, OK: it's potato sausage. We call it something different, and it's not really a big deal—we don't eat it as much as we used to. Blood sausage: we were served that in school, and I hated it. All it is is pork blood and wheat—who would want to eat that? It was eaten during the famished times. But in school, when they made us eat blood sausage, that was not a popular day.

Open-faced sandwiches are a modern thing, then, a tenuous link between the Midwest and Scandinavia as it is now—not as it was more than one hundred years ago.

At Takk for Maten restaurant in Duluth, the open-faced sandwich is making a comeback. The restaurant's smorrebrod plate comes with three options: a bacon and turkey sandwich with cucumber that's light and crunchy, a sandwich featuring cones of turkey cold cuts wrapped around mild cheese and served with mayo and sliced hard-boiled eggs, and a creamy egg with gravlax salmon served on a cranberry bread. The bread is fluffier than at Ingebretsen's or at one of Larsen's sandwich-making demonstrations, but the spirit is right.

Living Life Open-faced

Open-faced sandwiches, more than any other sandwich in this book, represent a lifestyle shift from the way we normally eat. On one hand, they slow you down, forcing the use of fork and knife, and on the other,

Open-faced sandwiches from Takk for Maten, Duluth

they're remarkably versatile and easy to manage. If you've got bread and butter, almost anything—cooked shrimp, chives from the garden, hard-boiled eggs, luncheon meat, leftover lettuce from a salad, dill from the farmers market, canned tuna fish, radishes—becomes fodder for a colorful luncheon or dinner meal. In hot weather, they're cool. During the holidays, a big spread can dazzle. And they're dynamite for feeding groups. A large batch of sandwiches can be quickly assembled just before company arrives.

"When you set the table at home, it's not like you make these sandwiches for people, unless it's a very formal occasion," notes Johnson.

> You have the different toppings; you might have the sausage, the cheese, the herring, the liver pâté—lots of different things. You take a slice of bread—a white bread, a rye bread, crackers. You make up your mind: what kind of bread would you like, would you like mayo, would you like butter? . . . So you sit there and you make your own sandwich with what you want to have on it. You sit there and talk: "Oh, I think I'm going to have sliced eggs on this one" . . . Or "I'm going to have pâté and cucumbers."

Larsen often hosts on a more formal level, premaking the sandwiches to impress. "What I do if I have company, with this kind of food, is I make it all up, so it's ready," says Larsen. "I have [a] tray of each one, and I bring people to the kitchen and say, 'Come see what you're going to have.' And they look so amazing. It's an easy way to entertain."

Dill-Cured Salmon Open-faced Sandwich

Makes 10–12 servings

Homemade gravlax

Contributed by Kirsten Larsen, from Danish Sandwiches: Only One Slice

Sugar- and Dill-Cured Salmon

(Gravad laks med dild sauce)

Gravlaks, gravet laks, gravad laks: call it what you like, but make sure to prepare it. The cured salmon—every fish-lover's favorite—must be sliced thin and served with a sauce. A Swedish invention, gravlax is now found in all Scandinavian countries, where you can buy it ready made in most delicatessens or supermarkets. About this simple but effective recipe for cured salmon, Kirsten Larsen notes, "When you look at the recipe, you can twist it any way you like: you can make it more salty, you can make it sweeter, you can add more dill. Some people pour aquavit on it while it's curing."

¼ cup coarse (kosher) salt
¼ cup brown sugar
2 tablespoons white or black peppercorns, crushed
1 large bunch (4–6 ounces) fresh dill
3 pounds fresh Atlantic salmon, tail or center cut, cleaned and scaled

1. In a small bowl, combine salt, sugar, and crushed peppercorns. Set aside. If the dill is not very pungent, crush or chop it to release the flavor. Set aside.
2. Cut salmon fillet in half lengthwise by running a sharp knife along backbone. Remove bones, using a small pliers if needed.

3. Line bottom of a 2- to 3-inch-deep glass, enamel, or stainless-steel baking dish with one-third of the dill. Sprinkle one-quarter of the salt mixture on the dill. Add half the salmon, skin side down, to the dish. Sprinkle one-quarter of salt mixture onto fish. Place one-third of dill on fish and sprinkle one-quarter of salt mixture on dill. Place other half of fish on top, skin side up, and sprinkle remaining salt mixture on fish. Add remaining dill to top.
4. Cover dish tightly, ensuring that dill and fish are pressed firmly together. Refrigerate 36 to 48 hours, turning dish every 12 hours.
5. When curing is finished, remove salmon from marinade and discard marinade, scrape away dill and seasonings, pat dry with paper towel, and place salmon on carving board. Slice thinly on the diagonal, detaching each slice from and then discarding the skin. Set aside until ready to use.

Dill Mustard Sauce

4 tablespoons Dijon-style mustard
1 teaspoon dry mustard
6 tablespoons brown sugar
1 tablespoon white vinegar
⅓ cup peanut oil
5 tablespoons chopped fresh dill
2 tablespoons dry dill flakes

In a small, deep bowl, mix mustards, sugar, and vinegar to a paste-like consistency. Using a wire whisk, slowly beat in oil until a mayonnaise-like emulsion forms. Stir in chopped dill and dill flakes. (Alternatively, place all ingredients [mustards through dill flakes] in bowl of food processor or blender, cover, and process until a smooth sauce forms, about 1 to 2 minutes.) Refrigerate, covered, up to 1 week.

Rye Bread with Yeast (Quick Method)

(Hurtigbagt rugbrød med gær)

This type of rye bread is quicker to make than rye bread baked with sourdough; however, this dough must rise for 1½ to 2 hours and bake for 1¾ hours.

4 tablespoons (2 ounces) dry yeast
3 cups lukewarm water

4 cups rye flour
2 teaspoons salt
2 tablespoons dark corn syrup
1½ cups wheat flour

1. Combine first five ingredients (yeast through corn syrup) to form a dough. On a lightly floured surface, knead dough with wheat flour until shiny and resilient. (Alternatively, using a standing mixer fitted with a dough hook, combine all ingredients [yeast through wheat flour] and mix at low speed until shiny and resilient.)

2. Place dough in a 2-quart greased bread pan and allow to rise, covered, in a warm, draft-free place 1½ to 2 hours. Adjust oven rack to lowest position and place bread pan in cold oven. Set temperature to 350°F and bake approximately 1¾ hours. Remove loaf from oven and cool, covered with a kitchen towel, on a wire rack overnight. Slice for sandwiches.

Assembly

Butter
Lettuce leaves
Fresh dill (optional)

Butter a piece of rye bread. Drape a piece of lettuce atop bread. Add slices of cured salmon. Spoon dill mustard sauce on top. Sprinkle with fresh dill, if desired. Enjoy.

Swedish Meatball and Beet Root Open-faced Sandwich

Makes 1 serving

Contributed by the American Swedish Institute

This recipe is a great way to use leftover meatballs.

For each sandwich
Softened butter
1 slice sturdy whole-wheat bread
Lettuce leaf (the prettier the better!)

Ingebretsen's sandwich: ham, pasta salad, and asparagus

3 unpeeled cucumber slices
3–5 homemade Swedish meatballs, sliced into coins
1–2 tablespoons beet root salad (recipe follows)
2 thin strips yellow pepper
1 orange slice
Fresh parsley sprig

Lightly spread butter to cover bread; place bread on plate. Cover bread with lettuce. Arrange cucumber slices down one side of bread. Place meatball slices down center of bread, stacking pieces so they stay in place. Place a spoonful of beet root salad on the remaining side. Decorate sandwich with yellow pepper strips, twisted orange slice, and parsley sprig. Enjoy!

Beet Root Salad

4 slices pickled beets, finely chopped
Chopped red or yellow onion, to taste
1 tablespoon mayonnaise or Miracle Whip

In a small bowl, combine beets and onion (if using). Stir in a small amount of mayonnaise to hold salad together.

Makes 1 serving

Contributed by the American Swedish Institute

For each sandwich
Softened butter
1 slice sturdy whole-wheat or rye bread
Lettuce leaf (fancy red leaf preferred)
3 unpeeled cucumber slices
2 tomato slices
3–5 tail-off shrimp, cooked, peeled, and deveined
½ hard-cooked egg, sliced
Dollop mayonnaise
1 lemon slice
Fresh dill sprig

Lightly spread butter to cover bread; place bread on plate. Cover bread with lettuce. Arrange cucumber and tomato slices down one side of bread. Place shrimp down center of bread. Place egg slices down remaining side. Top shrimp with a spoonful of mayonnaise. Decorate sandwich with lemon twist and dill sprig. Enjoy!

11 Bratwurst, Beef Commercials, Mayslack's Roast Beef, and More
The Outtakes

JAMES NORTON

$\mathcal{When}\ \mathcal{putting}\ \mathcal{together}$ *Minnesota Lunch,* my coauthors and I faced the challenge of narrowing down a long list of candidates to a select few. This final chapter collects a few notable sandwiches that didn't make the cut but deserve mention for their Minnesota ties and distinctive flavors.

The Bratwurst

A perfect food accompaniment to a tall stein of beer, the bratwurst can typically be found wherever Germans have settled—which means most of the state of Minnesota, the southern half in particular. Bratwurst come in a wide range of varieties, but the upper midwestern classic tends to be made from pork, precooked by boiling in beer, and then finished on the grill. Condiments include sauerkraut and hot mustard. Put ketchup on a brat if you must, but know that doing so may earn you glowers from traditionalists.

Popularized in Sheboygan County, Wisconsin, in the 1920s, the brat on a bun has become one of the staples of German American soul food, cropping up at meat markets and German restaurants throughout the state and region. (The Ukrainian sausage merchant Kramarczuk's in Minneapolis does a mean classic brat in addition to more exotic varieties such as curry brats, wild rice brats, and a spicy cherry brat called a "cherry bomb.")

If you're looking for the ideal specimen, head to New Ulm, where German heritage starts with the welcome sign, ricochets through the street names, and radiates from the town's restaurants. Veigel's Kaiserhoff, an old 3.2 bar converted into a German restaurant in 1938, should be your destination: the bratwurst is picture perfect, and pastoral murals and dark wood décor create an ideal atmosphere for a lunch of beer and sausage. Soaked in Schell's original beer before being grilled, the Kaiserhoff brat has a real snap to it—in terms of both flavor and the texture of the casing—and a tender, savory, balanced interior. The bun was buttered and toasted, and the sandwich arrived with a serious house-made sauerkraut that lent additional flavor. A chat with the waitress revealed that the Kaiserhoff's brats come from Deutschland Meats, Inc., in nearby Sanborn; the processor also has a location in Lindstrom.

The Beef Commercial

If you want insight into hearty prairie eating, look no further than the beef commercial sandwich. An open-faced combination of fork-tender roast beef, mashed potatoes, and gravy, the sandwich crops up on menus from the Dakotas through western Wisconsin but only takes on the enigmatic "commercial" name in central southern Minnesota. (It has reportedly turned up on the menu at the large Wisconsin-based Culver's chain under this name at least once, but as a special.)

The blog "Beef, Bread, Mashed Potatoes, and Gravy" may be the best existing source of information about these scarcely documented sandwiches, pointing to how little has been written about them. The blog's author, Jean Brislance, the only person to tout the sandwich on an ongoing basis, was too modest to consent to a sit-down interview or be considered an expert on the dish. He did provide some insight via e-mail:

> It is a fine example of Midwestern peasant food, if you will—a filling meal born out of necessity and economy where you take something cheap and make it taste good. I also think this is one of the great, and somewhat unheralded, culinary mysteries of Minnesota! . . . You can almost draw a line from the Twin Cities straight west to the Minnesota border. Then, [from there] if you go just about anywhere west of Interstate 35 and north of Interstate 90 in southern Minnesota, this pocket in the southern part of the state is, for the most part, beef commercial territory . . . I have yet to discover anyone who can say definitively where this regional difference for the name of the sandwich came from. My

mom grew up in this area of southern MN and remembers these sandwiches fondly—and she has no idea why they are named as such.

An article published by Minnesota 2020, a nonpartisan think tank, discusses the sandwich in some detail, mentioning that Wall Drug in Wall, South Dakota, at one point served it, but also slips into a Proustian trance vis-à-vis the perfect rendition of the dish: "Executed poorly, a beef commercial becomes sodden protein-starch-fat gloop. Executed properly, say at Dorothy's Café in Walnut Grove, Minn., in 1979, it's sublime. Dorothy Rabe ran Dorothy's for an eternity. She did it all, 18 hours a day, from scratch. She roasted her own beef, mashed her own potatoes and made a mean beef gravy.

"At least that's how I remember it."

A newsletter for the Comprehensive Advanced Life Support educational program pinpoints Windom as "Home of the Beef Commercial," which it describes as "a Central Minnesota delicacy (otherwise known as a hot roast beef sandwich with gravy)." Whether this assessment should be taken as gospel is debatable at best, but it points to the sandwich's popularity in the region.

Contributed by Michael Sundt, owner, Sunni's Grille, Howard Lake

Hot Beef Commercial

Makes 8–10 servings

Pot Roast

When roasting, Michael Sundt uses a beef base in his stock to preserve meaty flavor. For a similar effect, use a broth whose first ingredient is beef.

5 pounds beef chuck roast
1 tablespoon Lawry's seasoning
3 tablespoons oil, divided

3 large carrots, peeled and cut into large chunks
6 celery ribs
1 large yellow onion, peeled and quartered
6 garlic cloves, peeled
8 cups beef broth

1. Preheat oven to 350°F. Season roast evenly with Lawry's. In a large pan over medium-high heat, warm 1½ tablespoons oil and add vegetables (carrots through garlic), stirring to sear. Remove vegetables to roasting pan. In same pan, heat remaining oil and add seasoned roast, turning to sear on all sides. Add roast to roasting pan and cover with beef broth.
2. Roast, covered, 2 to 3 hours, until meat is tender and pulls apart effortlessly. Carefully remove meat from liquid and set aside. Strain vegetables from stock: discard vegetables and set aside stock for gravy.

Mashed Potatoes

2½ pounds baby red potatoes, cooked and drained
⅓ cup butter, melted
¼ cup half-and-half
1 tablespoon horseradish
2 tablespoons fresh grated Parmesan
Salt and white pepper to taste

Place potatoes in a large bowl. Using a hand mixer, combine butter with potatoes. Add remaining ingredients (half-and-half through salt and pepper) and continue mixing until desired consistency. Set aside.

Beef Gravy

½ cup butter
½ cup all-purpose flour

In a medium saucepan over medium heat, melt butter; add flour and simmer, stirring occasionally, until roux reaches the consistency of oatmeal. Remove from heat. In a medium bowl, whisk roux into reserved strained broth to thicken. Strain gravy to remove lumps. Set aside.

Assembly

Softened butter
Thick-cut sourdough bread

Butter bread and lightly grill in a skillet set over medium heat. Remove bread slices to plate and top with sliced roast. Place mashed potatoes alongside and smother everything in gravy. Serve.

SPAM

Whole books can and have been written about SPAM, the Minnesota-born, shelf-stable, pork-based, canned meat that helped get the country through World War II while defining the modern cuisine of Hawaii in the process. Austin, Minnesota, is the home of Hormel and the birthplace, in 1937, of SPAM, its name originally a contraction of "spiced ham." Austin is proximate to a great deal of hog raising (both in Minnesota and nearby Iowa), and the plant itself is next to a body of water called Mill Pond. Ice cut from the pond in winter helped keep founder George Hormel's meat products cool and sanitary in an era when many competitors cut corners with sometimes deadly results.

SPAM is as pliable gastronomically as it is physically, adapting to its surroundings wherever it's served. While it crops up as sushi in Hawaii, Minnesota incarnations include sandwiches on kaiser rolls and SPAM benedict, as featured in *Taste of the Midwest* by Dan Kaercher, who made the pilgrimage to Austin to visit the SPAM Museum. SPAM is truly a folk food, albeit one that sees little to no action on restaurant menus outside of Austin. Its domain is the home front, where it typically turns up in sandwich form. One notable exception: the Minnesota State Fair, where the SPAM people sell sandwiches and other delicacies featuring their iconic processed meat.

And while many view SPAM as a nostalgic food from a bygone era, the recent recession turned out to be a godsend to the thrifty meat product. A 2008 *New York Times* article described a SPAM boom triggered by cost-conscious consumers: "Slumped in chairs at the union hall after making 149,950 cans of SPAM on the day shift, several workers said they had been through boom times before—but nothing like this. SPAM 'seems to do well when hard times hit,' said Dan Bartel, business agent for the union local. 'We'll probably see SPAM lines instead of soup lines.'"

Stan Mayslack strikes a wrestler's pose, circa 1950

Mayslack's Roast Beef

"Sure, you'll eat around 1000 more calories than you probably need and reek of garlic for a day and a half. But while eating this fine sandwich you'll have a moment. Try it. Go hungry."

Blogger and community activist **ED KOHLER**, writing about Mayslack's Original on *The Deets*

If forced to pick one single sandwich that comes up most often when the topic of Minnesota originals is mentioned, the well-versed Twin Citizen would probably pick Mayslack's notorious Original. The Northeast Minneapolis bar has been slinging these mammoth sandwiches since 1955, under the supervision of its founder and owner, professional wrestler Stan Myslajek.

According to the menu: THE ORIGINAL $9.25

The storied sandwich that only Stan Mayslack could make popular. A sandwich piled so high with roast beef. Slow roasted for 8 hours in garlic & other juices so the beef just melts in your mouth. Served with onions, banana peppers, coleslaw & some of that awesome au jus.

The sandwich starts, briefly, as something that can be lifted and eaten with your hands, but it quickly implodes into a lake of beef and jus. Although the Original is overwhelmingly identified with its home in Northeast, when a former owner of Mayslack's opened a place called Moe's in Mounds View in June 2006, he included on the menu "Mayslack's Famous Roast Beef." Whether the sandwich will forever remain proprietary, bound up in a couple of locations, or whether public demand will set it free to become one of the state's dominant hand foods is a question future generations will need to resolve.

Tacos al Pastor

Colored by a derivative of the achiote tree and flavored by a variable mixture of spices and red wine vinegar (Coca Cola sometimes plays a role as a marinade), tacos al pastor is one of the most distinctive and ravishingly good Mexican foods available in the Twin Cities. Taqueria La Hacienda on Lake Street in Minneapolis does one of the best. The vertically spit-roasted pork (think gyro meat) is moist, delicate, and rich with smoky, sweet, subtle flavor, and it comes served with lime and cilantro on the tiny soft tortillas.

Midwestern Mexican food gets little respect from either coast, but the existence of authentic Mexican eats in Minnesota is inevitable: with large numbers of immigrants comes food made by native Mexicans for native Mexicans. If you're primarily familiar with tacos as seventy-nine-cent menu items that come wrapped in paper or ground-beef bombs made with a grocery store–formulated spice mix, your first bite into a real taco al pastor will be a revelation.

photo by BECCA DILLEY

*Tacos al Pastor, Taqueria La Hacienda,
Mercado Central, Minneapolis*

Acknowledgments

James Norton

I'm enormously grateful to the many chefs and home cooks who shared the recipes that appear throughout this book. My personal thanks to Brent Pilrain of Roman Market, Chris Olson, and the Dame of Sandwiches, Kirsten Larsen. My esteemed colleague Sue Doeden distinguished herself with her hospitality and assistance during the trip to Bemidji undertaken by myself and Becca Dilley. Iron Range writer Aaron Brown was exceedingly helpful, thoughtful, and patient beyond belief, and I owe him a debt of gratitude. Thanks to Rick Nelson and Teddy Hobbins for breaking bread with me and sharing their wisdom and knowledge. To the churches in Hibbing and Pequot Lakes that opened their doors to us, we are grateful.

The collective staff and readership of the *Heavy Table* suffered as I was driven to distraction by this project, and I beg their forgiveness. Elizabeth Mead Cavert Scheibel was an invaluable help to us, and all the authors are grateful for her good work. Pamela McClanahan and Shannon Pennefeather at the Minnesota Historical Society Press gave us this opportunity to tell these stories, and I'm deeply grateful to them for their faith and support.

As editor of this project, I also extend deep thank-yous of cosmic seriousness to my collaborators, Susan Pagani, Lori Writer, Jill Lewis, and Katie Cannon. And to contributing photographer Becca Dilley (who is also my wife), thank you for everything. First and foremost for your photos and steadfast support, but also—importantly—for putting up with a preoccupied and stress-prone husband for the duration of the project.

Jill Lewis

A heartfelt thank-you is due to Dennis Larson and Brooke Dillon at the Minnesota State Fair; Steve Olson and Lara Durben at the Minnesota Turkey Growers Association; Professor Sally Noll at the University of Minnesota–

Twin Cities; Mike Langmo of Lakewood Turkey Farm; Jessi Wood of Humble Roots Heritage Farm; Marilyn McAlpine; Drew Levin; and Kathryn Koutsky for their generosity of time and knowledge and their patience.

The entire *Minnesota Lunch* team of contributors deserves a shout-out for their brainstorming prowess, enthusiasm for collaboration, and endless appetite for sandwiches. Special thanks to Jim Norton for his guidance and encouragement from book conception to delivery, and to Katie Cannon for her dedication to getting the perfect shot and her willingness to taste test turkey sandwiches at a moment's notice. Finally, Uriel and Nathan Lewis endured numerous iterations of turkey sandwiches and nights when my attention was diverted to the computer instead of them. To them I am most grateful.

Susan Pagani

I would like to thank all of the folks I interviewed, not only for their wonderful stories and insight but also for accommodating my day job and meeting in the odd hours. I am especially grateful to Susan Wakefield at the Betty Crocker Archives as well as to Barbara Rostad and her crack team of research librarians. Cheers also to Mary Bartz and Mary Gunderson for sharing their incredible knowledge of Minnesota culinary history and indulging some long-winded, thoughtful conversations about ground beef. My deep appreciation to Vic Stark and his well-appointed fish shack for taking such good care of us and to Heidi Losleben for helping me make a few very critical connections. For testing recipes and then feeding me the results, I am indebted to Laura and Marcus Arneson, James and Maggie Manion, and Maria and Scott Thorpe—a special thanks to the latter two for hooking me up, so to speak, with the fishing community. And for reasons that need not be stated, I must thank William and our spotted dog for their love and encouragement.

Lori Writer

I am deeply indebted to all who generously opened their Rolodexes, data banks, memory banks, and kitchens to me: Aminah Amatullah; Isaac Becker, 112 Eatery; Carol Brumwell, LDA Minnesota; Sara Chute; Karen Cross, Black Cat Natural Foods; Phuong Dao, Vietnamese Community of Minnesota; Zahra Dirir; Dr. Saeed Fahia, Confederation of Somali Community in MN; Abdi Gelle, Dur Dur Bakery and Grocery; Nur Hamed, Dur Dur Bakery and Grocery; Jamal Hashi, Safari Express Restaurant; MayKao

Hang; Linda Haug, Café Twenty Eight; Raghavan Iyer; Asher Miller, 20.21 Restaurant; Martin Mohammed, the African Chamber of Commerce; Gail Mollner, Blackbird Café; Diana Nguyen, the Tea Garden; Ha Nguyen, Que Nha Restaurant; Nick Nguyen, the Tea Garden; Peter Phan Nguyen, Ala Francaise Bakery; Thu Nguyen, Que Nha Restaurant; Thuy Nguyen, Vina Restaurant, Richfield; Tron Nguyen, Vietnam Center; Lynne Olver, www. foodtimeline.org; Tam Phan; Thanh-Mai Phan; Abdi Roble, the Somali Documentary Project; Sara Rohde; Barbara J. Ronningen, Minnesota State Demographic Center; Doug Rutledge, the Somali Documentary Project; Chris Stevens, Blackbird Café; Jan Stone; John Stone; Sharon Stone; Caroline Nguyen Ticarro-Parker, Catalyst Foundation; Hai Truong, Ngon Vietnamese Bistro; Sameh Wadi, Saffron Restaurant and Lounge; Rachel Walstad, Lutheran Social Services of Minnesota.

Thank you to recipe testers (and the adventurous tasters in their households) Erica Bell, Chad Stoltenberg, Jan Stone, and Kari Winter.

I have incredible awe for the efficient and robust resource that, despite budget cuts, is the St. Paul Public Library.

Last but never least, my eternal gratitude to my friends and family for their loving support and for enduring my distractedness; to my cat, who naps on everything I write, whether it's good or not; and, especially, to my husband, who makes me happy every day.

Source Notes

The Fried Walleye Sandwich

Minnesota Department of Natural Resources.

Smith, Doug. "Minnesota Fishing Licenses Soar." *Minneapolis Star Tribune*, June 5, 2010.

The Vietnamese Bánh Mì Sandwich

Bladhold, Linda. *The Asian Grocery Store Demystified: A Food Lover's Guide to All the Best Ingredients.* Los Angeles: Renaissance Books, 1999.

Davidson, Alan. *The Oxford Companion to Food.* New York: Oxford University Press, 1999.

Mason, Susan R. "The Indochinese: Vietnamese, Ethnic Chinese, Hmong, Lao, Cambodians" and "The Chinese," in *They Chose Minnesota: A Survey of The State's Ethnic Groups.* Ed. June Drenning Holmquist. St. Paul: Minnesota Historical Society Press, 1981.

Mercury, Becky. *American Sandwich: Great Eats from All 50 States.* Salt Lake City, UT: Gibbs Smith, 2004.

Ngo, Bach, and Gloria Zimmerman. *The Classic Cuisine of Vietnam: 150 Authentic Recipes from the Three Distinctive Culinary Regions of Vietnam.* New York: Penguin Books USA Inc., 1979.

Nguyen, Am. "The Vietnamese and Economic Development in Minnesota," in *20 Years After—The Resettlement of the Vietnamese Refugees in Minnesota.* Ed. Quang Vu and Bien Chu. Hopkins, MN: Vietnamese Community of Minnesota, 1997.

Nguyen, Andrea. *Into the Vietnamese Kitchen: Treasured Foodways, Modern Flavors.* Berkeley, CA: Ten Speed Press, 2006.

Olver, Lynne. http://www.foodtimeline.org (accessed Aug. 2010).

Phan, Tam. "A Contribution to the American Culture: The Vietnamese Food," in *20 Years After—The Resettlement of the Vietnamese Refugees in Minnesota.* Ed. Quang Vu and Bien Chu. Hopkins, MN: Vietnamese Community of Minnesota, 1997.

Routhier, Nicole. *The Foods of Vietnam.* New York: Stewart, Tabori & Chang, 1989.

Ruhlman, Michael, and Brian Polcyn. *Charcuterie: The Craft of Salting, Smoking, and Curing.* New York: W. W. Norton & Company, 2005.

Thorne, John, and Matt Lewis Thorne. *Pot on the Fire: Further Exploits of a Renegade Cook.* New York: North Point Press, 2000.

Pasties and Porketta

Brown, Aaron. *Overburden: Modern Life on the Iron Range.* Duluth: Red Step Press, 2008.

Burckhardt, Ann L. *A Cook's Tour of Minnesota: A Portrait of the Festivals, Specialties, Places, and People Behind the State's Great Food Traditions.* St. Paul: Minnesota Historical Society Press, 2004.

Carlson, Scott. "Tasty Pasties: Lilya Aims to Bring Iron Range Staple to Twin Cities." *Finance and Commerce,* May 18, 2010.

Dooley, Beth, and Lucia Watson. *Savoring the Seasons of the Northern Heartland.* New York: Knopf, 1994.

Enger, Leif. "A History of Timbering in Minnesota." Our State, Our Forests Series. Minnesota Public Radio, November 16, 1998, http://news.minnesota.public radio.org/features/199811/16_engerl_history-m/ (accessed Sept. 2010).

Gauper, Beth. "A Pocket of Cornwall Preserved in Mineral Point." *St. Paul Pioneer Press,* Oct. 2, 1994.

Klobuchar, Jim. "Don't Be a Patsy: Know Your Pasties." *Minneapolis Star Tribune,* Sept. 24, 1986.

Mancina-Batinich, Mary Ellen. *Italian Voices: Making Minnesota Our Home.* St. Paul: Minnesota Historical Society Press, 2007.

Northeastern Minnesota Development Association. "Taconite and Northeastern Minnesota: The Present—The Future." Report. 1965.

Ode, Kim. "When Pride in the Old Ways Is No Longer Enough: Brotherson's Meats, Serving Its Minneapolis Neighborhood Since 1939, Bows to the Competition and Closes Its Doors." *Minneapolis Star Tribune,* Dec. 2, 2000.

Ostman, Eleanor. "Mom's Recipes among Those in 'savoring the Seasons.'" *St. Paul Pioneer Press,* Nov. 6, 1994.

Renewing the Countryside. *The Minnesota Homegrown Cookbook: Local Food, Local Restaurants, Local Recipes.* St. Paul, MN: Voyageur Press, 2008.

Tevlin, Jon. "Home-cooked on the Iron Range." *Minneapolis Star Tribune,* July 24, 2002.

Wilkowske, Tom. "From I-Falls to Ironwood to the Twin Ports, the Northland Runs on Pasty Pride." *Duluth News-Tribune,* Oct. 19, 2000.

The State Fair Turkey Sandwich

Koutsky, Kathryn Strand, and Linda Koutsky. *Minnesota State Fair: An Illustrated History*. Minneapolis, MN: Coffee House Press, 2007.

Marling, Karal Ann. *Blue Ribbon: A Social and Pictorial History of the Minnesota State Fair*. St. Paul: Minnesota Historical Society Press, 1990.

The Hot Dago

Boxmeyer, Don. *A Knack for Knowing Things: Stories from St. Paul Neighborhoods and Beyond*. St. Paul: Minnesota Historical Society Press, 2003.

Coleman, Nick. "Guerin Still Comes Out Swinging, Even after Guilty Plea." *St. Paul Pioneer Press,* Aug. 7, 2000.

Coppola, Francis Ford, dir. *The Godfather*. Paramount Pictures. 1972. Film.

Long, Donna Tabbert. *Tastes of Minnesota: A Food Lover's Tour*. Black Earth, WI: Trails Media Group, Inc., 2001.

Mancina-Batinich, Mary Ellen. *Italian Voices: Making Minnesota Our Home*. St. Paul: Minnesota Historical Society Press, 2007.

Scott, Charles P. G. *Transactions of the American Philological Association* 23 (1892), including *The Popular Science Monthly* 38 (Nov. 1890–Apr. 1891).

Sitaramiah, Gita. "Hot Sandwich, Hot Topic: In St. Paul, It's Called a Hot Dago." *St. Paul Pioneer Press,* Oct. 10, 2003.

Soucheray, Joe. "Anti-Bias Agency Leaps into Action!" *St. Paul Pioneer Press,* Mar. 15, 1991.

———. "'Hot' Sandwich Needs Code Word." *St. Paul Pioneer Press,* Apr. 10, 1991.

———. "One Sandwich, Hold the Reason." *St. Paul Pioneer Press,* June 24, 2007.

The Mexican Torta

Falcón, Adrienne, and Peter Rode. "Hidden Dreams, Hidden Lives: New Hispanic Immigrants in Minnesota." St. Paul and Minneapolis, MN: Urban Coalition and Sin Fronteras, Sept. 1992.

Fernandez, Enrique. "Our Search for a Good Cuban Sandwich Takes a Surprising Turn." *Miami Herald,* Aug. 2007.

Gibson, Campbell, and Kay Jung. "Historical Census Statistics on Population Totals by Race, 1970 to 1990, and by Hispanic Origins, 1970 to 1990, for the United States Regions, Divisions and States." Population Division, U.S. Census Bureau. Washington, DC, Sept. 2002.

Huse, Andrew. "Welcome to Cuban Sandwich City." *Cigar City Magazine* 1.2 (2005).

Jenkins, Kathie. "From Burritos to Quesadillas: A Wrap-up of Terms." *St. Paul Pioneer Press,* Nov. 5, 1999.

Pilcher, Jeffrey M. *¡Que vivan los tamales! Food and the Making of Mexican Identity*. Albuquerque: University of New Mexico Press, 1998.

U.S. Census Bureau. Census of Population and Housing, SF1. Washington, DC: GPO, 2000.

Valdés, Dionicio. *Mexicans in Minnesota*. St. Paul: Minnesota Historical Society Press, 2005.

The Meat Loaf Sandwich

Daniels, Frank. *The Collector's Guide to Cookbooks*. Paducah, KY: Collectors Books, 2005.

Fisher, Carol. *The American Cookbook: A History*. Jefferson, NC: McFarland & Company, Inc., 2006.

Funding Universe website, http://www.fundinguniverse.com/ (accessed Sept. 2010).

General Mills company website, http://www.generalmills.com/ (accessed Sept. 2010).

"Packers Put Up the Price of Beef." *New York Times,* Aug. 12, 1911.

The Sambusa

Abisalam, Adam. *Somalia and the Somalis: A Handbook for Teachers*. St. Paul, MN: St. Paul Public Schools, ELL Programs, 2005.

Ali, Barlin. *Somali Cuisine*. Bloomington, IN: AuthorHouse, 2007.

Davidson, Alan. *The Oxford Companion to Food*. New York: Oxford University Press, 1999.

Farid, Mohamed, and Don McMahan. *Accommodating and Educating Somali Students in Minnesota Schools: A Handbook for Teachers and Administrators*. St. Paul, MN: Hamline University Press, 2004.

Roble, Adbi, and Doug Rutledge. *The Somali Diaspora: A Journey Away*. Minneapolis: University of Minnesota Press, 2008.

The Ju(i)cy Lucy

The Cook's Country Cookbook. Brookline, MA: America's Test Kitchen, 2008.

Grumdahl, Dara Moskowitz. "A Tribe Called Lucy." City *Pages,* Aug. 12, 1998.

Iggers, Jeremy. "The Original 5-8 Club: Home of the Juicy Lucy!" *Secrets of the City,* Sept. 4, 2008, http://www.secretsofthecity.com/ (accessed Sept. 2010).

Writer, Lori. "Casper and Runyon's Nook in Highland Park." *The Heavy Table,* Feb. 11, 2009, http://heavytable.com/ (accessed Sept. 2010).

The Scandinavian Open-faced Sandwich

Anderson, Philip J., and Dag Blank. *Swedes in the Twin Cities: Immigrant Life and Minnesota's Urban Frontier*. St. Paul: Minnesota Historical Society Press, 2001.

Brown, Dale. *The Cooking of Scandinavia*. New York: Time-Life Books, 1968.

Lampe, Agnete. *Swedish Smorgasbord*. Stockholm: A.B. Lindquists Förlag, 1953.

Larsen, Kirsten. *Danish Sandwiches: Only One Slice*. Minneapolis, MN: the author, 1995.

Ojakangas, Beatrice. *The Finnish Cookbook*. New York: Crown Publishers, 1964.

Bratwurst, Beef Commercials, Mayslack's Roast Beef, and More

Brislance, Jean. *Beef, Bread, Mashed Potatoes, and Gravy*, beefcommercialsand wich.blogspot.com/ (accessed Sept. 2010).

Comprehensive Advanced Life Support Update 9.3 (July 20, 2004).

Flanagan, Marie. "Mayslack's: A Veritable Agglomeration of Beef and Jus." *Reetsyburger's Refuge*, June 1, 2009, http://www.reetsyburger.com/ (accessed Sept. 2010).

Hanson, Eric. "Classic Mayslack's Sandwich Moves to Mounds View." *Minneapolis Star Tribune*, Sept. 27, 2006.

Kaercher, Dan. *Taste of the Midwest: 12 States, 101 Recipes, 150 Meals, 8,207 Miles and Millions of Memories*. Guilford, CT: Globe Pequot, 2006.

Martin, Andrew. "SPAM Turns Serious and Hormel Turns Out More." *New York Times*, Nov. 14, 2008.

Raichlen, Steven. *Steven Raichlen's Healthy Latin Cooking: 200 Sizzling Recipes from Mexico*. Emmaus, PA: Rodale Books, 2000.

Van Hecke, John. "'Just Okay' is not Minnesotan." *Minnesota 2020 Journal* (Sept. 21, 2007).

Contributor Bios

JILL LEWIS is a Minneapolis-based public relations counselor and free-lance writer who has found that the only thing better than eating good food is writing about good food. She is a regular contributor to the *Heavy Table,* an online magazine covering the Upper Midwest food scene, and is the cofounder of the cheese-centric blog *Cheese and Champagne.* Her work has also appeared in the *Star Tribune*'s weekly *Vita.mn* and in *Culture* magazine. Jill lives in St. Louis Park with her husband and two young sons.

JAMES NORTON is a food writer currently dedicated to telling the stories of midwestern artisans. Born in Madison, Wisconsin, Norton has lived in Boston, New York City, and now Minneapolis, where he writes about food for CHOW.com and the *Heavy Table.* He and wife Becca Dilley are coauthors of the Midwest Book Award–winning *The Master Cheesemakers of Wisconsin.*

SUSAN PAGANI is a food writer and journalist. Her writing has appeared in the *East Bay Express, San Antonio Current, Heavy Table,* and *Vita.mn,* and at the Santa Cruz Actors Theatre. This is her first book project. She lives in Minneapolis with her husband and their quirky dog, Ella.

LORI WRITER has been a food fanatic ever since a fourth-grade field trip to San Francisco's Chinatown sparked a lifelong curiosity about unfamiliar cuisines. Her nightstand is stacked with cookbooks and her glove box is stuffed with take-out menus. Writer has been published in the *San Francisco Chronicle* and *Vita.mn* and as a contributing writer for the *Heavy Table.*

KATIE CANNON is a Twin Cities–based portrait and editorial photographer. She is a regular contributor to the *Heavy Table,* and her work has appeared in *Twin Cities Metro* magazine and *Vita.mn* and on NBC Kare11/Metromix.

BECCA DILLEY is a food and wedding photographer based in Minneapolis. Her work has appeared on Salon.com and in *Saveur,* the *Star Tribune, Minnesota Bride,* the *Heavy Table,* and *The Master Cheesemakers of Wisconsin.*

Index

Picture Credits

Katie Cannon: 2 (middle), 7, 8, 10, 13, 17, 18, 22, 28, 31, 32, 33, 36, 39, 82, 85, 86, 89, 91, 92, 94, 101, 116, 119, 121, 124–25, 126, 127, 129, 133, 141, 142, 146, 150, 153, 156, 159, 160, 161, 166, 167, 168, 169

Becca Dilley: ii, x, 2 (left and right), 3, 37, 38, 52, 57, 58, 60, 63, 65, 68, 76, 99, 104, 107, 109, 110, 111, 175, 177, 178, 181, 183, 185, 188, 191, 193, 195, 196, 199, 207

From the collections of the Minnesota Historical Society: 145, 190, 206

Minnesota Lunch was designed and set in type by Judy Gilats at Peregrine Graphics Services. The text type is PMN Caecilia and the display face is House-A-Rama. Printed by Sheridan Books, Ann Arbor, Michigan.